# A-Z
# MARKETING

# A-Z MARKETING

**Alok Satsangi**

**CENTRUM PRESS**
NEW DELHI-110002 (INDIA)

**CENTRUM PRESS**

**H.O.:** 4360/4, Ansari Road, Daryaganj,
New Delhi-110 002 (India)
Ph.: 23278000, 23261597

**B.O.:** No. 1015, Ist Main Road, BSK IIIrd Stage
IIIrd Phase, IIIrd Block,
Bangalore - 560 085 (India)
Tel.: 080-41723429
*Visit us at*: www.centrumpress.com

*A-Z Marketing*



First Edition, 2009

ISBN 978-93-80106-25-0

PRINTED IN INDIA

---

*Printed at* Salasar Imaging Systems, Delhi-110035 (India)

# Contents

# Preface

Since publication of this book, several major developments have come to be of outstanding interest to those professionally engaged in marketing education and management. Some of the most important may be summarized as follows:

(1) Critical appraisals within institutions of higher learning of the nature, objectives, and effectiveness of undergraduate and graduate education in marketing;

(2) A growing awareness within the business community of the totality of the marketing process and of the necessity of adapting marketing activities within the firm to rapid changes within a highly dynamic business and economic environment;

(3) The broadening interdisciplinary character of marketing thought and action; and

(4) The increasing realization on the part of business leaders and educators that the raison for all marketing effort is the satisfaction of needs and wants of customers.

The managerial viewpoint is nevertheless accorded its due place, along with an appraisal from a broader perspective. The result, in the authors' judgment, is a balanced treatment—one which recognizes as prerequisite for marketing leadership true understanding that comes from acquisition of accumulated basic knowledge as well as from the development of skills that may be acquired in various decision-making approaches to the subject.

Author

## Chapter 1

# Marketing Fundamentals

Almost every American has some conception of his country's technological prowess. It is easy to take for granted a continuing stream of inventions and innovations that enable our manufacturing, agricultural, and extractive industries to pour forth a constantly growing supply of products, increasingly varied in assortment and better adapted to the gratification of consumer and industrial-user wants. Not so well understood is the significance of marketing which raises our living standards and provides us the means of meeting these standards.

It is not surprising that the ordinary person has little appreciation of the role that marketing plays in our society, for it is only since about the 1920's that deserved attention has been given to marketing as a field of scientific study. It was not until the 1950's that widespread business awareness of the strategic significance of marketing was widely reflected in the prominence given to a marketing concept or a marketing orientation in the organization of even many of our most progressive companies.

As one moves through the pages of this book, one will have an opportunity to learn a great deal about marketing. At the outset, it is important to obtain a grasp of the nature and scope of the subject and to get an understanding of the way in which marketing conceptions have changed with the times.

## MARKETING AS A FIELD OF KNOWLEDGE

The subject of marketing as a field of human knowledge by giving attention to:

- The meaning of marketing and its major role in the production of economic values,
- The historical development of modern marketing, and
- The evolution of the scientific study of marketing.

*MARKETING—MARKETS—PRODUCTION*

Marketing meets the needs of markets by producing economic values which, while not so tangible, are qualitatively just as real and quantitatively more significant than those produced in agriculture, mining, and manufacturing.

## THE MEANING OF MARKETING

It is not easy to define marketing in a manner that is satisfactory to everyone. To illustrate from but a single area of consumption, the housewife does her marketing when she goes to a supermarket to buy food and household items. The supermarket is doing its marketing partly by bringing products to the store where they are available to meet the housewife's needs. Food processing companies do their marketing by planning products to meet consumer needs and moving these products through channels of trade so that they are available in stores, after being publicized through various media of communication. The farmer does his marketing by moving his produce from farm to market, which may consist of wholesale middlemen or processing companies. Each one of these persons or organizations is engaged in marketing, but each is doing only a small part of the total job encompassed by the marketing process. Clearly, for purposes of objective study and clarity of understanding marketing as a significant social process, it is essential to take a viewpoint which is much broader than that of any participating party.

Marketing is essentially a process like farming, manufacturing, mining, or construction. As such, it is basically functional in character and may, therefore, be defined *as the performance of all activities necessary for ascertaining the needs and wants of markets, planning product availability, effecting transfers in ownership of products, providing for their physical distribution, and facilitating the entire marketing process.* It thus embraces the entire group of functions performed and services rendered in the acquisition or distribution of products for further processing, for business or institutional use, or for ultimate consumption. The various methods by which these functions and services are performed, together with the institutions concerned and the policies adopted, are necessarily an integral part of the subject of marketing. For various pertinent reasons, the scope of this book is limited to marketing activities as they apply to goods and services other than real estate and financial securities.

## THE MARKET

Intelligent marketing, as indicated above, begins with a consideration of the wants and needs of customers in the market. A market is a *point, place,* or *sphere* in which transfers in the ownership of goods are effected. Actual presence of goods is not essential since the principal characteristic is change of title. In fact, some markets are often devoted largely to the exchange of title to goods rather than to physical transfer of merchandise. Nevertheless, goods tend to be concentrated at trading points. Consequently, *a market may be defined as a sphere within which price-making forces operate and in which exchanges of title tend to be accompanied by the actual movement of the goods affected.*

On a more general plane, the market is the mechanism by which the valuable resources of our society are allocated among the various alternative ends that compete for their use. From the point of view of society, the basic criterion of a good market is efficiency. If the market is inefficient and does not help to maximize consumer satisfactions, then society cannot be content with it. We will never have markets that operate at *optimum* efficiency in the economic sense, because society also places upon markets demands of a noneconomic character. While society seems to desire highly competitive markets, it is also strongly concerned with the welfare and security of individuals. Society wants only efficient middlemen to serve it, but still it desires freedom of entrance for participation in the market as a characteristic of American enterprise. Demands for efficiency or cost reduction are made upon manufacturers and middlemen. At the same time, society insists upon extensive varieties of goods, broad assortments of particular kinds of merchandise, and numerous services, all of which are expensive to provide.

**Attributes of Desirable Markets**

In spite of conflict between economic and noneconomic goals, it is possible to indicate some attributes which make a market socially desirable, as follows:

- Goods and services wanted by society are produced and offered in the right quantities and qualities.
- Desired goods and services are made available at the time and place that they are wanted.
- A fair price is charged for goods marketed. This is a price which in the long run covers the cost of making the goods and providing for their effective distribution.
- Adequate and reliable market information is provided to market participants, both producers (including marketing agencies) and consumers.
- Institutions performing marketing functions are dynamic, modifying their character or offerings in response to changes in customer needs.
- The market is regulated by law to some extent to prevent abuse and for the ultimate welfare of society.

**Various Conceptions**

The foregoing criteria are useful in judging markets in various specific senses in which the term is popularly used. The term sometimes is employed with a *geographical* connotation. Thus it may relate to a highly localized area, as in the case of a municipal retail market, or it may embrace a region, a country, or even the whole world. "There is a world market for grain" and "Los Angeles is a fastgrowing market" are expressions illustrating the point. Furthermore, the term market may relate to a place maintained by an *organization* for the purpose of facilitating buying and selling for its membership, as illustrated by produce exchanges and boards of trade. It may refer to the sphere in which price-making forces of a single *commodity* operate, or it may embrace a large variety of products. Thus, one may speak of the cotton market being brisk or sluggish, or the market for cigarettes being affected adversely by medical reports on cancer causes.

The term market is also commonly used to refer to individuals or firms that may be the potential users or buyers of a product, with obvious emphasis upon the demand side of exchange opportunity. Marketing strategy of many companies is based upon the knowledge that it is impossible to please everyone with the same thing. It is thus common to think of markets as consisting of relatively homogeneous groups of potential customers with similar interests, needs, wants, or other attributes. Consequently, one may refer to various consumer markets as "the teen-age market," "the Negro market," "the bridal market," or "the suburban family market." Sellers often distinguish among various categories of business buyers as, for example, "the variety store market," "the drugstore market," or the "motel and hotel market." Again, a market may be viewed in terms of level of operation as wholesale or retail.

It is thus apparent that a market may be conceived of in several ways and may often consist of a combination of all of them. First, it may mean a geographical area. Second, it may relate to a body or organization of buyers and sellers, possibly on a given plane in the distribution system. Third, it may apply to a combination of forces which determine price and exchange opportunity, in which sense the economist usually discusses the types of markets that exist under monopoly, pure competition, and imperfect competition. Fourth, it may be used to designate potential demand for products or services by classifying or enumerating prospective or actual buyers or users. It is in this last sense that the businessman would think of planning to meet the needs of the market.

In considering market structure and its performance for certain legal purposes or for economic analysis, the concept *relevant market* takes on special significance. In general, it refers to the "area" of effective competition. The *area* may, however, involve products and their cross-elasticities or ready substitutability, a geographic environment of an extremely limited local scope or as wide as the entire United States, a given segment of the total market that is of special or unique import to the problem at hand, a given level or plane of the distributive system, or a combination of two or more of these factors.

## NATURE OF PRODUCT, PRODUCTION, AND ECONOMIC VALUE

As explained above, marketing is concerned with the availability of products to meet needs. Many consumers and businessmen do not understand the significance of marketing because of a narrow and erroneous conception of the essence of a product and of production. A common misconception is to regard a product as a physical thing, thinking of it in terms of form, shape, dimensions, component parts, materials used in construction, etc., and to think of production in terms of the process of contributing these physical attributes.

Basically, however, a product is not a physical thing but consists of the satisfactions or benefits that may be derived from its use or consumption. In this sense, marketing effort is a part of the economic value of every product or service and is so treated in the computations of gross national product and certain of its sectors or segments.

One of the least understood characteristics of marketing activities is their productive nature. [1] It is unfortunate that the term "production" is used in two different ways, causing considerable ambiguity and confusion. In one sense, it is used to denote the *result of industrial activity*, as in referring to the output of farms, factories, or mines. On the other hand, it is more appropriately used in referring to the *whole productive process*, and it is in this sense that it will be used in this discussion and throughout this book.

Economists generally define production as the creation of economic values, which are the *capacities of goods* and *services to satisfy human wants*. Economic value may be described as the characteristics of a good or service which induce people to sacrifice their efforts, either past or present, to obtain it. Value is largely dependent upon utility. The only practical way to measure the utilities or satisfactions created by the productive process is through the expression of values in market prices which form the basis for exchange.

A brief explanation of different kinds of utilities demonstrates how production has been narrowly construed and associated chiefly with industrial activity, and how marketing activity is just as productive and is, in fact, responsible for a very major share of the value of individual products and services and of the total gross national product created annually in the economy.

One type of utility, *form utility,* consist of the conversion or *transformation* of scarce resources to increasingly satisfying states. This may be illustrated by the conversion of copper ore to ingots, to rods, to wire, to part of the ignition apparatus, to part of the internal-combustion engine, and to part of the automobile. As the ore moved from mine to smelting plant, to rolling mill, to wire mill, to electrical machinery plant, to automobile engine plant, and finally to automobile assembly plant, it acquired additional value at each stage because at each point of its progress it was in a more satisfying or more useful state. No one would question whether value was added (i.e., utility created), even when the copper wire may not itself have been changed in form as when it was made part of the ignition apparatus. Nevertheless, all are regarded as part of the transformation or form utility phase of the productive process. At each of these stages value was added, even though no consumer satisfactions whatever had yet been realized and were, in fact, still far in the offing.

In the foregoing illustration it cannot be assumed that the only utility created was that of a change in form through manufacturing activity. The ingots may have been *transferred* from the smelting and refining plant to a rolling mill that was far removed in *space;* and this may have been done *at times* when the mill could best handle the ingots. Furthermore, the two plants may have been under different *ownership,* which would involve not only place and time transfers, but also transfers between persons or firms, thereby creating what are known as *place, time,* and *possession* utilities. The same type of transfers may have been involved in the subsequent stages involving the wire mill, electrical machinery plant, engine plant, and automobile assembly plant.

The example calls attention to the productive character of marketing, even in connection with the creation of what is commonly regarded as *form* utility. This may be demonstrated further in connection with finished consumer goods as, for example, canned soup or fountain pens. Under modern conditions, such goods are mass produced in tremendous quantities. They would have practically no value if it were required that they be used by the people who made them and at the place and time of manufacture. The goods are of no value whatever *to the final consumer* until they are (1) in his *possession,* (2) at his home or other place of consumption, and (3) available *when* he wants to use them.

To illustrate further, when a wholesaler purchases goods from a manufacturer and resells them to a retailer, valuable *possession* utility is created involving two transfers of title with the movement of goods through the accepted channel of trade. When the wholesaler has the goods shipped to him from the factory and delivers them to the retailer, the goods are transferred nearer the place of consumption and further values are added through the creation of *place* utility. Finally, when the wholesaler and the retailer store the goods in the warehouse or on the store's display shelf until wanted by final consumers, the goods are made more useful or satisfying through the addition of *time* utility.

To create all these kinds of utilities, other functions must be performed by both wholesaler and retailer. Illustrative are financing of inventories and receivables, assuming the risk of price changes, advertising and displaying merchandise to make its existence known to those who may have use for it, and keeping informed about market trends and conditions. From the foregoing, it is clear that those who have to do with the movement of goods through channels of trade create utilities, add value to products, and are thus an integral and major part of the productive process. Unfortunately, such a point of view has not always been shared by many economists who, until fairly recent years, tended to confine their discussions of production almost exclusively to the form utility aspects, especially with reference to farming or manufacturing. The tendency in modern economic writings is to give more appropriate recognition to production in the broader, truer, and more meaningful sense. Among those who have given careful study to the matter, it is now well accepted that marketing is a major aspect of the economic process and, hence, the study of marketing is the study of an aspect of economics. As a consequence, it is expected that the future will bring more widespread appreciation of the essential nature of marketing effort and of the value added to products by the creation of time, place, and possession utilities in the marketing process.

## HISTORICAL DEVELOPMENT OF MODERN MARKETING

From earliest history, man has been dependent upon agriculture and upon some forms, however crude, of handicraft or manufacturing activity. Only in very recent times have people, especially in the United States, lived in an economy dominated by marketing-oriented organizations. The rather youthful character of our marketing system as it exists today may be better understood by giving very brief attention to historical changes from primitive times, through the emergence of a middleman system, down to current marketing conceptions.

### EARLY DEVELOPMENTS

The origin of marketing is lost in antiquity. Certainly there is ample evidence of the existence of trade among the ancient Egyptians. Numerous references to trade are to be found in the Old Testament, and the Phoenicians in their heyday were regarded as a nation of wholesalers. Both wholesale and retail trade were well developed during the era of Greek supremacy and in the period of Roman domination.

To be sure, articles traded in the early days of civilization were few. They were restricted largely to luxuries purchased by the rich, due to the costliness and dangers of transportation and the low standards of living. Differentiation of production in the various parts of a country and deficiencies in essentials such as common salt and spices in certain countries also stimulated trade, but in relatively few items. Even as late as the year 1000, villages were characterized by their agrarian, independent nature and by economic self-sufficiency. In every village attempts were made, by methods now considered crude and wasteful, to raise the necessary food supply and to produce other necessaries of existence. With the fall of the Roman Empire, trade seems to have suffered an eclipse for some centuries.

Beginning with the latter part of the Middle Ages the advance from the manorial or village system to the town was rapid. The town became a place of craftsmen and traders. In this handicraft stage, skilled workers set themselves up in their homes as craftsmen, making goods to order. Enterprising craftsmen began to use apprentices and often produced a surplus which was sold at local markets or fairs. This resulted in the organization of markets and in the holding of fairs at periodic intervals. Craftsmen soon organized into guilds, which controlled both manufacturing and marketing by minute regulations, much to the detriment of progress in both. The domestic system, whereby the products of the craftsmen were sold by businessmen, superseded the handicraft stage. With increased protection by stronger and more stable governments, towns grew rapidly and markets gradually expanded. Toward the close of the fifteenth century a period of discoveries began. It resulted in marked improvements in maritime transportation, thereby supplying an added impetus to commerce. With the development of national governments, guilds finally outlived their usefulness, and during the early part of the sixteenth century mercantilism became the guiding principle of state policy. In brief, mercantilists argued that a country could become opulent if it sold more merchandise and services to foreigners than it bought from them. Only in this way could it increase its stock of precious metals that was received in payment required by a "favorable balance of trade" and which, at that time, was considered the ultimate desideratum. Naturally, this movement stimulated commerce to no small degree.

## THE INDUSTRIAL REVOLUTION

In the latter part of the eighteenth century the Industrial Revolution began to usher in marked improvements in form utility production. These were continued throughout the early part of the nineteenth century, but were greatly accelerated in the United States in the period following the Civil War. The domestic stage of manufacture was supplanted almost entirely by factories in which large numbers of specialized workers were employed. Elaborate steam- or motor-driven machinery replaced handicraft methods. Industry became localized, largescale output became the goal of manufacturers, and a minute division of labor began to be considered an essential prerequisite to efficient operation.

Specialization reached such a point that whole communities or areas sometimes devoted a major part of their energy to the making of a single commodity. Thus, Pittsburgh and Gary became known for iron and steel products; Detroit for automobiles; Wisconsin for cheese and other dairy products; California, Florida, and the Rio Grande valley for citrus fruits; and so on. As a result, the geographical chasm separating farm or factory and consumer widened considerably. The agricultural producer, the processor, or the manufacturer cannot ordinarily seek out the final consumer or user of his wares. He finds it more economical to devote his major effort to physical production, where he is presumably of maximum service, and for the most part allows a marketing system to dispose of his finished goods and even to assemble his raw materials for him. Similarly, the consumer or business user finds that any attempt on his part to purchase the numerous commodities necessary to satisfy his increasing and varied wants, directly from their makers, is the height of absurdity. He is, therefore, only too glad in the vast majority of cases to be relieved of the necessity of buying direct and to let the marketing system do it for him.

## EFFECT OF INDUSTRIAL REVOLUTION

It thus becomes obvious that the present middleman system is the outgrowth of changed conditions, the outcome of a growing civilization and industrial progress. As long as towns were economically self-sufficient, producer-consumer contact was feasible except for trade between countries. As soon, however, as localized, large-scale physical production developed, and cities grew in importance, maladjustments made their appearance, marketing risks increased, and an elaborate middleman system was called into existence to bridge over the ever-widening gap that separated the consumer or business user from the manufacturer. To these factors may be added the constant pressure to increase both the scale of industrial output and production for sale instead of own use, both of which are direct results of our factory system.

## NEED FOR MIDDLEMEN

From this brief historical sketch it is apparent that few, if any, middlemen existed in primitive society—a condition that still obtains in underdeveloped parts of the globe. There is hardly any surplus to exchange in primitive or highly underdeveloped communities. Each family is making practically all that is used in the home. Whenever any surplus of products of the soil, chase, or craftsman's art becomes available, the members of the tribe or village effect exchanges directly among themselves. Even during the early part of the handicraft stage in Europe, consumers either visited the shops of craftsmen or the latter abandoned their loom or bench at frequent intervals in order to find buyers for their wares.

On the other hand, whenever a country advanced in civilization, trade flourished as it did in ancient Sumeria, Babylonia, Phoenicia, and Egypt. In later years the Persians, Greeks, and Romans engaged in trade to a considerable extent, which decreased in importance as these nations declined in power. In modern times the ascendancy of trade resulted largely from the Industrial Revolution. This presented in its early days what appeared to be insuperable marketing problems. Marketing functions were therefore shifted more and more to middlemen who specialized in their performance, so that in the latter part of the nineteenth century the basis for the present system of marketing was fairly well established.

Even today in the transfer of title to goods, direct contact may be established. Manufacturers sometimes buy raw materials directly from original producers, and they often purchase semimanufactured goods, parts, equipment, and supplies direct. Similarly, the consuming public buys a limited amount of merchandise direct from farmer or manufacturer. The bulk of farm products and manufactured goods, however, is bought and sold indirectly through one or more middlemen. *Middlemen are, then, individuals, firms, or corporations that stand between prime producers and ultimate consumers, assume title or assist directly in its transfer, and receive a profit for the risks they assume in addition to being paid for the cost of their services or take whatever losses are incident to the assumption of an entrepreneur's functions.* Salesmen are excluded from this group, for they are not in business for themselves and, consequently, assume none of the risks of entrepreneurs and receive no profit, nor do they sustain losses from their sales efforts as such.

## CLASSIFICATION OF MIDDLEMEN

Undoubtedly the most useful classification of middlemen is that based on ownership of the goods. From both legal and practical aspects the relationship to the transfer of title is a most significant factor in defining the position of any group of middlemen. On this basis, *all middlemen can be divided into merchant and functional middlemen. Merchant middlemen buy the goods outright and necessarily take title to them.* Wholesalers and retailers are common examples. *Functional,* or nonmerchant, middlemen ordinarily assist directly in effecting a change in ownership, but they *do not themselves take title to the goods in which they deal. They specialized in the performance of a single marketing function or of a limited number of such functions,* one of which is usually related to the transfer of title. Functional middlemen are best represented by auction companies, brokers, commission houses, manufacturers' agents, and selling agents.

Growing out of the major distinction between merchant and functional middlemen is a difference in degree of risk. All middlemen bear entrepreneurial risks, since they are in business for themselves and they may or may not be successful in securing the necessary volume for profitable operation. Merchant middlemen must, however, bear the additional risk resulting from the uncertain ability to dispose of the goods they own at remunerative prices. Functional middlemen, on the other hand, act for others in the purchase or sale of goods; hence the risks of a changing price level and of uncertain demand or supply conditions are borne by the principals in whom title to the goods vests.

There are, of course, other organizations, institutions, or agencies which facilitate the performance of marketing functions by acting in some specialized capacity. They are not, however, generally regarded as middlemen or as strictly marketing institutions, chiefly because they render no direct assistance in the transfer of title to goods—a characteristic peculiar to all bona fide middlemen and marketing organizations. Among these are railroads, commercial banks, insurance companies, ordinary warehouses, cold storage plants, marketing research agencies, inspectors, and graders. To the extent that they perform distributive and selling functions in certain lines of merchandise, warehouses may be classed among the functional middlemen, and to that extent they constitute an integral part of the marketing system.

## EVOLUTION OF THE MARKETING CONCEPT IN INDUSTRY

Even though marketing functions have long been performed and a middleman system of marketing was well established in the last century, great changes have taken place in the significance attached to marketing by all kinds of companies. In general, this has been a transition from emphasis on selling what a company had to the producing of goods and services that are wanted by the customers that made up the demand side of the market. In the marketing literature of the late 1950's and early 1960's, the newer emphasis has been described as *the marketing concept, marketing orientation, or marketing management philosophy.*

## Example of Transition

The evolution may be illustrated by the experience of a well-known manufacturer, The Pillsbury Company, which, like many other organizations, moved through four eras of emphasis. First, there was the era of *manufacturing dominance.* The company was founded in 1869 by Charles A. Pillsbury on the basis of availability of high-quality wheat and proximity of water power. Major concern was with manufacturing—not marketing. According to a company executive, company philosophy in the era of manufacturing dominance might be stated as follows: "We are professional flour millers. Blessed with a supply of the finest North American wheat, plenty of water power, and excellent milling machinery, we produce flour of the highest quality. Our *basic function is to mill high-quality flour,* and of course (and almost incidentally), we must hire salesmen to sell it, just as we hire accountants to keep our books."

The second era was one of *sales orientation.* By the 1930's, competition had become more significant and the problems of reaching the market had grown much more complex. Company officials became somewhat aware of consumer wants and needs, and formed a commercial research department to develop facts about markets. More attention was given to strengthening the distributing organization, consisting of wholesale and retail grocers. Company philosophy in this era is described as follows: "We are a flour milling company, manufacturing a number of products for the consumer market. We must have a first-rate sales organization which *can dispose of all the products we can make* at a favorable price. We must back up this sales force with consumer advertising and market intelligence. We .want our salesmen and our dealers to have all the tools they need for *moving the output of our plants to the consumer.*"

A third era of *marketing orientation* did not begin until the early 1950's. The company had experienced substantial post-World War II sales growth in new products, principally cake mixes. It realized that it could produce hundreds of new products, and faced the necessity of selecting the best ones. It was considered essential to build into the company organization *a new function* which would coordinate the heretofore separate company responsibilities of selling, advertising, marketing research, and product planning, and provide guidance for other areas. This function was called "marketing," and marketing developed the criteria for determining which products to market. Emphasis shifted from manufacturing and mere sales considerations to a determination of which products would best fit the needs of the company's customers. Company policy for the 1950's was stated as follows: "We make and sell products *for consumers.*"

At the beginning of the 1960's the company was moving into a fourth era of *marketing control,* described by a company official as follows: "Marketing today sets company operating policy short-term. It will come to influence long-range policy more and more.... At Pillsbury, as our fourth era progresses, marketing will become the basic motivating force for the entire corporation. Soon it will be true that every activity of the corporation—from finance to sales to production—is aimed at satisfying the needs and desires of the consumer."

## Other Examples—Structure to Process

While it has been commonplace to identify our marketing *system,* or structure of marketing institutions, primarily with commodity distribution industries—namely, wholesale and retail middlemen—it is clear from the foregoing example that marketing, when considered as a process represents an important activity in manufacturing firms as well, and that the emphasis upon a marketing conception as the *raison d'être* for the manufacturing company as well as the middleman is a relatively recent innovation. Several additional examples formulated to guide business policy in the 1960's illustrate similar conceptions of a marketing basis for business. At The B. F. Goodrich Company, the marketing program is defined as "the process of defining, anticipating, and creating customer needs and wants, and of organizing all the resources of the company to satisfy them at greater total profit to the company and to the customer".

A General Electric Company executive has pointed out a different kind of transition in the orientation of American business in terms of characteristic objectives, "... first, from a focus on profit for the owner to a striving for market position and success against competition, and most recently to a focus on growth in which there is a continuing planned effort to enlarge the size of the market.... So the principal task of the marketing function in a management team wedded to the marketing concept is not so much to be skillful in making the customer do what suits the interests of the business as to be skillful in conceiving and then making the business do what suits the interests of the customer".

In a somewhat similar vein, the President of General Foods Corporation has stated, "Instead of trying to market what it is easiest for us to make, we must find out much more about what the consumer is willing to buy in other words, we must apply our creativeness more intelligently to *people,* and their wants and needs, rather than to *products*".

These examples, while revealing some variation, illustrate several elements common to the so-called modern marketing concept:

- That marketing begins and ends with the needs and wants of customers, not with the goals or objectives of the business organization;
- That marketing is a social process with many participants, not just what one organization might do;
- That marketing is a much broader conception than the mere selling of goods and services, having also to do with research, product and inventory planning, purchasing, physical distribution, and various

facilitating services or activities. Indeed, the above quotations from recent statements by prominent company officials indicate that the business community, to a much greater extent than was formerly the case, views marketing more nearly as it has been viewed for some time in certain of the more widely accepted marketing textbooks and in many university courses on the subject.

## EVOLUTION OF SCIENTIFIC STUDY OF MARKETING

In the wake of the Industrial Revolution and the gradual development of a complex and specialized middleman system of distribution, there has been growing general interest in marketing activities and in institutions. This interest has been responsible for increasing attention to the study of marketing, with a gradual transition from the descriptive to more analytical methods of inquiry, and the development of a theoretical framework.

### EARLY LITERATURE

Early marketing literature consists of authoritative writings which appeared during the period running roughly from the beginning of this century to about 1920. Also during this period formal courses in marketing began to make an appearance in universities, although relatively few such courses were offered until after World War I. In most early books the treatment was almost altogether qualitative. The descriptive method predominated, interspersed with brief analytical discussions of more or less *theoretical* significance. Newness of the subject and lack of quantitative data were, no doubt, responsible for a state of affairs characterized largely by discussions of "what" and "how" in relation to marketing functions and institutions.

### DEFINITIONS AND QUANTITATIVE EMPHASIS

Shortcomings of the descriptive method and the prevailing qualitative treatments were not unrecognized by early students, some of whom are still important contributors in the field. It was generally held that before a classified and systematized body of marketing knowledge could be developed, the subject matter would first have to be defined. Without a correct definition of the elements of which marketing is composed, scientific study of it is impossible. Furthermore, no reasonably accurate quantitative measurement of any phase of marketing can be obtained without first defining its components and delimiting the field of investigation.

The greatest single impetus to the quantitative approach was that of the first Census of Business, taken for the year 1929. It provided a complete enumeration of business establishments, with numerous classifications, including geographical, kind of business, method of operation, legal ownership, sales volume size, and other bases. For the first time, there was a fairly complete picture of the complicated marketing system —one revealing how goods move through channels of distribution to consumption, the relative importance of the different channels, the kind of services performed and costs incurred in the marketing process, and many other hitherto unknown characteristics. Subsequent Censuses of Business have been taken for seven different years and covering a total period of three decades. In the chapters that follow liberal use is made of these data, for they provide the most comprehensive available picture of our marketing *system* and the trends exhibited in the progress of its development.

Another contribution of the first Census of Business was the clarification of many concepts. An important prerequisite to the enumeration and classification of business firms was a careful definition of marketing terminology. Further impetus for precise terminology was provided by various federal and state laws enacted during the 1930's for the purpose of regulating trade practices. For example, some laws dealt with brokerage fees, with taxes on retail units of chain stores, with advertising allowances, with resale price maintenance, etc. In order to enforce such laws, it was essential to state exactly what was meant by each such term so that there would be more or less uniform interpretation. Various pressures for better and clearer definitions have resulted in substantial agreement regarding much of important marketing terminology. As a consequence, the collection, interpretation, and dissemination of data have been facilitated, and many misunderstandings and erroneous conclusions, formerly commonplace, have been avoided or at least minimized.

## EMPHASIS ON PRINCIPLES

The shift in emphasis from the descriptive and qualitative to the quantitative meant that the study of marketing became more *factual*, at least to the extent that it was made in terms of *facts or empirical realities relevant to marketing problems or situations*, i.e., in terms of things, events, or conditions the reality of which (physical, material, psychological, or sociological) is indisputable and manifest (objectively or subjectively as in the case of opinion and expectational research) in marketing experience or which experience indicates may be inferred with certainty.

Marketing *facts* are basic to the formulation of marketing principles. After all, *a marketing principle is an explanatory statement of general truth, derived from a study of facts set up in a cause and effect relationship, that always applies under given conditions or assumptions.*

The assembly of facts in a concrete way and the detailed and comprehensive analysis of them have led to a knowledge of marketing no longer based largely on mere conjecture or on pure deductive reasoning. They have also aided greatly in the development of marketing principles, which are in the nature of significant generalizations derived from a careful analysis of facts and verified in experience. These may be sharply contrasted with *policies, which are rules of action adopted by operating organizations for the purpose of insuring uniformity of procedure under similar circumstances confronting such organizations.* Being man-made and created by persons for a specific purpose, policies may be changed drastically almost at will, while principles change only gradually, if at all, so long as the conditions or assumptions remain unaltered. That there are many principles in the field of marketing goes without question. For example, who would deny the general truth or validity of the following principle? "Since quantities involved in wholesale dealings are so large that even a small change in price becomes significant, and since wholesale organizations are generally more informed with respect to changes in demand and supply conditions and all or most of them receive such information more or less simultaneously, *wholesale prices fluctuate more frequently but less violently than do retail prices.*" Often only the statement of the general truth is made without setting forth the reasons or the sets of facts arranged in a cause and effect relationship, but such a statement is in the nature of a principle nevertheless. A few marketing principles are thus cited below, with varying degrees of brevity, to illustrate their existence and nature:

"Technical products of high unit value tend to have a short channel of distribution."

"As the income of a family increases, the proportion spent by it for food decreases."

"The success of a consumers' cooperative rests, in addition to efficient business management, upon its proximity to a sufficiently large, homogeneous, economy-minded membership willing to subordinate individual tastes and actions to group welfare."

"Because the marketing functions are inherent in the marketing process and must be performed by someone, elimination of the middleman results merely in the transfer or shifting of functions and not in their elimination."

"So long as a given type of marketing institution continues to perform essential functions in a reasonably efficient manner, its existence is economically justified and its continuity is well assured."

"In a competitive economic order it is impossible for an organization continually and generally to undersell all its competitors."

"Unless the use of loss-leaders results in an increase in total volume otherwise not attainable for the user, it tends inevitably to lead to a recoupment of the losses on other items that must of necessity be overpriced." Emphasis on principles tends to enhance our understanding and thus leads to more effective marketing. It also tends to subordinate descriptive material to the analytical. When a sufficient body of principles is adequately developed, it becomes possible to supplement our knowledge of marketing practice with that derived from the development of sound theory.

## MARKETING THEORY

Since the late 1940's, considerable discussion has been devoted to the nature of the generalizations thus far developed in marketing. A number of scholarly writers, while usually acknowledging the existence of principles as explained above, have lamented the lack of a more theoretical approach. When due consideration is given to the newness of scientific investigation of marketing, it appears to the authors that at least reasonable progress has been made in the formulation of sound theory.

### Nature of Existing Theory

While subject to a variety of meanings in common usage, the term *theory*, for purposes of this discussion, is defined to mean *a related or coherent group of facts, principles, and hypotheses*. A hypothesis is a conjectural explanation of variation, a tentative supposition provisionally adopted to explain certain facts and to guide research that might verify or disprove the hypothesis. Where a related body of principles has been developed to explain a class of marketing phenomena, a theory pertaining to such phenomena exists. In areas where the number of definitely formulated principles is at present too limited to afford a complete explanation, available knowledge may be supplemented with hypotheses, and a theory thereby developed. Viewed in this light, there can be no doubt as to the existence of theory in marketing. Certainly there are many areas in the literature characterized by a group of related principles and hypotheses which have been generally agreed upon even though not fully verified. Illustrative are those pertaining to the selection of channels of distribution, marketing functions, cooperative marketing, price determination, and consumer behavior.

## Further Prospects for Theoretical Development

The field of marketing is so vast and is composed of such a large number of complex and varied elements that the development of a body of generalizations so inclusive as to be properly described as "the theory of marketing" appears highly improbable. Instead of one theory, it appears more likely that marketing theory, when more fully developed, will consist of numerous complementary theories of limited scope, built upon the formulation of additional principles, just as there are in economic theory a number of theories of wages, of rent, and of interest. Attention to the theoretical aspects of marketing by leading thinkers in the field is therefore highly desirable because it raises important questions which point the way to further investigation of debatable issues. This gives direction to the application of scientific inquiry in areas of marketing hitherto inadequately explored in an objective manner through fundamental research, and it should contribute to the future development of a more complete and integrated body of marketing knowledge.

It is likely that future contributions to theory will be influenced substantially by two tendencies:

- Greater interest in the contributions that other disciplines can make to marketing knowledge
- Advances in methods and techniques of quantitative analysis.

As indicated earlier, marketing is basically a part of the field of economics, but there are no limits of an economic character to the field of marketing. In the development of the literature, students have also made considerable use of history, psychology, demography, sociology, anthropology, and political science. This interest was greatly accelerated in the late 1950's with the result that businessmen as well as scholars have become more concerned with the contributions that other disciplines can make to our understanding of marketing.

More sophisticated techniques of quantitative analysis, supplemented by high-speed electronic computers, have made possible many new approaches to marketing research. The increasing use of such computers in large business firms has resulted in the availability of many kinds of data that were previously nonexistent or not available in a form suitable for analysis. At the same time, computers have afforded the scholar a means of subjecting hypotheses to rigorous mathematical analysis, with fruitful results in some areas, particularly in relation to physical distribution of commodities.

The nature of the contributions of other disciplines, both in the social sciences and in quantitative analysis, will be illustrated at appropriate points in later portions of this book.

## Is Marketing a Science or an Art

There has been much controversy as to whether marketing is a science or only an art, or more of one and less of the other, depending upon one's frame of reference, understanding of the distinction between the two, and the bias from which the matter is viewed. Under proper scrutiny, however, the controversy tends to dissolve into thin air.

Certainly marketing is one of the social sciences and is a science in the commonly accepted meaning of being a body of accumulated and systematized knowledge. It is equally certain that in more and more studies of the subject the scientific method is employed, the results of which are reflected in the rapidly developing literature of the field. On this point, the following excerpts from a highly authoritative treatment of the subject seem pertinent:

*The classification of facts, the recognition of their sequence and relative significance is the function of science,* and the habit of forming a judgment upon these facts unbiased by personal feeling is characteristic of what may be termed the scientific frame of mind. The scientific method of examining facts is not peculiar to one class of phenomena... it is applicable to social as well as to physical problems. The scientific method is one and the same in all branches.

The field of science is unlimited; its material is endless,

every group of natural phenomena, every phase of social life, every stage of past or present development is material for science. *The unity of all science consists alone in its method, not in its material.* The man who classifies facts of any kind whatever, who sees their mutual relation and describes their sequences, is applying the scientific method and is a man of science. This view has been shared by leading scientists many years before, as exemplified by the following:

The application of Scientific Method cannot be restricted to the sphere of lifeless objects. We must sooner or later have strict sciences of those mental and social phenomena, which, if comparison be possible, are of more interest to us than purely material phenomena.

To be sure, not all leading scientists today would agree with the broad use of the term science as indicated by the above quotations. Nevertheless, even those who object to such wide usage of the term, as in the case of the author of the following quotations, admit that the term science might well be applied to such social areas as marketing:

Of course, one can arbitrarily define the word science in such way as to exclude all the "social sciences," or include all phases of the work of social scientists. There may be merits in a definition, however, such as the one I suggest in that it focuses attention on those aspects of the natural sciences which have been most characteristic of the phenomenal growth of the last three centuries. It neither includes or excludes any of the disciplines usually classified under the heading social science. Rather it suggests that portions of many if not all these disciplines may fall within the scope of the definition—and the areas thus embraced will continually widen.

The performance of marketing functions is also an art in the nature of a skill that can be acquired by experience, study, or observation. Within the business organization, for example, the manager of marketing activities must go about his job of making many kinds of business decisions without the benefit of all the relevant facts that he would like to have. Even when considerable research has provided the information for the evaluation of possible courses of action, *artful* judgment is still required for decision making, especially when considerations of the long-run future are involved. Essentially, there need be no conflict between marketing as a science in terms of a field of knowledge and marketing as an art in the field of practical application. As allegedly stated by Jevons, "A science teaches us to *know,* and an art to *do,* and all the more perfected sciences lead to the creation of corresponding useful arts."

# Chapter 2

# Importance of Marketing

In order to gain a better appreciation of the role of marketing in our economy and in the everyday lives of all our people, it is necessary to obtain a clear picture or conception of marketing and its scope. This may be done by giving consideration both to certain quantitative measures and to some basic conceptual factors that are indicative of the nature and probable extent of the marketing task.

## QUANTITATIVE MEASURES

At any given time, the importance and magnitude of the marketing task may be approximated by a number of quantitative measures, including the following:

- Personal consumption expenditures
- The gross national product
- Volume of trade transacted
- Vastness of the institutional structure for the performance of marketing activities
- Employment in marketing, or the persons who do the job
- Value added by marketing

### PERSONAL CONSUMPTION EXPENDITURES

In any given year, total personal consumption expenditures reflect the level of living of our people. At the same time they indicate to a large extent the magnitude of the marketing task because, except for housing, government, and certain business expenditures, they mark the end result of all economic effort including that of marketing and represent the value of goods and services currently delivered by the nation's economy to its people for use and absorption. In a sense, they also furnish a basis for judging our capacity to consume under given economic and business conditions and thus aid, in a very general way, but in a restricted sense, in measuring the marketing task.

In 1960, personal consumption expenditures amounted to $329 billion, an increase of 297 per cent over the level of $79 billion reported for 1929, the most prosperous year in our pre-World War II history.

Much of this increase may be attributed, however, to the higher price level prevailing in the later year. The Consumer Price Index of the U.S. Bureau of Labor Statistics was, in fact, 73 per cent higher in 1960 than in 1929. When proper statistical adjustments are made to compensate for the effects of price level changes, the result is that the increase in constant dollars or in real volume was still 141 per cent over 1929. Thus, over three decades, it is evident that the marketing task had more than doubled.

## GROSS NATIONAL PRODUCT

The *total national output* of goods and services produced by our economy and expressed on an annual basis at current market prices or in constant dollars is known as the gross national product or more familiarly as GNP It is a fairly comprehensive measure of the total marketing task that involves relatively little duplication, since GNP is made up of values added or of the aggregate of all *final* purchases when combined with the change in business inventories rather than of the sum of all transactions.

The largest group of final purchasers is to be found in the consumption market as expressed in terms of personal consumption expenditures which comprise, since 1947, an average of 66 per cent of GNP and a range of 63 to 70 per cent. This is usually referred to as the consumer market. It includes all goods and services, except homes, purchased by ultimate consumers and involves dealings in various wholesale markets as well as at the retail level. The marketing task, however, is by no means confined to the consumer area. Beginning with the 1950's the second most important market area has been that involving government purchases of goods and services, which account for about 20 per cent of GNP. Historically, the role of government as a provider of defense and other public services has tended to grow in importance.

The third market comprised in the GNP total consists of gross private domestic investment and covers expenditures for residential construction, on business plant and equipment, and changes in business inventories. This segment accounts for about 14 or 15 per cent of GNP. The remainder of GNP is made up of net exports of goods and services, if any, an of personal savings.

From the above it is quite clear that a large part of the marketing task is necessarily related to other than consumer goods since in 1960, for example, GNP was about 54 per cent greater than the amount of personal consumption expenditures. It involves the marketing of goods and services to the government, marketing activities by the government, the marketing of goods and services for business use, the marketing of new construction and its components, etc.

## VOLUME OF TRADE

Data on personal consumption expenditures or gross national product do not fully reflect the scope of the marketing task because in our complex order of economic specialization, it is usually necessary, before goods reach their ultimate destination, that they change hands and ownership two or more times in their movement through channels of trade.

In ascertaining the *total volume of trade* transacted, it is first necessary to determine the value of goods marketed by original producers in agricultural or extractive industries, by manufacturers or processors, and by importers. To this must be added the sales of wholesale establishments and retail stores, and sales and other receipts of personal, business, and repair service establishments. The sum of all of these figures includes considerable duplication in value because manufacturing companies, for example, obtain supplies of raw materials from agricultural and extractive industries, and their value is again reflected in sales of manufactured goods. Value previously contributed by manufacturing and extractive industries is again included in sales of wholesale establishments. All previous contributions are included in retail store and service establishment sales data, along with that value which is added by the functions performed in these particular businesses and by the transportation agencies in moving the goods to them.

The total volume of trade varies from one year to another, depending upon the physical output of the nation's economy and the price level that happens to prevail. What is of special significance to the student of marketing is the fact that the marketing system must provide facilities to accommodate a volume of trade several times as great as the aggregate of total production or expenditures for current ultimate consumption.

## VASTNESS OF MARKETING STRUCTURE

Another way of gauging the importance of marketing is to ascertain the character of the intsitutional structure which has evolved to perform the marketing functions. To be sure, all kinds of business establishments are engaged in marketing goods and services. Agricultural producers, manufacturing establishments or factories, mines, wells, and quarries in the extractive industries are not, however, usually included within the scope of the institutional structure for marketing. While concerned with marketing in varying degrees, their primary contribution is usually that of creating form utility.

If attention is confined to establishments that are engaged principally in marketing goods and services (commonly referred to as the "distributive trades"), the record is still very impressive. There were in 1958, according to the Census of Business, 1,788,325 retail establishments, 290,018 wholesale establishments, and some 975,250 business service, personal service, and repair establishments. Thus, the total number of establishments primarily engaged in marketing amounts to something in excess of 3 million. Even this is a very conservative appraisal because it does not include any transportation agencies, banks and other financial institutions, radio and television broadcasting companies, legal firms, accounting firms, and many other businesses whose work is principally or substantially that of facilitating the marketing process.

## EMPLOYMENT IN MARKETING STRUCTURE

Still another criterion is the number of people employed in marketing. This is impossible to determine exactly because so many people in the agricultural, extractive, and manufacturing industries are engaged in the performance of marketing functions. The number so employed, or the portion of time devoted to marketing by those who have a variety of duties, has never been ascertained with any degree of accuracy.

If attention is again confined merely to marketing establishments or the so-called distributive trades, employment within this specialized segment of the economy in 1958 amounted to some 17 million persons, of which 9.7 million were engaged in retailing nearly 3 million in wholesaling, and 3.8 million in the various service industries enumerated in the Census of Business. Employment in such marketing establishments was slightly more than one-fourth the total number of persons employed that year.

Over the long run, the proportion of the civilian labor force employed in marketing has exhibited an upward secular trend as work on farms and in factories has become more mechanized and more specialized, on the one hand, and the task of marketing has increased in magnitude and complexity, on the other. In one major research study it was indicated that the number of persons employed in the distribution or marketing of commodities was, in 1950, more than four times greater, *relative to the number engaged in the production of commodities*, than it was in 1870.

## VALUE ADDED BY MARKETING

The most meaningful manner of judging the importance of marketing is by measuring the value that is added by the performance of marketing functions. Since widespread interest in such measurement is of recent origin, accurate data regarding the total contribution of marketing are yet to be compiled. Reasonably comprehensive, though incomplete, estimates are available for value added in the process of marketing finished consumer goods, as indicated by the spread between the value of commodities leaving the distributive system and their value when they entered it. This measures the value contributed by retailers and by wholesalers (when commodities are handled by them) between the time of sale by manufacturer and the time of sale to ultimate consumer. For all consumer goods, the total value added by such marketing establishments amounts to about 37 per cent of the final retail price.

Such measurements greatly understate the *total value contributed in the marketing process* because they do not take into account the value added by marketing raw materials from farm to factory, by marketing manufacturing equipment from one manufacturer to another, by marketing semimanufactured goods and parts between different stages of manufacture, by marketing raw materials and supplies which enter into the creation of services in the service industries, and by the marketing of consumer goods by others than retailers and wholesalers. They do, nevertheless, help to visualize the importance of marketing in our economy.

While the foregoing discussion may serve to indicate quantitatively the significance of marketing, it does not reflect adequately its complexity. Certain basic concepts may prove helpful in this regard and should also contribute to an understanding of the contents of subsequent chapters. The basic conceptual factors to be introduced include:

- Variety and classes of products marketed
- Marketing functions
- Channels of distribution

## VARIETY AND CLASSES OF PRODUCTS

Owing to the hundreds of thousands of articles moving daily through arteries of commerce, it is impractical to analyze the characteristics of each commodity or product; hence, goods are classified to make the study of marketing comprehensible.

## CLASSIFICATION OF PRODUCTS

The following classification of products (goods and services) is significant because of differences in origin, destination, distributive channels, and special marketing problems:

- Consumer Products
  - Agricultural commodities
  - Products of extractive industries
  - Manufactured goods
- Convenience goods
  - Shopping goods
  - Specialty goods
- Consumer services
- Industrial Products
  - Agricultural commodities (raw materials)
  - Products of extractive industries
- Raw materials
- Supplies
- Manufactured goods
  - Semimanufactured goods
  - Parts
  - Machinery (installations)
  - Equipment
  - Supplies
- Business services

The basic classification is according to *destination*. Industrial products are purchased by business units, not for personal consumption, but to assist in, or to enter into, the production of other goods or services.

In contrast with consumer products, they are usually marketed under conditions where transactions involve large amounts; they are often purchased according to specifications; and they are more subject to the influence of business fluctuations. Consumer products, on the other hand, are purchased by people because of the satisfactions they are expected to yield. They are bought by the ultimate consumer usually in small quantities, often without careful advance planning, and commonly on the basis of nonrational or emotional considerations.

The secondary classification is according to *origin.* Because of vagaries of nature and other factors, the quantity and quality of agricultural production are not easily controlled; because of numerous relatively small producers, there are unusual problems of assembling for shipment to markets; partly resulting from the acceptance of agriculture as a way of life as well as a form of business operation, more problems of social control and public assistance arise. Products of extractive industries (e.g., mining, quarrying) are, in a sense, a gift of nature. Thus, freedom of location is limited, and there are unusual problems of grading and transportation to markets. Manufactured products are in marked contrast, since quality can be controlled in relation to standards; quantity can be adjusted to market demand; and plant location decisions can be made on the basis of marketing as well as manufacturing cost factors. Special marketing considerations associated with various subclassifications shown above are indicated in the following more detailed discussion.

## PRODUCTS OF AGRICULTURE AND EXTRACTIVE INDUSTRIES

Agriculture supplies a large proportion of the world's foodstuffs and industrial raw materials. Many products, such as certain fruits and vegetables are ready for consumption when leaving the farm. Others, such as grain, livestock, and textile fibers, are raw materials and must pass through one or more manufacturing processes. Certain products at the time of leaving the farm may function either as raw materials or as consumer goods. Products of extractive industries, such as mining, lumbering, and fishing, also consist of both consumer goods and raw materials. Some coal, for example, leaves mines destined for the household, but a much larger tonnage becomes raw material or supplies for industry. The distribution of consumer goods often differs from that used in marketing raw materials, and the marketing mechanism for raw materials from the farm frequently differs from that used in the distribution of raw materials from the extractive industries.

For example, the extent to which middlemen are used in marketing raw materials depends upon such factors as the number of processing stages through which the material goes, its ultimate uses, and the scale of production and consumption. In general, raw materials from farms, with the exception of those sold to local users, pass through the hands of more middlemen than do products of forests and mines, largely because of the smaller scale of agricultural production. Consumer goods from farms frequently must be concentrated by local shippers for economical transportation, whereas manufactured consumer goods, because of larger scale of production, go through no such concentrating process.

## SEMIMANUFACTURED GOODS AND PARTS

Semimanufactured goods, such as pig iron, copper, most flour, and lumber, represent commodities which enter into other products before use by the final consumer or the business user. Some parts are like semimanufactured goods, since they must go through another manufacturing process, assembling, before they are ready for use. Examples include automotive parts and electric motors that become part of household appliances. From another point of view, parts must be separately considered because they have a double market, the so-called "after market" (repair or replacement market) and the original equipment market, whereas semimanufactures are intended only for industrial use. The scale of semimanufactured goods marketing is large, the number of users is small, and sale is usually made directly from maker to user.

## MACHINERY, EQUIPMENT, AND SUPPLIES

Machinery, equipment, and supplies do not become a part of the finished product. Oil, stationery, office equipment, machinery, and store fixtures are familiar examples. Marketing methods and channels differ widely. Much machinery is manufactured to order of user and sold directly to him. In some cases, such as machine installations, if the seller has important patent rights, the purchaser has little choice of source of supply. Selling costs may be quite low. On the other hand, maximum selling costs may be experienced in the sale of equipment where the seller faces the task of converting reluctant and uninformed buyers to customers for his products.

## CONSUMER GOODS

The term consumer goods, as applied to the entire range of commodities used by final consumers, embraces three classes, namely: convenience goods, shopping goods, and specialty goods.

### Convenience Goods

Convenience goods are articles which consumers purchase with a minimum of searching, measured either in terms of time or money spent in shopping, because the probable gain or satisfaction from making comparisons of alternatives is ordinarily slight. Such purchases usually involve a small unit price. The consumer is familiar with the goods wanted, demand is clearly defined as soon as a want is recognized, and prompt satisfaction is desired. The demands of the consumer with respect to such merchandise lead him to expect ready accessibility. Tobacco, drugs, confectionery products, some hardware, and staple groceries are good examples.

Once a consumer recognizes that his stock of cigarettes is low, he wishes to replenish it with the least possible trouble. The individual purchase is small and frequent. The buyer knows the particular kind desired, and it is convenient to find a seller at no great distance from where he is at the time when his want is recognized. This explains why cigarettes are sold in so many stores. Thus, a tobacco manufacturer, to realize maximum sales, must have wide distribution. The difficulty of selling directly to thousands of retailers—many of them small—leads him to employ wholesalers who can more effectively distribute to the retail trade. With many stores handling convenience goods, the volume of sales for any designated item in the average store tends to be small, and the store must sell numerous individual items. With thousands of retailers, each buying small quantities of any one manufacturer's goods, wholesalers become an important distributive factor. The retailer whose stocks include items produced by hundreds of different manufacturers would find it difficult and very expensive to buy directly from manufacturers. Much time would be consumed in buying and accounting, and transportation costs on many small shipments would be excessive. Moreover, most manufacturers of convenience goods would be unable or unwilling to assume the burdens and risks of direct selling.

Some manufacturers of extensive lines of related products do, however, find it practicable to deal directly with retailers, particularly the larger outlets. Certain grocery and drug product manufacturers, for example, can sell directly to retailers since the size of the typical order is increased by the number of related items which are offered for sale together. Nevertheless, most manufacturers of convenience goods find it best to sell through wholesalers, and most retailers of such merchandise regard the wholesaler as their logical source of supply.

The neighborhood store, whether operated by the owner or of the chain store type, and whether operated singly or as part of a group of stores in a shopping center, is the outstanding outlet for convenience goods. Convenience of customers, however, calls for retail distribution of such goods not only in stores of residential neighborhoods and in shopping centers but also in downtown stores. The housewife may find the neighborhood drygoods or variety store, for example, a great convenience in purchasing such articles as thread, pins, and needles. On the other hand, if she happens to be shopping downtown and has purchased material for a dress, she may find it more convenient to buy thread and needles in the same store. Because of the frequency of purchase and use of convenience goods, the consumer ordinarily is reasonably well informed regarding the characteristics of at least several brands of each type. For this reason, the shopper needs little or no assistance from salespeople. Hence, selfservice merchandising techniques have attained the highest degree of development in marketing convenience goods.

## Shopping Goods

Shopping goods are in contrast with convenience goods in that the consumer has a relatively large potential gain or satisfaction by making price, quality, or style comparisons among alternative sellers or among alternative items within a particular store before making a purchase. The shopper's concept of what to buy and where to buy it is not clearly defined when a want is recognized. The shopper wants to examine the offerings of a number of stores and make a decision on the basis of actual comparison. The purchase is of sufficient magnitude or significance to warrant some expenditure of time and effort in shopping.

Shopping goods are not purchased, by most persons, as frequently as are convenience goods. Convenience in buying is overshadowed by the desire to institute comparisons, which are facilitated by a grouping of the stores selling shopping goods. The most important groupings are to be found in downtown business districts and in large or so-called "regional" shopping centers where department stores and specialty stores in the apparel and home furnishings lines abound. Neighborhood stores cannot ordinarily build a large enough volume in shopping lines, because the limited sales potential in any one neighborhood does not permit these stores to carry sufficient assortments of merchandise to provide a basis for comparisons.

The retail distribution of shopping goods contrasts sharply with that of convenience goods in many ways, especially in number of outlets. Shopping goods tend to be sold at a relatively small number of large or specialized retail stores, while convenience goods, other than those handled by a supermarket, are generally sold in a large number of relatively small stores. Since the department stores and most specialized stores selling shopping goods are centrally located, eithed in downtown shopping or in large shopping centers, they draw their patronage from a wide territory and are often large institutions. The sales volume of typical shopping goods stores permits direct dealing with manufacturers. Moreover, many manufacturers of shopping goods, such as women's clothing, make a relatively full line of goods so that their *unit of sale* is large enough to make direct selling feasible.

## Specialty Goods

Specialty goods are those that have some particular attraction other than price, which induces the consumer to put forth special effort to visit the store handling them. The attraction lies in special qualities which differentiate the goods from similar merchandise with the result that the consumer does not care to make comparisons before purchasing, or it may reside in the distinctive characteristics of the store handling the merchandise. Specialty goods contrast with convenience goods in that their purchase is sufficiently important to induce the consumer to visit rather inaccessible sources of supply, if necessary, and to postpone action until the store can be visited.

Some of the prestige brands of men's clothing, major household appliances, sporting goods equipment, and electronic equipment are examples of products often purchased as specialty goods. Many men confine their clothing purchases to a single manufacturer's line and habitually patronize the same retailer. To them the particular brand has distinctive and favored characteristics. They will take the trouble to visit a downtown store, partly because they strongly prefer a special brand and because they buy at considerable intervals of time.

While specialty goods are ordinarily of high unit value, this is not necessarily the situation. The test lies in the strength of the preferences which exist for the distinctive qualities of a particular good or outlet. These qualities may be unique physical attributes of a product, or they may consist of differentiations in the psychological realm, such as the prestige associated with a brand name or the personality of the retail enterprise. For example, some men have such strong preferences for a particular brand of cigars or smoking tobacco that they go to considerable trouble to visit out-of-the-way stores where the brand is sold. If they refuse to accept substitutes when the desired brand is not available and are willing to expend considerable effort in making purchases, then the article must be considered a specialty good, even if there are other products with exactly the same characteristics and capable of producing the same physical satisfactions.

The manufacturer of a specialty good may find it unnecessary to have a wide retail distribution. In fact, there may be distinct advantages in limiting distribution to one or a few selected outlets in each city. Such a practice may simplify selling problems, and at the same time encourage selected retailers to market the line aggressively and furnish desirable service to consumers. Because consumers seek out the local dealer, the limited number of retail outlets may prove no detriment to the manufacturer. The small number of stores necessary for effective distribution encourages the manufacturer to sell directly to the retail trade.

## Some Reservations

The classification of merchandise discussed above is subject to several qualifications. Obviously, it is based upon buying habits of consumers. Not all consumers buy the same kind of merchandise in the same way. One man may buy a suit of clothes only after comparing prices, qualities, and styles of several manufacturers. For him clothing is a shopping good. Another man may habitually buy a certain manufacturer's brand, and for him clothing is a specialty. One woman may shop for laundry equipment while another may insist on a particular brand. Hosiery may be a convenience good for one individual, a shopping good for another, and a specialty for a third. Any one consumer's habit of buying and the dominant motives in buying are subject to change. An individual who shops for clothing may chance to buy a brand which pleases him and has such distinctive features that, thereafter, he may confine his purchases to the particular brand. For him, this brand of clothing has become a specialty. Furthermore, there are numerous commodities which are difficult to classify, being of a borderline nature. Besides, the habits of consumers as a group may undergo important changes. There is more of a tendency on the part of consumers to shop for groceries now than in the past, largely because of the automobile and the frequent concentration of several supermarkets within a shopping center. Thus, a specialty good may in time become a convenience good, as illustrated by prepared baby foods which were first handled through drugstores and later through the grocery trade, or it may become a shopping good. The latter case is illustrated by the electrical appliance market. When a new appliance is first developed, the number of competitive makes is naturally very limited, and each is likely to enjoy the advantage of being purchased as a specialty good. The Bendix automatic washing machine, for example, was the first appliance of this type and was originally sold entirely as a specialty good. When the product proved popular, other manufacturers entered the field. Now, with a number of nationally advertised and distributors' private brands of completely automatic washing machines, most customers make comparisons regarding prices, terms of sale, construction features, style, operation methods, and so on, before buying. Thus, a given product may move from the shopping to the specialty or to the convenience category, from the specialty category to that of convenience, or from the convenience to the shopping classification, but very seldom from the convenience class to the specialty field. In spite of these reservations, the classification of consumer goods on the basis of consumer shopping habits *as a whole* is practical and useful and provides an excellent starting point in the solution of numerous complex marketing problems.

## SERVICES

The marketing of services is, in many respects, similar to the marketing of tangible commodities, but certain distinctions are important. Services, like commodities, are destined for business use or for ultimate consumption, but it is often difficult to classify them on this basis. To cite one example, the business firm and the ultimate consumer may require identical types of banking services, such as a checking account or a single payment loan, but for quite different reasons. As is the case with industrial goods, business services must be marketed on the basis of their significance in the productive process. In other words, business services become part of the expense structure of a firm, and their cost must be recovered in the price of other goods and services. Ultimate consumers, on the other hand, buy services for the same motivation that is involved in buying tangible goods, namely, the satisfaction derived as an individual or family user.

The complexity of service marketing is indicated by a listing of a few common types of service enterprises. These include such personal service establishments, as barber and beauty shops, automobile and other repair establishments, amusement and recreation organizations, hotels and motels, financial institutions, and storage and transportation companies, and such business services as accounting firms, advertising agencies, credit bureaus, consulting and legal firms, and research organizations.

In spite of this complexity, certain generalizations are noteworthy. One distinctive feature of service marketing is that the product cannot, in most instances, be separated readily from the producer, in contrast to tangible commodities. So it is ordinarily impossible to distinguish clearly between the creation of a service and the marketing of it. Since services are ordinarily produced as wanted, there is no problem of physical supply. Still, it is essential that services be available at the times and places wanted. Thus marketers of services are concerned with providing time and place utility, which are the contributions of the transportation and storage functions of marketing.

While there is usually no tangible product directly involved in marketing services, there is often some tangible evidence of service performed, and the marketing of many services is closely related to the marketing of goods. Tangible evidence of a service may be illustrated by insurance policies, by reports prepared by accounting or consulting firms, and by legal briefs. Telephones and air-conditioning units are examples of products closely related to the marketing of different kinds of public utility services.

Since services are usually marketed as they are created, channels of distribution are commonly direct. In some cases, however, middlemen are significant, as illustrated by agents or brokers who sell insurance, securities, travel service, or theatre tickets. Some service establishments market on a wholesale basis. Illustrative are certain laundries, cleaners, and repair establishments that sell through regular retail establishments to the ultimate consumer, who has no direct contact with the firm actually producing the service.

The classification of convenience, shopping, and specialty goods may be applied to consumer services with the same import and reservations as indicated in the preceding section. For example, personal services, such as dry cleaning or shoe repair, are commonly purchased on a convenience basis, although some people will buy them on the basis of the highly specialized appeal of a particular producer. House painting or carpet cleaning are illustrative of services often bought after considerable shopping effort to compare prices and expected quality of work. Various highly technical services, such as termite treatment for homes, are commonly marketed on a specialty basis.

## MARKETING FUNCTIONS

One of the best ways to obtain an appreciation of the nature and extent of the marketing task is through an understanding of the basic functions which are the essence of the marketing process.

### MARKETING FUNCTIONS DEFINED AND LISTED

*A marketing function may be defined as a major economic activity which is inherent in the marketing process, pervades it, and which, through a continuous division of labor, tends to become specialized.* In this sense a marketing function is not a technique, a tool, or a special activity that may be properly considered as but a part or phase of some more basic function. Specialization may be intraorganizational or interorganizational—the former is illustrated by the existence of salesmen or buyers in a marketing company and the latter by companies that specialize in the performance of a particular function or aspect of a function.

The major functions which are recognized when marketing is viewed as a social process may be quite different from specific marketing activities which are performed by individual companies. Some writers have listed numerous detailed marketing activities of manufacturers or middlemen, and have proceeded to call them marketing functions, thus confusing the activities of selected individual enterprises with marketing functions, even though some of the activities are not universal in their application or inevitable, and despite the fact that marketing functions are also being performed daily by farmers and consumers. Others have set down the numerous *activities* involved in marketing a given commodity and have labeled them marketing functions. This method, too, is subject to the objection that many of the activities in connection with a specific commodity are but part of a major marketing function or are not universally applicable.For the sake of simplicity and clarity, the authors have confined their statement of functions to those *major activities that must be performed in the marketing of all products*. These functions are:

- Buying
- Selling
- Transportation
- Storage
- Standardization and grading
- Financing
- Risk bearing
- Marketing information

The first two of these functions are known as the *functions of exchange,* for they are directly concerned with the change in ownership. They are complementary in the sense that both are involved in every transaction. For every sale there is a purchase and for every purchase there must be a sale. Transportation and storage are the *functions of supply,* frequently referred to as *physical distribution,* both having to do with the actual, physical handling of goods incident to their movement from places of plenty to places of relative scarcity or to their storage from times of plenty to times of scarcity, or with the provision of services at times and at places as needed. The remaining functions, namely, standardization, financing, risk bearing, and the collection and dissemination of marketing information, are *facilitating functions,* inasmuch as each of them aids in the performance of all of the other marketing functions.

To some critics it may appear that certain activities are not covered by these eight functions. The so-called function of *assembling* goods in large quantities for economical shipment and handling or from different sources for the purpose of providing an assortment of merchandise may, upon closer analysis, well be considered but a part of the buying function. Similarly, the so-called function of *dividing* large quantities into the smaller amounts required by customers is but a small part of the selling function; while *packaging,* which is sometimes named as a separate marketing function, is often but coincidental to the function of grading and standardization and may at times even be regarded as a manufacturing rather than marketing operation. It is therefore believed that practically all activities of those engaged in marketing are embraced in the functions herein outlined.

## CHANNELS OF DISTRIBUTION

Still another method of judging the magnitude and complexity of the marketing task is by giving consideration to the multiplicity of channels through which products move from origin to destination.

### CHANNEL OF DISTRIBUTION DEFINED

*The course taken in the transfer of title to a product constitutes its channel of distribution.* The title may be transferred directly, as when the product is bought or sold outright, or indirectly, as when the transaction is negotiated through a functional middleman such as an agent or broker who does not himself actually take title to it. It is the *route taken by the title to a product in its passage from its first owner,* the agricultural producer or manufacturer as the case may be, *to the last owner,* the ultimate consumer or the business user. The links in the channel or chain of distribution of necessity include both such owners inasmuch as they always participate to some extent in the marketing process.

## VERTICAL ASPECTS

Normally, the channel of distribution is viewed vertically, that is, from the standpoint of the various *types* of links of which it is composed. It is concerned with the number of levels through which the title to goods is passed in the flow from source to final destination. For example, a manufacturer may sell direct to consumers, or he may utilize different types of middlemen who perform a variety of functions at different stages in the flow of title transfer. The most common vertical variations in channels for consumer and industrial goods, respectively.

The simplest channel is obviously that where manufacturers sell direct to consumers. This is sometimes accomplished by those who make a wide line of related merchandise, the sales of which can support the operation of company-owned retail establishments. Stores operated by some manufacturers of paint or of men's clothing are illustrative. The direct channel is also used by manufacturers of articles that have qualities sufficiently distinctive to make possible mail-order sales. A third method of direct sale is through house-to-house salesmen.

A number of situations account for the manufacturer-retailer-consumer channel. Many manufacturers of men's and women's clothing sell direct to retailers, because the retailers handling such goods ordinarily purchase in fairly large quantities. This may be true because the stores are large, as in the case of department stores, or because they specialize in a limited line of merchandise. The channel is also used by some manufacturers of perishable commodities. The meat packing industry is illustrative; here, sale to retailers through company-owned branches is common because of the financial strength of large producers and because of the special storage and handling requirements of the commodity. A less direct channel is to use agents or brokers to contact the retail trade. Such a channel is usually favored by small or specialized manufacturers who cannot afford to maintain their own sales organizations. Sales may be made more economically through agents or brokers because their costs of distribution are spread over the product lines of several manufacturers. This channel is generally used in contacting large retailing organizations, such as chain stores, department stores, and larger specialty stores.

The manufacturer-wholesaler-retailer-consumer channel is most common in the distribution of convenience goods to independent retail stores. Most manufacturers of tobacco, hardware, drugs, groceries, and other convenience goods have only a few products in their line of merchandise and cannot economically contact the thousands of retail stores needed for adequate distribution. Consequently, they call upon wholesalers who stock merchandise and cultivate the entire retail market, even in the remotest regions. Then there are numerous companies whose potential sales volume is so small or whose business is of such a seasonal nature that they cannot develop a sales organization to contact even wholesalers. This accounts in large measure for the use of agents and brokers who serve as substitutes for a manufacturer's own selling organization. In the canned fruit and vegetable industry, for example, many small manufacturers market through food brokers, who render a comparable service to other grocery product companies, including many flour millers and beet sugar refining companies.

In marketing business or industrial goods, direct manufacturer-user relationships are more common. Industrial installations usually involve sales of high unit value and require factory-trained sales engineers for effective sale and service. Semimanufactured goods, such as sheet steel and parts, like motors for washing machines, are usually sold in large individual contracts. Consequently, many manufacturers of such items are able to sell direct. Producers of standardized equipment and tools of the type used in numerous factories often find it more economical to distribute through industrial wholesalers. Operating in a manner similar to the consumer goods wholesaler, but selling to industrial users rather than to retail stores, these organizations are to be found in all principal cities and are known by such terms as *industrial distributors, mill supply houses, equipment distributors,* and so on. Short-line manufacturers of industrial goods often use agents and brokers for the same reason that these functional middlemen are used in consumer goods marketing.

**Marketing Establishments of Integrated Firms**

An important vertical phase of channels—namely, the position of marketing establishments that are owned and operated by integrated companies. Examples are manufacturer-owned retail stores, manufacturer-owned wholesale branches, warehouses, or petroleum bulk tank distributing stations, and retailer-owned wholesale warehouses. According to a strict interpretation of the definition of the term *channel of distribution,* one may question the inclusion of such establishments in a discussion of channels. Actually, there is no *legal* transfer of title between factory and manufacturer-owned sales branch or retail store, nor is there any between the chain store warehouse and retail units in the same organization.

Since, however, the census is taken on the basis of establishments and the information must be published for individual industries and lines of trade and by states and local areas, it is necessary that each reporting *unit* of a multiple-unit organization report as though it were operated as an independent establishment. That procedure is followed by the Bureau of the Census, even when goods are transferred from one plant of a manufacturing company to another for further processing; and while they are designated as *interplant transfers,* they are viewed as in the nature of sales or shipments. Furthermore, manufacturers' wholesale branches and chain store warehouses operate similar to independent wholesale establishments of the same character, and manufacturers' own retail stores operate similar to independent or chain retail stores of the same type and character. *Functionally,* therefore, such establishments operating on the same level are fairly identical irrespective of differences in ownership. Failure to consider them as links in the chain of distribution would lead to confusion when comparing one channel with another or in comparing costs of distributing through alternative channels. From a practical standpoint, therefore, transfers of goods to different kinds of establishments within an integrated company must be considered in the nature of sales.

## HORIZONTAL ASPECTS

Many manufacturers also have important alternatives to consider with regard to the *horizontal* aspects of different levels in the channel. On any given level (wholesale or retail) there are many different kinds of establishments when classified by line of goods handled or by method of operation. Although the situation varies considerably from one line of goods to another, the character of the problem may be illustrated with an example. Prepared baby foods were originally marketed as specialty goods and were sold chiefly through drugstores, because they were purchased by mothers upon the advice of pediatricians or general medical practitioners who prescribed feeding programs for babies. When the first mass producer of such goods began to sell them through the grocery trade, a different channel was used even though it may have comprised the same types of links.

More recently, this was illustrated by the change made by another manufacturer of such items who primarily produced drug merchandise and hence found it natural to sell also the few baby food items through such line of business. This manufacturer originally distributed these products through wholesale drug firms who, in turn, sold them to the retail drug trade. As such products became more widespread in use, they were purchased by the housewife as convenience goods and mostly in retail grocery outlets. Because wholesale druggists did not have contact with retail grocery outlets, many wholesale grocers purchased the products from wholesale druggists and in this unnatural manner the items eventually found their way to the retail grocer. The marketing pattern changed to such an extent that about 85 per cent of total consumer purchases of these baby foods was being made from grocery stores. When this was recognized by the manufacturer, a decision was made to simplify the channel of distribution by making the product directly available to wholesale grocery organizations.

This change was fraught with real significance. National distribution was formerly accomplished by direct dealings at the most with only about 300 wholesale drug firms. Wholesale grocers, however, are much more numerous. It would be essential to contact at least about 3,000 such firms to provide dense nation-wide coverage among retail grocery outlets. This called for basic marketing changes. Since it was not feasible for the manufacturer to expand his own sales organization to the extent necessary to handle such a large number of channel contacts, food brokers were employed to sell from the manufacturer to wholesale grocery organizations. Thus, a decision to modify the channel horizontally on the wholesale level, by shifting from drug wholesalers to grocery wholesalers, was a channel problem of very great importance. Even in the absence of the introduction of brokers, the shift from drug to grocery wholesale outlets was of sufficient significance to constitute a change in the channel of distribution.

Horizontal modifications of channels have become increasingly important. In former decades, it was rather common to find that there was a single natural channel for many kinds of commodities. Especially since the middle 1940's, however, there has been considerable diversification of merchandise lines by many kinds of stores. Many drug items, toilet goods, and housewares are now sold in food stores, especially of the supermarket type. The modern large drugstore sells many items of general merchandise not formerly part of drugstore retailing. Many automobile accessory stores have become rather complete hard-line stores, handling all kinds of household appliances, hardware, lawn and garden supplies, and housewares. Such changes, sometimes popularly described as "scrambled merchandising," have increased the complexity of horizontal aspects of many manufacturers' distribution efforts.

## OTHER CHANNEL VARIATIONS

There are additional reasons which complicate the channel question. Many manufacturers find it necessary or desirable to use more than one kind of channel (in the vertical or horizontal sense) for the same product. The vertical aspect is particularly true of commodities which have a double market. Automotive tires are an important example. That portion of the industry's output which is sold for original equipment on new cars is distributed direct from tire factories to automobile manufacturers. Tires for replacement equipment on cars on the road are sold principally through manufacturers' branches to retailers, or through regular wholesalers to retailers. Some manufacturers have different products that require separate distribution channels. Illustrative is the meat packing industry. In addition to meat sales to retail stores, the industry is confronted with the problems of selling numerous types of by-products to different classes of customers, each of which poses a special channel-selection problem.

Finally, some manufacturers find it feasible to use different channels in different parts of the country. Many manufacturers of factory machinery and store equipment sell direct to industrial consumers in regions where customers are highly concentrated but rely on manufacturers' agents for effecting sales in those areas where potential customers are widely scattered.

The foregoing discussion has been concerned with the distribution of manufactured goods. Channels for agricultural commodities involve a greater multiplicity of types of middlemen. Distribution of such goods is more complicated because they come from large numbers of small producers. In local growers' markets, various types of assembling middlemen are found. These include independent cash buyers of farm products, trucker-buyers, and the assembling agencies of cooperative marketing associations. Then there are also unique types of concentrating agencies in the major city wholesale markets. Of particular importance are the fruit and vegetable auctions found in a number of our leading cities.

## SELECTION OF CHANNELS

It must not be assumed that every manufacturer has a wide range of alternatives to consider in selecting channels. Many middlemen, particularly wholesalers and retailers who handle a wide range of merchandise items, regard themselves as purchasing agents for a group of customers rather than as distributing organizations for manufacturers. At any given time, they are likely to be stocking what they consider to be the maximum feasible number of items in a particular classification. Thus, a manufacturer often finds it difficult to obtain distribution among new outlets. The point is that the channel of distribution may be determined as much by the middleman, acting as a buyer, as it is by the manufacturer, acting as a seller.

Another factor which limits freedom in selection consists of changes in consumer buying habits. As illustrated in a preceding section, the trend toward consumer buying of baby food items in food stores forced a drug firm to market its baby food items through such outlets, even though from a standpoint of operating convenience and utilization of an existing sales organization, it would have preferred to continue distribution through the drug trade. No manufacturer of a highly competitive product can maintain his historic share of market by confining his distribution to types of outlets which are of decreasing relative importance for a class of products. In the last analysis, the relative importance of different channels for consumer and industrial goods items is determined by the buying decisions of ultimate consumers and business purchasers, respectively.

Moreover, in some cases a variety of types of middlemen is not available. In certain lines, such as high-fashion apparel, wholesalers are of such limited significance that they do not constitute a practical alternative. In other cases, such as elaborate industrial machinery, the requirements of each potential customer are so unique that a direct manufacturer-to-user channel is dictated by unalterable circumstances.

Nevertheless, many manufacturing sellers have considerable freedom in channel selection. Whether to sell direct or to utilize the services of one or a number of types of middlemen is often a perplexing question of marketing strategy. The manufacturer may also be faced with determining whether one channel will suffice, or whether two or more different channels are required because of differences in the products made or markets served. Finally, he may have to decide upon the kinds of business or lines of trade through which his goods should move, which will, in turn, determine not only the types of links to be used but the number of links. Cases abound where such decisions have been reached in a haphazard manner. To approach this problem scientifically, it is essential to know how various products are distributed and what factors govern the choice of given channels.

Chapter 3

# Population Factors and Consumptions

Critical determinants of the magnitude and the character of consumer demand include the total population of the country and its composition in terms of various demographic factors. The total potential demand of the national economy is naturally closely related to the total number of people whose wants call for satisfaction. Consumer demand for broad categories of expenditures (e.g., food, clothing, transportation), also for specific classes of products (e.g., alcoholic beverages, sport jackets, motorcycles), depends in some substantial measure upon population factors, such as age levels, geographic distribution, mobility, and educational level.

## POPULATION CHARACTERISTICS AND MARKET SEGMENTS

While changes in the total population indicate some aspects of the nature of total demand, few if any products are demanded equally by all types of persons. The total national market consists of many individual segments, some of which can be distinguished on the basis of population characteristics. Accordingly, knowledge of past and probable future changes in the composition of the population, as discussed below, is of crucial significance to marketing management.

### SIZE OF FAMILY

Family size has an important bearing upon the character of consumption. Small families may maintain a fairly high living standard on an income which would support only a relatively low standard for a family with more dependents. Over the course of this century to about 1950, the average size of family tended to decline. This trend, together with rising personal income levels, contributed to marked expansions in markets for durable goods, education, health services, and recreation, since the small family needs to spend less of its income for basic requirements of food, clothing, and shelter.

An accelerated birth rate beginning in the late 1940's provided indications of a possible reversal of the long-run trend of declining family size. Actually, this may be more of a statistical illusion than a reflection of preference for families of larger size. Economic conditions in these years favored earlier marriages and an advancement in the age at which typical parents have their first, second, or third children. There has also been a substantial decline in the proportion of childless families. In other words, the tendency has been for more couples to have children and to have them sooner. This increases the "statistical" average size of family, without any significant change in actual family size among families with children. Current child bearing, as in former eras, is inversely related to income level, educational level, and status within the occupational hierarchy, but the differences among socioeconomic groups have narrowed appreciably. The national market has become somewhat more homogeneous with respect to the attribute of family size, rather than dispersed so widely around the modal experience.

The increased birth rate has contributed to a changing character of demand. Infants' and children's stores have prospered, as well as those selling toys and games. By the late 1950's many families that were started in the post—World War II years of the late 1940's had outgrown their small homes or apartments, and this resulted in a growing demand for three- and four-bedroom residences and the necessary furnishings for them.

## AGE GROUPS

Changing composition of the population by age groups

is reflected by the data in Table. In the early part of this century the United States was a nation of youth. More than one-third of the population was under 15 years of age in 1900, but this proportion declined to one-fourth by 1940. Since that time it increased to about 31 per cent in 1960 because of the high birth rates in the 1940's and 1950's.

Over a long period the death rate has been steadily declining, due, in large measure, to lower infant mortality, better balanced and more adequate diets, improved medical care, reduced occupational hazards, and greater control of certain infectious and contagious diseases. As a consequence, the proportion of the population over 65 years of age more than doubled between 1900 and 1960, giving the population a more mature character. This has resulted in greater demand for goods and services especially wanted by or suited to the aged. Because older people are particularly prone to sickness, accidents, and other disabilities, manufacturers and distributors of certain drugs and disability devices have experienced expanding markets. Many of the aged are not able to provide for their own support. Aid for their benefit has become recognized as a public responsibility. Governmental and industry-sponsored pension plans pro vide a widening stream of fixed income, and this helps to stabilize the total purchasing power.

Because birth rates in the past have varied considerably from year to year, the distribution of population by age groups is very uneven and it changes continuously. The previously unequalled number of 3.7 million births in 1947, followed by more than 3.5 million births in each of the two succeeding years, was accompanied by an unprecedented demand for infant layettes in those years and by a similar demand for shoes for threeyear-old children in 1950. The even greater birth rates of a prolific population in some of the succeeding years has continued to expand markets for such products.

The impact of the post-World War II "baby bulge" in the population was felt in the elementary school system in the early 1950's, as the babies became children, giving rise to greater needs for grade school equipment, textbooks, and supplies. The same wave passes through high school and college years in the early and middle 1960's with benefits, among numerous others, to manufacturers and retailers of teen-age and junior size apparel.

Abnormally low birth rates in the serious depression years of the 1930's resulted in a situation where there was an unusually low number of teen-agers during the late 1940's and a decline in the number of persons between the ages 20 and 24 between 1950 and 1960. On the other hand, post-World War II infants will be entering the labor market, marrying, and starting families in the years 1965-70, giving rise to unparalleled potential demand for housing and home furnishings.

## GEOGRAPHIC DISTRIBUTION

Markets are often considered as segmented regions due to widely varying population characteristics, environmental influences, and differing competitive pressures among major geographic areas of the nation. Each region may pose different marketing problems and each also may have experienced peculiar growth trends.

During this century, growth in the New England, North Central, and the Southern states along the eastern seaboard has failed to keep pace with, the national trend. The result is a declining *proportion* of the total population in each of these areas. On the other hand, regional migrations have accounted for substantial increases in the proportion residing in the West South Central, Mountain, and Pacific states.

These shifts are not only related to the distribution of market potentials for products which are in widespread use everywhere, but are also of great significance in explaining changes in consumption of products that are related to climatic differences and the varying cultural and social patterns in the several regions.

California, Florida, and Texas are three of the states experiencing very large population increases as a result of migrations from other states. The warmer climate and more leisurely life in these areas have contributed to greater demand for comfortable and colorful sportswear. Other products affected by regional population shifts include convertible automobiles, sunglasses, gas floor heaters for installation in homes not requiring central heating plants, and men's lightweight topcoats.

## RURAL-URBAN MIGRATION

Originally and for many years the inhabitants of the United States were primarily an agricultural people. For some decades there has been a steady decline in the percentage of people living on farms and in rural areas. By 1960 only about 12 per cent of the population actually lived on farms; nearly 70 per cent resided in cities or other urban places; the remainder lived in rural nonfarm areas.

This trend has important marketing consequences. Mechanization of agriculture has contributed to a declining farm population, a decline in mass farm markets, and a drastic alteration in the pattern of consumer demand originating on remaining farms. Our cities, housing the majority of the population, are market places where more than three-fourths of total retail trade is transacted. Although rural dwellers make numerous visits to cities, the urban population constitutes the dominant market for consumer goods.

Varying degrees of urbanization apply in different regions. New York, Massachusetts, New Jersey, Rhode Island, and California are the most urbanized, with more than four-fifths of their populations living in urban places. By way of contrast, Mississippi, Arkansas, North Dakota, South Dakota, North Carolina, and West Virginia are the most rural, with only about one-third or less of their populations being urban. This, of course, is one of the many factors helping to explain interregional variances in consumer behavior and in marketing plans and methods.

## SUBURBAN LIVING

Demand for many products has been modified substantially by growth in suburban living. Between 1950 and 1960, population increases in the suburban or outlying regions of the nation's 212 major metropolitan areas were, on the average, about 5 times as great as population growth in the central cities. In many metropolitan areas, where the total land area of the city was fully utilized years ago, the central city actually experienced a decline in population, in part due to relocations necessitated by expressway construction and other urban improvements, with resulting abnormally high rates of suburban population growth.

In the exodus to the suburbs, the tendency has been for middle income families to abandon the central city to upper income (and usually older) families and to the very poor. In spite of the fact that many suburbs contain considerable industry and commercial activity, suburban areas for the most part are residential in nature, and are often referred to as "bedroom" or "dormitory" communities. In the early stages of population flow to a suburban region, land values are based largely upon chance location factors, with scenic qualities playing an important role. As a suburban area becomes more built up, access to arterial highways and to important community services such as schools and shopping facilities becomes dominant. Most newer suburban areas reflect the influence of massive or at least large-scale real estate developments and some degree of community planning. Similarity in architectural designs and price class of homes, as well as newness of community, have tended to make most newer suburbs quite homogeneous with respect to socioeconomic characteristics, and the suburb thus became a popular topic of sociological comment.

Suburban movement has been accompanied by substantial increases in home ownership. Over the period 1900-40, the proportion of home-owning families was relatively stable at about 40 per cent, but increased to 55 per cent in 1950 and to 62 per cent in 1960. Wider home ownership and greater interest in family life have brought many changes in consumption patterns. Less interest in public spectator amusements has been accompanied by increased expenditures for television, phonographs and records, magazines and books. Demand for many kinds of products has multiplied many times. Illustrative are porch and lawn furniture, power lawnmowers, garden tools and supplies, outdoor cooking equipment, and second and even third family cars. This trend has also accounted for the development of large, planned suburban shopping centers.

In the largest metropolitan areas, where suburban communities are the greatest distance from the central city, many suburban families have revolted against their way of life and have returned to the city. Among the contributing factors are dissatisfaction with time and expense of daily commuting to work, attainment of a stage in the life cycle where children are no longer at home, cost and effort involved in lawn and yard maintenance, and dislike of the distance from central city cultural and entertainment facilities. Construction of attractive new housing in slum clearance and urban renewal areas has made the central city more attractive for many families. While movements back to the city have been moderate in relation to the outflow of population to the suburbs, they provide an indication of a possible change of trend which will be watched closely by those interested in consumer behavior.

## MOBILITY

In many countries it is common for members of the same family to live in the same home for several generations. The United States is in marked contrast. In a typical year about 20 per cent of our families move from one place of residence to another. Of the total movers, about twothirds change to another residence in the same county, about one-sixth to another residence in some other county in the same state, and about onesixth to another residence in another state. Over a period of years the cumulative effects are striking. They account in large measure for the changing geographic pattern of population distribution, for the rural to urban migration trend, and for the trend to suburban living and back again. A family that moves is likely to have different buying behavior and expenditure patterns during the year than a nonmoving family. In addition to moving expenses, there are usually requirements for new home furniture or household equipment. It has been found that the proportion of movers making major durable goods purchases in a year is nearly 50 per cent greater than the proportion for nonmovers.Population mobility has also accounted for the development of a large market for house trailers or so-called "mobile homes." Many of these are occupied by families of construction workers and others engaged in seasonal or other temporary types of employment, by retired persons or other itinerants who desire to move their own home with them, and by those who find the idea of living in a modern home trailer economical or appealing.

## EDUCATIONAL LEVEL

One of the most rapidly changing population characteristics is level of educational attainment. This is usually measured by the median years of school completed by persons 25 years of age or older, since by age 25 almost all persons have completed the amount of formal education to which they aspire or which they can afford. From 1940 to 1960 this figure increased from 8.6 years to 11, meaning that in the latter year one-half of the adult population had completed 11 years or more of formal education. During the same period the proportion of the adult population classified as functional illiterates (less than five years of elementary school) decreased by more than one-third, the proportion having attended or completed high school increased by more than one-half, and the proportion having completed college increased by about two-thirds. Since the educational attainment of the adult population is a function of schooling in youth, and because of much more widespread educational opportunities and requirements in recent years, the least-educated persons are heavily concentrated in the older ages. It is inevitable, therefore, that the average level of educational attainment will advance rapidly.

Educational attainment is highly correlated with income, with status or social position, with age, with place of residence, with many attitudes and opinions, and with other factors that are discussed here in Part II. It may be noted briefly, however, that the more highly educated consumer-buyer is a more sophisticated shopper, with different patterns of needs and wants growing in part out of higher levels of aspiration. Continuing advances in educational attainment will contribute to great modifications in responses to many kinds of product offerings and advertising and selling appeals.

## LEISURE

The consumption of many types of goods and services has been accelerated by greater leisure. Leisure is defined to mean any period of time which is free from obligatory pursuits and which is used by individuals for voluntary activities that produce personal satisfaction. At one time leisure was widely regarded as the privilege of the relatively few in the most fortunate economic circumstances. Among the factors contributing to increased opportunity for leisure for the average person are shorter working hours, a larger number of paid holidays, more and longer paid vacations, labor-saving products used in household operation, and earlier retirement. That all people do not take advantage of opportunity for leisure is evidenced by preference on the part of many to work overtime, the commonplace situation of "moonlighting" (holding two jobs), the employment of married women, and the desire of many persons at retirement age to continue in their occupations. Opportunity for leisure time activities has advanced considerably over recent decades, enhanced purchasing power has enabled the average individual to elect to engage in a much wider range of relatively expensive leisure pursuits, particularly those related to recreation, play, and educational activities.

## STATUS OF WOMEN IN RELATION TO MARKETING

Improvements in the economic and social status of women are matters of great marketing significance. Many changing consumption patterns are explained in part by the employment of women, the increase in their interests outside the home, and their outstanding role as purchasers.

## EMPLOYMENT OF WOMEN

The number and percentage of women, both single and married, who are gainfully employed have increased greatly. In 1900, only 17 per cent of the total labour force consisted of women, and of the women who were employed at that time, less than one-sixth were married. By 1959, 32 per cent of the labour force consisted of women, of which group 61 per cent was married. Since 1940 the proportion of single women in the labour force has tended to decline, partly due to prosperous conditions and better educational opportunities, which have reduced employment of teen-agers. Labour force participation by young married women has also dropped, due to trends toward early child bearing. Most of the female addition to the labour force has consisted of married women age 35 or over. Nearly one out of three wives over age 35 was in the work force in 1959, as compared with one out of eight in 1940. This reflects a tendency of women to seek gainful employment after their children are in school or have completed schooling.

Growing employment of women has greatly affected marketing by increasing family incomes and stimulating demand for clothing, education, recreation, investments, and luxury items. Pressure on the energies of women employed outside the home has helped to expand the market for labor-saving household devices, ready-made clothing, and prepared foods. The gainful employment of women has also been facilitated by release from certain former household tasks.

## WOMEN AS PURCHASERS

Improvement in economic status due to gainful employment and related advancement in political and social status, as well as a tendency to outlive and inherit from their husbands, has placed a large share of total income and wealth at the disposition of women. When we were predominantly an agricultural people and few women were employed outside the home, the bulk of the family purchases was made by men. Today, marketing executives think of the housewife as the family purchasing agent. In the great majority of families, women buy clothing for themselves and for the children, as well as food, housewares, home furnishings, and even much of the clothing worn by their husbands. To be sure, the housewife is influenced by the needs and wants of other members of the family and interprets these as she makes buying decisions. This explains the considerable amount of advertising directed to children, who can become quite vociferous in the expression of their wants, which are taken into account by the housewife in planning family purchases.

It is generally recognized that women exert a profound influence in the purchase of much merchandise even though the actual buying may be done by men. While men buy most automobiles, a woman's influence is often reflected in choice of body design, color, and interior appointments. The manufacturer and merchant must realize the importance of the woman purchaser and her far-reaching influence in the selection of goods and services. Merchandise must appeal to women, publicity must be adapted to their motivation, and the place of sale and the accompanying service must be adjusted to their needs, whims, and fancies.

Whether men, women, or the family are the usual purchasers of a given product is a question of importance to the marketing executive. Numerous scientific studies have revealed important differences between the sexes with respect to purchasing activity and reaction to advertising and selling appeals. Generally, but not in all individual cases, women are more interested in social situations and conventions, have stronger likes and dislikes, have a slower association and perception time, are more inclined toward introversion, are more open to suggestion, and are less self-sufficient and less dominant than men. The knowledge that these differences generally prevail has led to numerous consumer research studies, the purpose of which is to determine which member of the family usually buys a given product and the degree to which the purchaser is influenced by other members of the family in reaching buying decisions.

## Chpter 4

# Consumer Motivation

The nature of the consumer market is only partially explained by the size and characteristics of the population. Also essential is an understanding of consumer behavior—*what* people do—and consumer motivation—*why* they do it. The successful marketing organization must be concerned about needs and wants of consumers, consumer behavior patterns in satisfying their wants, motives that prompt them in making buying decisions, and attitudes that caused them to react favorably or unfavorably toward certain products or institutions.

### CONSUMER NEEDS AND WANTS

Much misunderstanding and some criticism of marketing stems from confusion regarding the needs as distinguished from the wants of people. For example, it is sometimes stated that people of former generations had everything they *needed.* Modern marketing activity is often criticized for making people "want things they don't need."

In the same sense, one may hear a person say that he "doesn't need" an automobile or a typewriter or a television set, meaning usually that he can get along without it. Similarly, a wage earner may be critical of selling effort which makes his wife want to buy household appliances or clothing when he believes that she "does not need them." When the word "need" is so used, it generally refers to something absolutely necessary or indispensable.

Another common meaning of *need is the lack of something requisite, desirable, or useful.* This is believed to be a more sensible interpretation. When needs are so considered, there is certainly no lack of them anywhere in the world. To be sure, some needs imply more urgency than others. All people require food to sustain life, and clothing and shelter for protection from the elements of nature. But they need much more than this.

They need all the goods and facilities for meeting the normal circumstances of life in the social group of which they are a part; they need protection against uncertainties and hazards which may threaten the pattern of life to which they have become accustomed or which they prefer; they need the means of improving their present pattern of living so that they may live with more dignity and greater enjoyment.

Life is so complex, its opportunities so varied, and our resources so limited, that it is apparent that most people will always need more things than they will be able to possess or afford. If such is the meaning of needs, then what is meant by wants? *To want a product is to recognize that it will satisfy a need.* Consumers are very directly conscious of many of their wants, but it is also true that they are made aware of others as a result of marketing activity. Marketing arouses, stimulates, modifies, or creates wants by making consumers aware or more conscious of their needs and by calling attention to specific products, services, or marketing institutions as the means of satisfying these needs.

While marketing institutions are very much concerned with arousing or creating wants, it is erroneous to interpret this in the sense of making people want things which they do not need. Actually, properly conceived selling effort stems from the premise that *wants arise out of needs*. The conversion of needs into wants is, however, often not a simple process. This may involve convincing the consumer, first, that some general kind of product or service will satisfy his want and, subsequently, that some individual brand or style number of a given product or service is the best specific solution to his problem. In order to accomplish this end, marketing organizations are dependent upon knowledge of *what* people *do* in providing for their consumption and *why*.

## CONSUMER BEHAVIOR AND MOTIVATION

Knowledge of how consumers behave is relatively easy to acquire through observation, descriptive research, or experiments. A firm interested in locating a new supermarket in a city can obtain a great deal of information about present consumer shopping habits in existing competitive stores by observing the number of automobiles parked at each one, ascertaining the number of check-out counters in operation at peak periods, noting the quantities of various types of perishable food items kept on display, and so on. One may observe consumer reactions to a new store or window display, to a new item placed on a restaurant menu, or to a change in customary hours of doing business.

Descriptive research, through analysis of internal records, often yields considerable data about consumer behavior. A middleman or manufacturer learns much about what products people prefer to others in his line by analyzing data in inventory control records. By studying sales and transaction data a department store can accumulate a wealth of information about shopping habits as related to departmental locations, changes in the weather, days of the week, or the timing of competitors' major promotional events. Survey research techniques are often used to describe behavior of consumers by finding out such things as what brands they prefer, when they made their most recent purchase of a particular item and where, or how many stores they visited before making a buying decision.

The manner in which people react to a situation is often tested experimentally. A chain organization may test the responsiveness of sales of certain items in relation to price by varying prices at different locations under controlled conditions and keeping careful records of results. A manufacturer considering a change in the color, style, or size of a product package may determine probable consumer reaction by carefully controlled tests in selected local markets before committing the firm to a drastic change.

Regardless of how much one knows about consumer behavior in a particular market or in relation to some product, service, price, or policy, this information is likely to be an inadequate basis for planning the marketing action which is most appropriate for a given situation, especially for long-run effects. To be reasonably sure that a product offering or a selling appeal will accomplish the purpose of satisfying wants, marketing organizations are dependent upon knowledge of consumer motivation. They are interested not only in the forces that motivate the consumerbuyer, who is often the housewife, but also in motivating other consumers who influence buying by expressions of their wants within the consuming unit which is usually the family.

## THEORIES OF CONSUMER MOTIVATION

Professional psychologists have made significant contributions toward understanding the motivations which underlie consumer behavior. Unfortunately for the marketing man, the application of psychology to the solution of marketing problems is no easy task. It is indeed perplexing because proponents of different schools of psychological thought often explain identical behavior patterns in totally disconnected or diametrically opposed terms. This may be illustrated by presenting briefly and in an oversimplified manner two apparently conflicting theories.

One theory visualizes the typical consumer as a rational person with certain goals or levels of aspiration. Her (or his) behavior in the market is likened to the solving of a problem by a logical process. The problem is how to achieve maximum satisfactions (come as close as possible to attaining personal or family goals) with limited funds and limitless wants. The process is complicated by a wide range of choices among products and sellers, by uncertainty about which choices will result in maximum satisfactions, by the necessity to plan purchases in advance of want, by the impossibility of doing all of the things one would like to do, and by a host of other considerations. Nevertheless, according to proponents of this theory, most consumers to the best of their ability attempt to balance their means with their wants in a manner that is consistent with their goals, and in a logical or reasoned way.

The fact that some consumers do things which other consumers deem stupid or silly does not invalidate the general idea. One group may have different aspirations or knowledge but both may be acting in a rational manner with respect to individual frames of reference.

Another theory sees the typical consumer as a creature of emotions who behaves irrationally more often than not. Proponents of this view hold that people have a great desire to behave as rational human beings and tend to seek rational explanations for their behavior. More often than not, however, such rational explanations are merely a cloak over deeprooted emotional motivations of which the consumer may not be aware. The consumer, according to this theory, is seen as a dynamic organism— changeable, suggestible, nonrational, and influenced more by symbols and overtones than by reason and logic.

Some critics of marketing, often overawed by the implications of this theory, see the typical consumer as a helpless creature who is unscrupulously manipulated by skilfully contrived appeals to emotions, with the result that she (or he) is tossed about without a course or means of selfpropulsion, as a balloon floating upon a stormy sea. Such critics often do not understand the true nature of product or the productive nature of marketing effort. At least, a tendency to react unfavorably to the efficient and productive use of tools of persuasion often reflects a primitive conception of product as a physical thing rather than as the total of all satisfactions that may be provided for use or consumption.

Both theories of consumer motivations have been oversimplified for purposes of illustrative introduction to the subject. If consumers were totally rational, they would not really be people or human; if they were totally emotional or nonrational and influenced altogether by symbolic appeals to nearly or actual subconscious considerations, then there would be little to distinguish them from other forms of animal life.

The subject of consumer motivations is actually much more complex than indicated above, no matter which theory one favors. Motivation in a particular situation is usually the result of a whole pattern or configuration of individual motivations which may fall into a number of different classifications.

## CONSUMER BUYING MOTIVES

Those responsible for marketing effort find it essential to be informed about major classes of buying motives and also specific motives within classes. Products vary in appeal to different individuals and to the same individual at different times. For example, a certain automobile may be bought by one person because of a careful study of its mechanical features and by another person purely because of a desire to imitate a social or business leader. A life insurance salesman may easily err by basing his appeal on a prospect's desire to protect his loved ones when that particular prospect might be more easily influenced by a consideration of insurance as an investment.

### SIGNIFICANCE TO ADVERTISING AND SELLING

Advertising is a means of mass communication. Since an individual advertisement presents the same appeals to a large number of consumers, success depends largely upon the degree to which chosen selling points (whether specified or implied by illustration or suggestions) are consistent with motives which are important to people in the particular market or market segment to which the advertisement is directed. Personal sales effort can be individualized. Thus, emphasis upon selling appeals which are in harmony with the motives of individual consumers is the essential consideration.

### PROBLEMS IN CLASSIFICATION

It is difficult to classify buying motives because a number of different types are usually involved in any specific buying decision. Some of these are likely to be of negligible influence while one or only a few may be really governing. A further complication is that ther *puchaser* may be someone other than the actual consumer. Many items are purchased as gifts. Numerous housewives are the routine purchasers of items of clothing and furnishings for their husbands and children. In all such cases, the determination of what shall be bought may be the result of the feelings and preferences of either the purchaser or the user, or a compromise involving both.

The classification of consumer buying motives is fraught with many difficulties. Every social situation is different and thus requires separate analysis for precise conclusions. There is actually no such thing as a universal set of explanatory motives, because individual motives are closely related to one another, are overlapping in meaning, and can be reclassified under a number of different headings. Nevertheless, the classifications discussed below, while by no means the only ones possible, do afford a realistic general picture of *consumer buying motives,* that is, the group of influences or motivating forces which determine *what* purchases will be made.

## PRIMARY AND SELECTIVE BUYING MOTIVES

Even a superficial study of the subject will reveal two distinct types of buying motives, primary and selective. *Primary buying motives* are those which induce an individual to buy a certain kind or general class of article or service. A housewife may decide that she wants a new rug for her home. The decision may be reached because of any one or a combination of several buying motives which unite to induce her to believe that a new rug should be substituted for one which has been in use. The decision to purchase the new rug is based upon primary buying motives. After this decision has been reached, it is necessary for the housewife to select from a number of types of rugs, any one of which might have rendered satisfactory service. The reasons which influence the decision to buy a particular rug from among several possibilities are known as *selective buying motives.*

Other illustrations may help to make this point clear. Assume that a housewife is considering the purchase of an electric washing machine. She may want the product because of a desire to lessen the time and labor in washing clothes. This is a primary buying motive. Unless it is offset by some stronger influence, it will sooner or later result in the purchase of some washing machine. Other primary motives may strengthen the desire until a definite decision has been reached to make the purchase. A particular make or brand of machine may then be selected from among those on the market. Other motives will determine which one is finally purchased. The decision may be based on the quality of the motor, on the preference of a certain kind of agitator, or may result from the cumulative influence of the past advertising of a certain machine.

The various motives which determine what *particular* article will be purchased after primary motives have created the basic desire for the article are known as selective motives. For instance, the consumer who drinks orange juice because of its health-giving qualities is swayed by a primary motive of health; but his decision to purchase Florida rather than California orange juice (or vice versa) is based on a selective motive. As technology made television, automatic clothes dryers, and other such products commer cially available, primary motives had to be aroused before selective motives could be brought into play and before such products could be marketed in substantial quantities.

## Emotional and Rational Motives

Every decision to purchase or not to purchase is the result of a mental reaction which may be considered *emotional* if the inspiration is based upon fundamental instincts with no or only a minimum of deliberation, or *rational* if characterized by a fairly reasoned consideration of the arguments for and against the proposed purchase. Obviously, many buying decisions are motivated by both emotional and rational considerations.

## Nature of Rational Motives

Everyone likes to buy things, and generally speaking, the normal individual likes to buy things for socially approved reasons. Before any purchase is made, the individual buyer must have reasons for buying which make sense to him as he understands them, and being a social creature, these reasons must also be of a nature that would make sense to many other people. A rational motive is one that is *self-approved*—a motive which the buyer, as a thinking person, believes to be correct or reasonable because it is in line with his own expectations or with what he expects society would consider to be reasonable and proper. The following list is suggestive of buying motives that would be considered rational for most consumers under usual circumstances:

- *Dependability,* as in seeking assurance that a fountain pen will be be ready for use under all circumstances, will hold a generous supply of ink, or will not leak
- *Low purchase price,* as monetary saving from buying a new automobile late in the model year, just before next year's models are introduced
- *Economy in use,* as in purchasing a small car with standard transmission to obtain maximum gasoline mileage
- *Money gain,* as in subscribing to a business magazine to become better informed and thereby increase opportunities for enlarged earnings
- *Convenience* in use of a product, as in the use of automatic timecontrol devices on modern kitchen ranges or "roll-on" applicator packages of deodorants

## Nature of Emotional Motives

Emotional motives are not necessarily irrational in the sense that they are contrary to reason or preposterous, but are nonrational to the extent that they do not result from a mental process of deliberation of reasons for and against a proposed buying action. An emotional motive involves little or no reasoned deliberation and may often be regarded as one which is not self-approved or socially acceptable, as defined above for rational motives, and for that reason is not likely to be admitted by an individual, or it may even be beyond his awareness as a motivating factor. The following list is suggestive of some common types of emotional motives:

- *Prestige,* or the desire to command admiration or be held in esteem, as in buying the very finest clothing, furniture, or workshop tools
- *Emulation,* as illustrated by favorable reactions to

testimonial advertisements in which famous personalities recommend the use of a product

- *Individuality*, or the desire to be markedly different, as illustrated by the college student who wears apparel of a nonconforming style, even though not of a prestige nature
- *Conformity* to social patterns of behavior, as illustrated by the high school girl who wears a certain kind of shoe or skirt because "all the other girls are wearing them"
- *Pleasure*, or the desire for a change from the drab monotony of daily duties, as through spectator or participant amusements, sports, and hobbies
- *Creativeness*, or the desire for self-expression which goes beyond the requirements of pleasurable pursuits, as illustrated by the appeal of do-it-yourself kits, art courses, etc.

## Rational and Emotional Motives in Combination

Rational motives tend to be more paramount in basic decisions (e.g., whether to live in an apartment or buy a home, whether to buy a new car or new carpeting for the home) and emotional factors tend to play a more important role in selective choices where it is more difficult to discriminate (e.g., what specific cigarettes, radio, or shirt to buy). In any kind of situation, however, both rational and emotional motives are likely to be working in combination.

A man may wish to subscribe to a certain highly regarded and relatively expensive business publication because it makes him feel important to receive it, but he needs a good common-sense reason, like improving his ability to solve business problems, before filling out the subscription order form. A woman may want to buy new household appliances primarily in order "to keep up" with her neighbors who are regarded as community leaders, but she is also likely to reason that modern time-saving devices will enable her to spend more time with her children or prepare food in a manner that will be more enjoyable to her family.

In determining just what marketing strategy to use in a given situation, it is essential to recognize that rational motives are self-approved and emotional motives are not usually of that species. Even when emotional motives are likely to be dominant, direct appeals to them are often avoided because the consumer is not willing to admit that they are the basis for his actions. In other words, the consumer is likely to react adversely to direct appeals to his fundamental instincts, whereas he can rationalize the situation if the emotional appeal is in the background-merely suggested by pictures, illustrations, symbols—and the selling message carries a clear-cut, rational reason for buying which is socially acceptable and therefore likely to be self-approved.

## Conscious and Dormant Motives

Any of the specific emotional or rational motives may be conscious or dormant. Conscious motives are clearly experienced by the consumer without being aroused through the instruments of marketing strategy. For example, a young executive who is anxious for a promotion may receive an invitation to a party likely to be attended by important company officials. He may immediately decide to purchase a new suit of clothes of a particular quality and style because he believes that this will add to his prestige, aid him in attaining his ambition in life, and because it is somewhat in conformity with the tastes and expectations of the executive group.

On the other hand, many motives are dormant in the sense that they are unrecognized until brought to the consumer's attention. As a result of marketing strategy, definite appeals are directed at the masses, at specific groups, or to individuals, which have the effect of creating wants by making people aware of certain needs which previously were not consciously felt. Illustrative is the case of a man who has been so engrossed in business and family cares as to make it impossible for him to give much time in life to any form of recreation. Properly worded appeals emphasizing the attraction of golf or the social contact of a good club may bring about the realization that he will be able to accomplish more if he devotes part of his time to some pleasurable pursuit. When this motive has been aroused, other recreational appeals will reach him with some force. Demand for many products depends on the possibility of arousing dormant or unconscious motives which can be appealed to by new articles or new uses for an old article. A household paint which can be easily applied appeals to those who wish to enhance the appearance of the home and furniture. The want, while present, had not been aroused until a specific article was presented for use. Electric floor polishers, when first placed on the market, met a ready demand since they appealed to the desire to save labor, a desire which is almost universal, and also to take pride in the appearance of one's home.

## Patronage Motives

Up to this point, the discussion has been concerned with motives which relate to choices among different types of products, including services and among different specific products within a class. *Motives which determine just where or from whom purchases will be made are known as patronage motives.* Appeals to these do not tend so much to arouse a desire for a product as to persuade the customer to buy it from one of several possible sources. Some common patronage motives are as follows:

- *Reputation of the seller* for reliability in all relations with customers
- *Supplementary services* which make shopping a more pleasurable or convenient experience, as illustrated by check-cashing, charge accounts, rest rooms, delivery, and so on
- *Product-connected services* relating to the installation or repair purchase of items, such as automobiles, major household appliances, electronic products, or clocks and watches
- *Variety of merchandise carried,* as in a department or variety store where it is possible for the consumer to satisfy a number of different needs on a single store visit

- *Breadth of assortments,* or the offering of a wide range of items in a given class which permits the consumer, for example in the case of dresses, to choose from many colors, styles, types of materials, and prices
- *Price,* an almost pervasive patronage motive, is reflected by appeals consistently made by nearly all kinds of retail establishments
- Special *sales promotion techniques,* such as trading stamps or premium plans, which give the consumer an incentive to make repeat purchases at a given establishment
- *Convenience of location,* unless offset by other factors, is a strong motivation which may apply within neighborhoods near the consumer's home or downtown in the case of small shops or service establishments located near other facilities which constitute a more dominant attraction
- *Ownership of establishment,* which is important to many people who have a strong belief in certain types of outlets and express their preferences by favoring the independent merchant or the chain store or the consumers' cooperative organization.

Like product buying motives, patronage motives usually work in combination. Each selling enterprise has a variety of potential appeals which collectively give it a sort of personality.

Consumers tend to be attracted or repelled, in most cases, by the composite personality attributes of an organization rather than by one patronage motive alone.

## MOTIVATION RESEARCH

The preceding discussion throws light, in a general way, on the nature of basic buying and patronage motives. It does not reveal, however, in a specific manner and with any degree of accuracy just what part given motives play in the consumer's decision to act or in the attitude he assumes. Yet this more specific knowledge is essential to the selection of selling appeals that are in harmony with consumer motivation and which make possible efficient performance of the marketing task. This desire to harmonize selling effort with buying interest of consumers has led many marketing organizations to engage in research aimed at discovering true consumer-buyer motivation in some measurable way.

To discover why consumers act as they do, different methods and types of techniques have been used for many years, ranging from mere observation and counting devices to elaborate questionnaire surveys. The latter have, in turn, ranged from simple types intended for extensive coverage to complex ones designed for depth interviews on an intensive basis. All of these have helped to unearth valuable "why" information concerning the actions and attitudes of ultimate consumers and to that extent must be regarded as a form of motivation research.

More recently emphasis has been placed on projective and other psychological or even psychiatric methods and techniques of consumer research, for which the all-embracing designation of motivation research was inappropriately appropriated. In fact, in some respects this type of research is not as scientific as some of the older methods and techniques, because the conclusions about an identical universe are not usually reproducible when studied by different practitioners whose interpretations and evaluations may differ substantially.

## NATURE OF MOTIVATION RESEARCH

In its true sense the task of motivation research is to find out just what makes people behave as they do, regardless of the technique or method used for the purpose. As a matter of fact, the term "motivation research" is equally applicable to all methods and techniques designed to discover reasons why people act or think the way they do, whether in the capacity of ultimate consumers, purchasing agents, store buyers, or in any other capacity. So far, however, the term has been applied principally to consumer motivation studies dealing with consumer buying and patronage motives, and with consumer attitudes. *An attitude may be defined as a tendency to respond favorably or unfavorably toward a person, an institution, a thing, or an idea.* An individual's attitude in any given situation is usually a result of a variety of past influences, including his assumptions or beliefs, his social frame of reference, and sensations or feelings that he has experienced.

Since an attitude is an effect of what one has experienced, it is also something of a prophet of future action in the sense that a consumer's conscious or unconscious feelings or moods largely determine whether and how he will react to certain selling appeals. For this reason, marketing researchers attempt to discover consumer attitudes and, whenever possible, to measure the magnitude of such reactions. Manufacturers and marketing institutions are interested not only in the motivations of their customers, but also in the attitudes of those who have not used, or have discontinued to use, their products.

Although research in consumer motivation has been popularized to a high degree in recent years, it is not essentially a new concept. Some marketing books devoted considerable attention to consumer motivation, and elaborate classifications of buying motives were presented in the early 1920's. Contemporary developments have included refinements in research methodology and increased appreciation, on the part of marketing executives, of the practical application of motivation knowledge to marketing problems. This may be better understood by giving brief attention to methods of motivation research and to actual illustrations of such research findings.

## MOTIVATION RESEARCH METHODS

Methods used to obtain information about consumer attitudes or buying behavior may be classified into three groups, namely, observation of consumer action, consumer surveys, and psychological approaches.

Most early classifications of buying motives depended largely upon careful observation of consumer reactions to different kinds of stimuli. If an advertisement stressed a selling appeal directed to a particular buying motive, and if this evoked considerable favorable response, then it was concluded that this particular motive was of considerable importance to consumers purchasing the product. In many instances a change in selling appeals provoked such a significant response that the importance of certain motives could be inferred with reasonable certainty. While this is an old method, it continues to be highly relevant in situations where consumer reaction to certain stimuli is quite pronounced. This may be illyustrated by reference to patronage motives under modern conditions. In the 1950's, discount houses grew in importance in many metropolitan markets. When such stores are located outside the main stream of shopping traffic and hence are relatively inaccessible to many consumers, and when they do not offer the usual range of customer services available in regular stores, it does not take an elaborate survey or psychological analysis to determine that price appeal constitutes the principal patronage motive.

Consumer surveys have often been utilized when consumer motivations cannot be inferred from direct observation of consumer actions in the market. This approach usually involves selection of a representative sample of the presumed market for a particular product. Consumers are asked to state why they buy particular products or patronize certain institutions or are asked to rank or evaluate given factors which are related to particular motives.

Analysis of such replies may reveal what motives or attitudes are of great importance to many consumers and which are of only incidental or no significance in the situation being investigated. Such surveys have revealed that consumers prefer to shop in downtown stores rather than in outlying shopping centers because of the broader assortments of merchandise available, the greater emphasis upon bargain or clearance sales, and the feasibility of combining shopping with other things that one may want to do. At the same time they have revealed that many prefer to shop in outlying centers because of lower cost for transportation, better parking facilities, more convenient store hours, ease of taking children on shopping trips, and other reasons. [7] In connection with selective buying motives, such surveys may reveal that most consumers buy one brand of a product rather than another because of a price differential, a reusable package, or some premium that is offered in connection with the product. Such surveys are a particularly appropriate method for motivation research in kinds of situations where consumers know why they have reacted in a given manner and when they are willing to state their reasons or attitudes.

More elaborate psychological approaches have become popular because of recognition that consumer behavior in some situations is a result of complex personality variables rather than a simple reaction to easily identified stimuli. Often, the consumer has given little systematic thought to buying situations and may not actually be aware of all the considerations that entered into his purchasing decisions. Moreover, consumers may know why they bought something or what their attitude is regarding a situation but are reluctant or unwilling to state their true motives or opinions when asked straightforward questions. Such circumstances have led to a number of refinements in research techniques, treatment of which is beyond the scope of this text. In general, they involve the use of probing procedures, depth interviewing, and other projective techniques that have been borrowed from the fields of per sonality studies and clinical psychology where they have been used for many years.

## MOTIVATION RESEARCH FINDINGS

Motivation research studies, whether of the general survey or psychological approach type, reveal that consumers often do not think in terms of general classifications of buying motives but rather in terms of quite specific features of a product or a service. From very concrete consumer reactions, it is necessary to form hypotheses or generalizations about the basic underlying motives. The nature of such findings and the character of their application to questions of marketing strategy are illustrated below.

### Product Examples

Several examples are presented to show how motivation

research findings have been applied in the marketing of specific goods or services.

- The State Farm Mutual Automobile Insurance Company attained a dominant position in its industry by advertising emphasis upon low cost. To broaden the company's appeal further, extensive motivation research was undertaken to learn more about why people buy automobile insurance and what qualities they look for in an insurance company. Techniques included large-sample consumer surveys supplemented by projective studies conducted by trained psychologists with a much smaller sample. The company learned that an insurance company may be unconsciously resented at the same time it is accepted as a protector of individual welfare; that even though people are generally happy not to have had an accident, they are inclined to resent the fact that they have had to pay for something on which they have had no opportunity to collect; and that policyholders are greatly interested in prompt, courteous and expert service. As a result of these findings, the company's advertising was changed. While low cost was still stressed, more emphasis was placed on providing answers to important questions which people have about automobile insurance, on illustrating the availability of desired services through convincing case histories, and on reflecting the size and stature of the company.
- Encouraged by its success with Wildroot Cream Oil Charlie, a hair conditioner for men, the Wildroot Company decided to produce a shampoo for women and call it Lady Wildroot. A research company was retained to make a study to determine how the proposed product should be marketed and whether the name was good or should be changed. A sample of 250 consumers was selected and interviewed on a nondirective basis. It was learned that the name was a major handicap. Through its advertising for Cream

Oil Charlie, the company had established a reputation as a "masculine" company and a concept of a special type of man as the ideal male. This male was forward and aggressive in the minds of women. They tended to resent the implication that by merely having a stock of hair smoothed down with cream oil, this type of man can prevail over them. These findings were validated by a test.

Two control groups of women were selected and members of each group were given bottles of the new product—some bottles labeled Lady Wildroot, the others by a quite different name. In the group testing Lady Wildroot, user comments were critical or negative, but in the other group the product was quite acceptable.

- In a study conducted by Social Research, Inc., for the *Chicago Tribune,* considerable light was shed upon primary and selective motives which are important to people in purchasing automobiles. It was found that the meanings which the automobile embodies are grouped around five central ideas:
  - A mechanical object which satisfies practical needs for transportation;
  - A sizable investment with an important place in family economics, partly in terms of original price but to a greater extent in relation to cost of operation and upkeep;
  - An indicator of the individual's social status, his position, his place in the scheme of things, and the role the car plays in social companionship, like family vacations, car pools, dates, etc.;
  - A symbol of self-control, signifying personal mastery, through a sense of power, with the thrill of speeding, or many other opportunities for showing personal superiorities;
  - As an avenue of self-expression, or a clearly understood way of conveying in our society the characteristics, feelings, and motives that typify

a particular individual. As a result of these findings, it was recommended that automobile advertising should appeal to two types of motivations:

- The foregoing basic wishes for ownership of automobiles in general
- Specific personality attributes of a particular brand which an individual purchaser can identify with his own understanding of himself, his social situation, and his aspirations.

- A prune growers' association, while suffering a continuing decline in sales, decided to find out what consumers thought about prunes. In detailed interviews it was learned that consumers thought prunes were dry and wrinkled—ugly things to behold; that they were believed to be without particular food value or were to be used only as a laxative. As a result of this research, marketing strategy was changed. Most prunes are now distributed in cans or glass jars. They appear on supermarket shelves as fat, juicy "prune plums." They are associated with fruit and with the quality of freshness. Sales have improved, bringing more consumer satisfaction with increasing consumption and with benefits to the producing industry.

## Concept of Brand Image

An important contribution of motivation research has been the development of the concept of "brand image." Brands, like types of products, are perceived by people as images. The image results from the total of all the impressions that the consumer receives from many sources: actual experience and hearsay about the brand, its packaging, its name, the company making it, the kind of stores in which it is sold, the types of people the consumer has seen using or buying the brand, what has been said in the advertising for the brand, the tone and format of the advertising, the type of advertising media used. The total of such impressions results in an image which tends to be similar for the consuming public at large, particularly for well-publicized brands, but different groups of consumers may have different attitudes toward it. For example, users of a given brand may think of it as "first and best on the market" while nonusers regard it as "an oldfashioned brand." Both groups, however, may agree that it is "an old, well-established brand.

The preceding example of Lady Wildroot illustrates the power of a brand image when attempting to market a new product under an established name. In another study dealing with brands of gasoline, it was found that motorists tended to think of Gulf, among other things, as a "friendly" gasoline. Such a notion was supported by name associations reminding people of the out-of-doors, "Gulf of Mexico," etc.; by the "sunny" yellow color used in the brand emblem; by a "friendly" approach in advertising copy (Go Gulf); and by the nature of an advertising program, "We the People," which, although off the air at the time of the study, had contributed to the brand image.

## Concept of Store Personality

Somewhat similar to the concept of brand image is the idea of store character or store personality. Individual patronage motives, as listed in a preceding section, sometimes are adequate to explain why a consumer will go to one store rather than another. It often happens, however, that many alternative establishments would be similarly ranked in regard to various specific patronage motives. In many metropolitan areas, for example, housewives have at their command a number of supermarkets which carry just about the same assortments and variety of merchandise, sell at comparable prices, render similar services, and are about equally convenient. Each organization is still likely to have a distinct personality based on the totality of all the impressions that consumers have of it. One store that, over-all, reflects an atmosphere of sophistication and elegance will tend to attract patrons who feel at home in such surroundings while it may not appeal to others who would be more comfortable in a store with a severely functional atmosphere. Some stores have clear-cut personalities because all of the things that the organization does make impressions of a consistent character. Others may have a vague or dull personality in the minds of consumers because advertising reflects one kind of personality, store layout another, and the nature of personal selling effort still a third, with the result that one kind of activity undermines rather than builds upon the impressions made by others.

Some studies have attempted to determine the personality attributes of people as well as the personality attributes of particular brands of products or stores. When the brands or stores actually used by people are matched with their own personalities, the findings are usually that people tend to select those brands or stores they conceive as being consistent with their own personalities, even though they are unable to describe their own personality attributes which are revealed by psychological testing.

## DYNAMICS OF MOTIVATION

The foregoing examples demonstrate that consumers have attitudes toward products and services which are directly influenced by the shortrun policies and plans of marketing executives in a particular company and by the action of persons employed in individual business establishments. While consumer attitudes toward the general question of branded merchandise are well grounded and relatively stable, attitudes toward a particular brand of a prepared food product may change radically and within a very short period of time merely as a result of a barely perceptible change in flavoring, the adoption of a new shape or type of container, or the modification of some other product characteristic. Likes and dislikes about a particular make of car may be drastically altered with the introduction of a new model with different style and engineering characteristics. Consumer attitudes toward a specific retail store may be considerably different before and after thorough modernization programs have been carried out in competing stores in the same shopping district. Such attitudes may also undergo rapid change if a lax personnel policy results in discourtesy on the part of salespeople, if a stricter customer return and adjustment policy is adopted, if the store begins to feature a price rather than a quality appeal, or for numerous other reasons.

Motivations of individuals are also influenced by a host of other considerations. To a large extent, personal motivations reflect values in society. As cultural values change, motivations are modified. In our country there has been a decline in Puritanism, or the feeling that it is wrong to get too much pleasure out of life. This has enabled many advertisers to make forceful and direct appeals to the motive of comfort which would not have been as appropriate in former generations. Individuals also tend to follow behavior patterns of socioeconomic classes to which they belong or to which they aspire. Everyone feels that there are certain things which "are all right for people like us," but which would not be appropriate for people in altogether different socioeconomic classifications. As one moves from one class to another, perhaps as a result of a successful business career, the family takes on a whole new set of motivating characteristics.

Each person is also influenced by close associates, friends or neighbors, who may be regarded as taste setters because they are intellectual, economically successful, travel a lot, or are social leaders.Because of the multitudinous product and source of supply choices open to consumers and the possibility of unexpected change in consumer attitudes, it is difficult to formulate generalizations about motivations which can be continuously applied in connection with the marketing of any specific product. The consumer's reaction at any given time is a function of a complex set of factors involving:

- The make-up of the individual
- The environmental situation as it exists at the time of the reaction. Many illuminating facts have come to light through motivations studies; but for the most part, to be of value from the standpoint of marketing management, they must be acted upon promptly after they become known. The mere application of the results in a large-scale marketing program

changes the environmental situation in which the consumer is expected to respond.Nevertheless, motivation research has made significant contributions to our understanding of consumer behavior. It has provided much insight into the nature of motives that influence behavior, the complexity of multiple motives in given situations, the importance of understanding motivation as a basis for predicting behavior, and the dynamics of motivation as affected by cultural change, social class status, and one's close associates.

Chapter 5

# Income and Consumption

The mere existence of *people* with *wants* does not create markets or make possible a high level of consumption. Also required is *purchasing power,* which enables consumers to translate wants into effective demand.

Consumers possess purchasing or spending power when they have income, wealth, or credit. In the long run, such power is limited to income, for it is income which provides *the continuing flow* of purchasing power while serving also as the source for accumulating wealth and as the principal basis for the use of consumer credit.

The relationship between consumption and income is analyzed in considerable detail. Attention is directed to the level of total income and total consumption, to particular categories of consumer expenditures, and to variations in consumer behavior by levels of family income. Wealth and credit, as supplementary forms of purchasing or spending power, along with other factors affecting consumption.

## TOTAL INCOME AND CONSUMPTION

In any given year, total consumer demand and the pattern of consumption are largely dependent upon the amount of income available for current consumption expenditures. The student of marketing and the marketing executive must understand the concepts underlying various statistical measures of the flow of income in our economy and their relationship to demand for various categories of goods and services.

## PRODUCTION, INCOME, AND CONSUMPTION

Essentially, *income arises out of production*. Production has been previously defined as the creation of economic values or utilities which, in turn, are the capacities of products to satisfy human wants and desires. Our wants are satisfied, adequately or inadequately, by the goods and services produced in the economy. From a broad viewpoint, then, it is the total production of goods and services that constitutes the income of society. From the standpoint of an individual, income is the amount that our system of exchange determines as the value of his contribution in the productive process, although income may be augmented in certain instances by transfer payments from the current or accumulated income of others as, for example, gifts, subsidies, social security benefits, and pension and relief payments.

The general level of economic activity is reflected in a very comprehensive manner by estimates of *gross national product*. This concept is a measure of the total market value of all goods and services produced in the economy. In addition to goods and services provided by the business system, an allowance is also made for the value of services rendered by the government.

All of the gross national product is not available for consumption. Part of it must be used to replace assets which are used up or consumed in the productive process. Buildings and equipment used in agriculture, manufacturing, and trade depreciate, and our stock of natural resources is depleted through the activity of the extractive industries. Adjustments to provide for depreciation, depletion, and accidental damage to fixed capital (as through fire or flood) are known as capital consumption allowances. These are deducted from gross national product to calculate *net national product*.

Some products are sold on the market at prices which exceed the incomes accruing to the manpower, capital, or land resources used in their production. The difference is due mainly to indirect taxes (sales, excise, property) paid by business to various government units. Such taxes do not, by current treatment in national income studies, constitute value added by production, but reflect arbitrary decisions of government as to the place or stage from which to procure revenue. Indirect taxes are subtracted from net national product to derive *net national income* which measures the total net value of services performed by the various groups participating in productive activities. It therefore constitutes the basis of the claims of the factors of production to income.

Individuals do not receive all of the net national income. Corporation income taxes are paid to the government out of the income to which stockholders have a claim. Employers' contributions to social security funds are paid out of the income to which labor has a claim. Many corporations do not pay out all of the available income after taxes, but retain part of the profits for reserves or for business expansion. This explains the reasons for these deductions in Table. Also certain additions are made because individuals receive transfer payments which do not result from their current role in the productive process. Illustrative are social security benefits, veterans' pensions, relief payments, and unemployment compensation. When the national income is adjusted to provide for these respective deductions and additions, the result is known as *personal income.*

Individuals cannot normally spend the total of their personal income, because they must pay income and other personal taxes to government units. When such taxes are deducted from personal income, the result is *disposable personal income.* This concept, which measures the amount available for spending and saving, is of utmost significance in analyzing variations in total consumption over periods of time and the nature of demand for various categories of consumption at any particular time.

## TREND IN PRODUCTION AND INCOME

Gross national product has increased rather steadily over the 14-year period 1947-60. If gross national product should continue to grow during the 1960's in line with the computed arithmetic trend for 1947-60, total production of over $700 billion would be realized by 1970; if production should increase at the average annual percentage rate of change actually experienced in 1947-60, the economy would be well past the $900-billion mark. An actual gross product in 1970 somewhere between these extremes is more probable, but unpredictable events such as a war, a program of major disarmament, or a prolonged depression could greatly alter the picture.

Economists, businessmen, and leaders in the field of public policy are greatly interested in projections of gross national product because of historical relationships between this measure and all of the net income concepts as well as consumption expenditures.

**Gross National Product and Consumption Expenditures**

In Table it is revealed that annual changes in gross national product are generally accompanied by changes in personal income and disposable personal income which are similar in direction and in annual rates of change. On a long-run basis, however, the relationship between gross national product and personal consumption expenditures has been modified substantially. This is highlighted by the following summary data:.

| Year | Personal Consumption Expenditures as Per Cent of Gross National Product |
|---|---|
| 1929 | 75.6 |
| 1939 | 74.2 |
| 1949 | 70.2 |
| 1959 | 64.9 |
| 1960 | 65.1 |

Over the same years government purchases of goods and services increased from 8.1 to about 20 per cent of gross national product. This is accounted for largely by higher levels of national defense expenditures and by expanded public services at federal, state, and local government levels, as illustrated by highway construction, health services, education and welfare expenditures, veterans' services and benefits, agricultural stabilization programs, conservation of resources, regulatory activities, and increased costs of government administration. As a consequence, the long-run trend has been for a reduction in the share of gross national product which goes directly to the consumer and is regulated by free and open choices of individual consumers through their actions in markets. An increasing proportion is allocated to end uses without direct consumer action, but by legislative decision at all levels of government.

In spite of the downward trend just indicated, the ratio of personal consumption expenditures to gross national product in recent years has been considerably more stable than in former periods. Throughout the 1950's, personal consumption expenditures have consistently amounted to about 65 per cent of total production, with only very minor variations from this average relationship. Stabilization of expenditures in relation to gross national product during the 1950's is explained in part by a rather consistent upward trend in total production—that is, a period generally characterized by rising, high-level economic activity. Moreover, stabilization of this relationship has been facilitated by the more widespread supplementation of personal income, including expanded unemployment compensation, social security benefits, and other so-called transfer payments.

## Disposable Income and Total Consumption

As may be observed in the, disposable personal income bears a closer relationship to total consumption expenditures than any of the more gross measures of national production or personal income. Longrange relationships between *personal income* and consumption are affected by changes in personal taxes, which have increased in significance, as well as by consumer buying decisions. The difference between *disposable income* and consumption expenditures, on the other hand, is determined altogether by consumer decisions to spend or to save.

The per cent of disposable personal income used for current consumption expenditures measures what is known as the *average propensity to consume.* In the aggregate, consumers tend to spend practically all of their disposable income on current consumption, saving only a small portion of it. Normally, the proportion expended for consumption tends to be about 93 to 95 per cent, although some variation may be observed from this general tendency. In the depression years 1932-33 consumption expenditures actually exceeded the amount of disposable personal income.

This period of economic stress was marked by the withdrawal of *savings* which were used for current consumption and by considerable indebtedness incurred for the same purpose; thus, instead of personal savings there were *dissavings*. After these worst of the depression years, current consumption returned to a level of approximately 95 per cent of disposable income and this relationship was maintained, with only minor variations, until the years of World War II. During those years the spread between personal income and disposable personal income increased with larger rates of personal income tax and a higher level of income payments which brought many individuals into higher tax brackets. Durable goods were not available in quantities, as numerous manufacturing concerns devoted their efforts to war production. Consumption of many types of nondurable goods was curtailed through rationing and other controls.

Appeals to patriotism encouraged savings through the purchase of war bonds. All these factors contributed to a declining level of personal consumption relative to disposable income and effectively bridled people's general propensity to consume. During World War II the proportion of disposable income expended upon current consumption was generally between 75 and 80 per cent. After the war the removal of artificial restrictions on consumption and the increasing supply of consumer goods of all kinds were accompanied by a return to a more normal relationship between disposable personal income and personal consumption expenditures, especially in the years 1948-50. Throughout the decade of the 1950's, generally a prosperous period characterized by a pattern of consistent increases in total disposable income, personal consumption expenditures were below what would have been regarded as normal in previous periods, but were quite stable at about 92 to 93 per cent of disposable income. From the foregoing analysis, it is apparent that except for highly abnormal periods such as severe economic depression or major war, the level of total consumption expenditures can be predicted with only a small margin of error, given the amount of disposable personal income.

## Disposable Income and Major Consumption Categories

The disposition of income according to major consumption categories, a matter of great marketing interest, is shown in terms of per cent of disposable income and in terms of per cent of personal consumption expenditures. In a general way, these data show what basic changes in consumer expenditure patterns have occurred over a decade during which many revolutionary developments have been witnessed.

Several characteristics of consumer spending are noteworthy. First, durable goods purchases, while commonly in the range of 12 to 14 per cent of disposable income, are somewhat more volatile than other categories. This is particularly observable by the data for 1958 (a recession year) and especially for the automotive component of durable goods purchases. Such expenditures are easily postponable and, therefore, are more subject to influence by the economic attitudes and expectations of consumers than are expenditures for nondurable goods and services.

## Sensitivity of Specific Types of Expenditures to Income Changes

While total *proportionate* expenditures by major consumption categories tend to remain relatively stable, this is not true of all their components. Consequently, if analysis is confined to broad categories and no attention is given to specific types of expenditures within each such category, much of the income-consumption relationship of great market ing significance is obscured or completely lost. For example, while it is of considerable import that expenditures for household operation are a fairly stable proportion of disposable income, the marketing executive in a particular company is interested in much more detailed data, such as the income-sensitivity of consumer expenditures for furniture, major appliances, floor coverings, fuel, or public utility services.

Such relationships are closely allied to an economic concept of demand elasticity, of which there are several forms. Historically, greatest emphasis has been devoted to *price elasticity of demand* which is concerned with changes in demand that are associated with price changes when other factors (including income and promotional efforts) are held constant. Demand for a product is said to be elastic in this sense if the increase or decrease in demand is greater than unity, that is, higher in proportion than the decrease in price or lower in proportion than the increase in price. Thus, if the price is reduced by 2 per cent and the demand for the product, in consequence of the price change, is increased by 2 per cent or less, the demand is inelastic; but if the demand is increased by much more than 2 per cent, it is elastic.

*Income elasticity of demand* is a concept which involves changes in demand that are related to changes in income, when prices, promotional efforts and other factors are held constant. The demand for a product is elastic if a change in income by, say, 4 per cent results in a changed demand for the product by more than 4 per cent. Some marketing scholars have also become interested in a concept of *promotional elasticity of demand*. In applying this concept one would attempt to measure the degree to which the demand for a product is sensitive to increases or decreases in the seller's promotional effort or expenditures, under conditions when the influences of price or income changes are held constant or are isolated.

It is almost impossible to measure precisely the elasticity of demand for a product in relation to price, to income, or to promotional effort. Serious practical problems are encountered when attempts are made to isolate the effects of a change in just one factor when, in a dynamic economy, all of them and still other factors affecting consumption are changing almost continuously. Income elasticity, which is the primary concern of the present discussion, has been approximated in research studies in which the sensitivity to income of specific types of expenditures is measured by a coefficient derived from correlating dollar expenditures with disposable personal income. *The coefficient of income sensitivity expresses the average per cent by which expenditures have varied, over a period of years, corresponding to a 1 per cent change in disposable income.*

Several comprehensive studies of the sensitivity of expenditures to income changes have been made by the Office of Business Economics of the U.S. Department of Commerce. Coefficients of sensitivity from the most recent such study, covering the 1947-58 period, are illustrated as follows:

| Item of Expenditure | Coefficient of Sensitivity |
|---|---|
| Personal consumption expenditures, total | 1.0 |
| New cars and net purchases of used cars | 1.2 |
| Tires, tubes, accessories and parts | 0.7 |
| Furniture | 1.0 |
| Kitchen and other houshold appliances | 0.8 |
| Other durable house furnishings | 0.4 |
| Jewelry and watches | 1.2 |
| Women's and children's clothing and accessories | 0.5 |
| Food | 0.8 |
| Tobacco products | 0.8 |
| Drug preparations and Sundries | 1.4 |
| Cleaning, dying, pressing, alteration services | 0.6 |
| Automobile repair and related services | 1.3 |
| Physicians' services | 1.1 |
| Shoes and other footwear | 0.4 |

The interpretation of these data may be illustrated by several examples. The coefficient of sensitivity for total consumption expenditures for the 1947-58 period was 1.0, which means that a i per cent increase in disposable income was accompanied, on the average, by a corresponding increase of I per cent in aggregate consumption expenditures. Items with higher ratios than 1.0 may be said to have higher than average income sensitivity, and those with lower ratios, lower than average sensitivity. For the specific category, "drug preparations and sundries," the coefficient is 1.4, meaning that a 10 per cent increase in disposable income should produce an increase of 14 per cent in total expenditures for such items. For "women's and children's clothing and accessories," with a coefficient of 0.5, a 10 per cent change in income would be accompanied, on the average, by a 5 per cent change in expenditures. These relationships were derived for a period (1947-58) of rising, high-level economic activity, and could be used realistically for predictive purposes only under conditions of comparable expectations. Their value as a forecasting tool under conditions markedly different from those experienced in this period remains uncertain.

Studies of sensitivity of expenditures to income changes have proved helpful in estimating demand. They have also led many consumer goods manufacturing companies, retailing organizations, and marketers of services to study their own sales carefully in relation to current estimates of disposable personal income, as published regularly in the *Survey of Current Business*. When judged in proper perspective, along with other factors that also influence consumption, such income sensitivity relationships not only have proved valuable for purposes of future estimation, but also permit the more realistic appraisal of the effectiveness of marketing efforts in current periods for which income is already accurately known.

## FAMILY EXPENDITURES BY INCOME LEVELS

Just as the people as a whole cannot, in the long run, consume more than the total national income, so it is with the individual or family unit. An individual may, by drawing on his accumulated savings or wealth or by means of credit, consume more for a limited time than he can purchase out of current income. Such a procedure ultimately exhausts his principal and his debt-paying power. Furthermore, most consumers have no substantial accumulation of wealth upon which to draw.

Generally speaking, therefore, the disposable income of the individual sets the limit of his consumption, just as the consumption of a people over a period of years finds its maximum limit in the national income. The income of the individual or of a family is, therefore, the prime factor in determining the standard of living for the family. Because living standards and expenditure patterns vary considerably with the amount of family income, the distribution of income among people is of great marketing significance. There is a strong tendency for most people with comparable incomes to effect a somewhat similar distribution of their incomes according to major divisions of expenditures normally incurred in the course of living. Moreover, as individuals or families move from one income level to another they tend in time to take on the standard of living of the new income group and to spend their income in somewhat the same way.

## Application of Generalizations on Family Income

The generalizations formulated above in regard to expenditure patterns by income level should not be confused with principles previously presented in regard to total disposable income for the entire country. For example, even though Engel's law with regard to food has been found valid in modern times, it does not follow that an increase in *aggregate disposable income* should inevitably result in a *lower national proportion* expended for food. Moderate annual changes in aggregate disposable income do not necessarily result in significant shifts in the proportions of families in different income groups.

Some annual changes in income, when measured in dollars of current value, are due primarily to inflationary or deflationary tendencies. Changes in the size of the labor force or number of families are other factors. Broad social and economic trends also influence the aggregate amounts expended for major categories of consumption over time. The generalizations stated within this section are used properly only for purposes of comparing the consumption pattern of *families* at different income levels—not for comparing *aggregate* expenditures for all families from one period of time to the next. Market analysts find such generalizations, and the data upon which they are based, particularly useful in determining the degree to which markets for certain products are concentrated in certain income classes. For such purposes, it is significant to know that family expenditures for home furnishings and equipment, while declining relatively in relation to size of income, are about three times as great in absolute amount at the over $10,000 level as they are at the $3,000-$3,999 level. Another useful application is in market area studies, as in evaluating trading areas of cities or of planned shopping centers. When local area levels of family income are determined, as may be done from census data or other sources, the potential market for individual categories of consumption expenditures can be approximated much more accurately than from a knowledge of population alone.

Such generalizations are also useful in family budget planning. In preparing a plan for family spending, knowledge of the manner in which other families with similar incomes spend their money may be of value to many. They also aid in determining how much is needed to support a family of a certain size in a given income status in matters of separations, divorces, and similar legal proceedings.

## CHANGES IN THE DISTRIBUTION OF FAMILY INCOME

Because of the foregoing established relationships between family income level and consumption, marketing executives are very much interested in average family income and the distribution of income among all families. Considerable discussion is regularly devoted to this question in the business press, but many articles leave a confusing picture, since data are often given for personal income before taxes and are stated in current dollars the exchange value of Which varies with changes in the price level. The truly significant question is that relating to changes occurring in the *distribution of real family purchasing power*. The lowest quintile, for example, contains the 20 per cent of all families that have the lowest family incomes. Income has been stated *ufler* incomc taxes, and appropriate statistical adjustments have been made to eliminate the effects of changes in the price level.

Between 1941 and 1950, when the average real purchasing power of all families increased by 17 per cent, the distribution of this *increase* was very unequal, tending to be concentrated heavily within the low-income groups. A number of factors contributed to this "leveling" process. Among the important considerations were changes in income tax laws which resulted in heavier tax liabilities for higher income groups, conditions of relatively full employment, a redistribution of the occupational structure with a resulting larger proportion of workers in higher-skilled and higher-paying occupations, and a tendency toward multi-wage-earner situations among families in the middle and lower income categories. Since 1950, increases in the level of real purchasing power have been much more evenly distributed among the entire population, with all quintiles experiencing a gain reasonably close to the average for all families.

During the 1950's, as compared with the pre-World War II era, the situation reflects a much greater equality of distribution at a higher level of family purchasing power. This has resulted in a more homogeneous market for consumer goods. It brought about significant increases in *discretionary buying power*, i.e., income not required for the purchase of the basic necessities of life, especially in the middle and lower income groups. Thus, large numbers of such families have entered the market for many kinds of goods and services which were formerly regarded as luxuries to be enjoyed only by a few. Illustrative are many kinds of major household appliances, radios and television, second telephone extensions in homes, long distance phone calls, fashionable wearing apparel, better cuts of meat, wide varieties of fresh fruits and vegetables and prepared food products, and all kinds of lawn and garden equipment and supplies. For this reason, trends in average family income levels and distribution are observed with great interest.

# Chapter 6

# Consumption Factors

Discussion of the ultimate consumer is a treatment of wealth and credit as supplementary forms of purchasing or spending power and as factors influencing consumer behavior. Consideration is then given to the manner in which the economic attitudes and expectations of consumers also influence buying behavior. Changing customs and social interest in fashion are additional factors examined in relation to consumption.

## WEALTH, CREDIT, AND ECONOMIC EXPECTATIONS

Even though disposable income is of primary significance, wealth and credit are of great importance in relation to consumption expenditures and hence are subjects of considerable interest to economists and marketing executives.

### MEANING OF WEALTH

There are differences of opinion as to just what constitutes wealth and how wealth is to be measured, whether in terms of physical resources or in terms of claims and rights. These differences to a large extent depend upon whether wealth is viewed socially or is considered from the standpoint of individuals.

#### Social or National Wealth

When considered from a social viewpoint, wealth is synonymous with the nation's stock of economic goods. Measurement of national wealth, then, requires identification of the nation's economic goods and determination of their value. Serious practical problems of measurement have given rise to different concepts of national wealth which vary in degrees of comprehensiveness.

The broadest concept includes all material and nonmaterial economic goods. When goods have a material form, their identification is simple. Many items, however, do not exist in material form but are economic nevertheless. Human skills and institutional arrangements such as the skill of a plumber or the established organizational structure of a manufacturing company are examples. Such things must be included in any *comprehensive* conception of the nation's wealth.

From a practical standpoint, however, it is not possible to compute a realistic monetary value for such nonmaterial resources. In fact, it is also practically impossible to determine the aggregate value of many kinds of material resources, especially land and natural resources which are not man-made and are limited in total supply. Changes in their total valuation are often due to increasing scarcity rather than to growing supply, or to new techniques of measurement or new knowledge relating to total available supply. Thus, when it comes to measuring wealth from a social viewpoint, it is often construed narrowly rather than comprehensively, being limited to man-made or reproducible material or tangible economic goods.

## Individual Wealth

All social wealth is owned ultimately by individuals, either as individuals or as members of some collective group, such as a municipality, state, or nation. In the preceding discussion of social wealth, no mention was made of *instruments,* such as mortgages, promissory notes, stocks, and bonds, which are merely *claims* upon wealth rather than wealth itself. Such instruments are excluded from social wealth to avoid duplication that would result when, for example, a mortgage upon a house is counted as wealth and the house also is enumerated as a material economic good of given value including that of the mortgage. Similar duplication in social wealth would result if a corporate bond were counted, because the bond is merely a claim upon assets held by the issuer. From the individual's viewpoint, however, the term wealth need not be confined to tangible economic goods; it may well consist of *all of an individual's net possessions external to himself,* including *claims* and *rights* to wealth as well as material goods to which he holds title. Since individuals have claims to the disposal of economic goods or services of such goods, the measurement of wealth and its distribution may take the form of an evaluation of the claims of individuals. This is often more feasible than the measurement of the value of economic goods, because such claims usually have an identifiable form and can be more easily evaluated than the goods to which the claims appertain.

## CONSUMPTION AND NATIONAL WEALTH

The total wealth of a people is an important indication of the potentialities of production and therefore of consumption. Estimates of the reproducible national wealth of the United States are as follows:

| Year | Billions of Current Dollars |
|---|---|
| 1900 | $59.1 |
| 1910 | 99.6 |
| 1920 | 264.6 |
| 1930 | 293.4 |
| 1940 | 331.2 |
| 1950 | 852.0 |
| 1958 | 1,366.9 |

These estimates include the value of nonfarm residential structures, other improvements upon real property, producers' durable equipment, consumer durable goods, inventories, monetary gold and silver, and net foreign assets. Not included are value of land or unreproducible natural resources such as waterways, petroleum reserves, or mineral deposits. While these exclusions result in an understatement of the total social wealth, they probably do not substantially affect the general trend. Estimates of national wealth in current dollars are, of course, substantially affected by a long-run inflationary bias. For purposes of this discussion, the effect of a changing price level can be ignored, since the objective is to relate the increase in wealth to increases in production and consumption, both of which are similarly affected. Over a period of nearly three decades, growth trends were as follows:

| Basis for Measurement | Ratio, 1958 to 1930 Values |
|---|---|
| Reproducible national wealth | 4.7 |
| Gross national product | 4.9 |
| Personal consumption expenditures | 4.1 |

Thus, on a long-run basis total production has corresponded very closely with increases in wealth. The increase in personal consumption expenditures, while somewhat below that of wealth, is also similar, with the lower ratio explained largely by a smaller proportion of gross national product used for personal consumption and a higher proportion for government expenditures, savings, etc.

## CONSUMPTION AND WEALTH DISTRIBUTION

While total wealth is an important factor affecting consumption, its *distribution* among the people also exercises a great influence in determining *total* consumption and in explaining certain aspects of consumer behavior. Unfortunately, there is a dearth of comparative historical data concerning the distribution of wealth. Nevertheless, two major factors indicate that a pronounced concentration in earlier years has been reduced in favor of at least somewhat more widespread distribution. First, public policy since the 1930's has been directed toward a reduction in wealth concentration. High rates of taxation upon large amounts of personal income have made the accumulation of substantial wealth more difficult. Further, heavy death taxes on large estates are an impediment to the perpetuation of great individual wealth and hence favor more widespread distribution. Second, increasing amounts of real disposable income among middle income and lower income groups in recent years have made it possible for millions of people to support a reasonably high standard of living without using all of their income for current consumption. This has resulted in significant, although modest, accumulations of assets among a broader range of families. By midcentury, ownership of, or an equity interest in, a home had become commonplace and home ownership continues to increase. Ownership of automobiles, other durable goods, corporate or government securities, and savings accounts is much more commonplace than was the case in former decades.

Possession of wealth influences consumer behavior in a number of ways. The amount and character of a person's assets often determine his economic interests and affect his social position and obligations. Great wealth is a claim to substantial income resulting from the productive employment of wealth, thereby making it possible for the wealthy to enjoy a high standard of living which cannot be supported by work alone, and to do so without any impairment of the wealth itself. The wealthy, as a class, represent a market for luxurious clothing, expensive automobiles, motor boats, travel, opera, objets d'art, and investments.

Purchases of such luxuries as sable coats, costly jewels, and private yachts are a byproduct of a marked concentration of wealth. A concentration of wealth in the hands of a small minority of the population not only creates a demand for luxury goods, but also sets standards in consumption which those of lesser wealth imitate. If the very wealthy build homes of a certain design, the style is likely to be reflected in the homes of the less wealthy. Similarly, the desire of the wealthy for distinctive custom-made clothing furnishes an important source of ideas for the mass production company, which, in copying or adapting unusual features, destroys the unique character of the original model.

On the other hand, a wide distribution of wealth promotes social stability. Those who have a share in the wealth of a community are naturally conservative and reluctant to risk the effects of rapid change. The attitude of the homeowner as compared with that of the renter illustrates the stabilizing effects of accumulations. The renter may demand superficial changes and frequent repairs, whereas the homeowner is more likely to install durable fixtures and equipment. During periods of economic recession the owner of even modest wealth contributes a certain stability to the market. He can continue to purchase on a conservative basis even though his income may be seriously reduced or temporarily eliminated.

Recognition of the general desirability of a widespread distribution of wealth has led to a number of proposed political and economic so-called reforms designed to generate a high level of prosperity by an artificial and enforced redistribution of wealth.

Such proposals have generally ignored the complicated nature of the modern production process in our economy. They reflect little evidence of understanding that a high rate of investment and incentives to make such investment are necessary in order that the economy may expand its level of production.

## LIQUIDITY OF WEALTH HELD BY INDIVIDUALS

Probably of as great importance as the distribution of total wealth is the *form* in which the individual wealth is held and the proportion of it that is liquid and thus more readily spendable. If substantial amounts are not only widely distributed among the people but are also in the form of savings and checking accounts, or in stocks or bonds which are readily convertible into cash, the effect on consumption is different than when such wealth is in real estate, farm land, industrial and commercial equipment, or in stocks of goods which must be maintained.

The total amount of *liquid* wealth and its distribution vary greatly with economic and other conditions. During periods of stress the total amount of such wealth is diminished and becomes more highly concentrated inasmuch as the limited accumulations of many people are rapidly exhausted. During periods of prosperity the total liquid wealth is increased and its distribution is more widespread. In periods of war or national emergency the purchase of government bonds, on the one hand, and the difficulty of securing durable consumer goods, on the other, tend to increase liquid asset holdings. The significance of liquid assets to consumption does not lie merely in changes in *total* holdings but rather in changes in the liquid asset position of millions of families, some of which are adding to their holdings while others are using their assets for current consumption.

Decreases in holdings are more frequent among spending units that experience a decline in income than among those whose income remains the same or increases.

*This means that families are more likely to draw upon their liquid reserves in order to maintain their standard of living than for purposes of raising it to a higher level.* Among families that have experienced increases in income, substantial withdrawals of liquid asset holdings for purposes of current spending are not commonplace, but they tend to occur with greater relative frequency among families characterized both by:

- Higher than average income
- Higher than average accumulations of liquid asset holdings.

Analyses of the purposes for which people use funds that are withdrawn from their liquid assets cast further light upon the relationship between the liquidity position of consumers and consumption. When consumers are asked why they accumulate assets, the traditional answer is that they do it in order to provide for "a rainy day."

This is borne out by the most frequently reported use of funds withdrawn from holdings, which is to pay for family emergencies and sickness. Other major uses in approximately the order of their importance are the following: purchases of durable goods; nondurable consumer goods and service expenditures, particularly among families experiencing reductions in current income; repairs and additions to homes; luxuries and travel; home purchases; moving expenses; education; investment in assets not classified as liquid; use for farm expenses and investment in farm machinery; the repair of automobiles and other durable goods; and the payment of debts.

# CUSTOM AND FASHION

## HABIT AND CUSTOM

Habits and customs of consumers are powerful influences directing, limiting, and controlling consumer behavior. Habits relate to the practices of individuals. When particular habits are common to a considerable group of people, we have a social custom. Man is so constituted that he tends to develop more or less firmly established habits or fixed types of reactions. Originally, most of the things which we buy frequently were chosen as the result of careful selection either by ourselves or by others who were or are now in a position to influence us. Repeated selection of the same article has resulted in the formation of habits which, while greatly economizing our time and energy, are substantial barriers to change.

Customs exert a profound influence upon the consumption of social groups, sections, and nations. In certain parts of Europe, social customs resulted in the peasantry wearing costumes which differentiated them from other economic and social groups. Similarly, within the United States every section has some peculiar customs which distinguish its consumption from that of other areas. Many differences in customs among various social groups and regions are economic in their origin while others have a religious or climatic foundation. The practice of abstaining from meat on Friday and of fasting during the Lenten season is custom of adherents to the Roman Catholic faith and influences the consumption of food products in varying degrees in different places according to the relative importance of members of this faith within the local or sectional population. Consumption of cigarettes, coffee, and carbonated and alcoholic beverages is relatively low in Utah, because the use of stimulants is prohibited by the tenets of the Mormon Church which has a very large membership in that state. It is customary for men to wear hats with relatively narrow brims in the New England and Middle Atlantic states and hats with wide brims in the Southwest. Per capita consumption of soft drinks is much greater in Florida than in Vermont. New York City women use many times as large a quantity of cosmetics as do Vermont women. In New England there is an unusually heavy per capita consumption of tea, while in southern Louisiana per capita coffee consumption is at a high level. French traditions dominate the cuisine of New Orleans, while Milwaukee foods show the Teutonic influence. In the same way, New England colonial architecture contrasts with the Spanish designs of California.

Many local customs tend to perpetuate themselves while others are subject to rapid disappearance. Where differences depend upon such substantial bases as climate and economic need, they tend to persist. Where they are founded in geographical or educational isolation they tend to disappear in these days of population mobility, high educational levels, large circulation of national magazines, motion pictures, and television.

## PREDICTING SOCIAL TRENDS

Changes in customs are frequently referred to as social trends. When the manufacturer or merchant adapts his merchandise and services in such a way as to bring them into conformity with a social trend, he is likely to experience maximum success. When his efforts go counter to a fundamental social trend, they are doomed to failure.

Recognition of this basic principle has resulted in considerable marketing interest in sociological research studies which attempt to differentiate social classes and leaders of social change. Future consumer behavior can be anticipated only partly by analyses of quantitative factors such as population growth, income levels, wealth, and credit. Also of great significance is the future nature of consumer behavior as influenced by changes in social values, motives, and ways of life. It is recognized that some people, much more than others, have a major role in influencing change in our culture. A common research problem, therefore, is the identification of those who may be regarded as "opinion-leaders" or "taste-makers." Such leaders, it is widely believed, presently think and act in a manner that will become characteristic of the general public in the future. Hence, identification of such leaders and determination of the nature of their current behavior are often regarded as a sort of index of social change and predictor of future consumer behavior.

## FASHION

People of all historical eras have been concerned to some extent with fashion. In other countries and in former generations in the United States, this interest was limited largely to the small proportion of the population that had the means to consume more than the basic necessities of life. Contemporary American living is characterized by an interest in fashion and style that seems to permeate the entire population.

In common usage the terms fashion and style are synonymous. Technically, however, there is an important distinction. *Style,* according to one of the pioneering authorities on the subject, is *"a characteristic or distinctive mode or method of expression, presentation or conception in the field of art."* In furniture, for example, one may speak of the Victorian or Regency styles or of such styles as Chippendale or Hepplewhite, the latter referring to two of the leading designers of furniture during the eighteenth century. *Fashion,* on the other hand, *is an accepted and popular style.* A certain style, therefore, may or may not be in fashion or fashionable at a given time. If the fashion is of relatively short duration, being accepted quickly and with exaggerated zeal and just as quickly disappearing, it is regarded as a *fad.* Ordinarily, only articles of the novelty type or matters of relatively unimportant style details are susceptible to faddist use.

Earlier in the century, discussions of fashion merchandising were confined almost exclusively to women's apparel. At that time, manufacturers and designers were much more successful in securing acceptance of their style creations by their own efforts than they have been since that time. For example, manufacturers of women's clothing would meet in conventions and reach an agreement as to the general character of apparel design for the forthcoming season. Merchants had little alternative to purchasing these designs, and the consuming public showed great docility in their acceptance. In later years the consumer has shown no hesitancy in rejecting offerings, and the plans of manufacturers and merchants have frequently met with ignominious failure.

In present-day America, fashion is almost universal. It is to be found not only in all women's wearing apparel but also in men's clothing and furnishings. It is present in furniture, home furnishings, automobiles, homes, modes of public transportation, foods and beverages, and in certain personal services. In fact, practically every phase of consumption has been touched by the wand of fashion. Moreover, fashion is of importance in the choice of the store from which to buy such goods. In purchasing style goods, consumers generally prefer to compare the offerings of several stores before making a final selection. That has been an important factor in the development of city shopping districts and in the growth of city stores at the expense of smaller town competitors.

With improvement in our economic well-being and constantly rising standards of living has come about a growing emphasis on fashion. Fashion consciousness has been further stimulated by the greater mobility of our population, the motion picture, wider periodical and newspaper circulations, and the greater fashion awareness of retail merchants.

*Fashion change* is, therefore, an accepted fact of our economy. The trend has been for a larger element of fashion in practically all goods we consume and services we use and for more rapid changes in fashion. The same factors that accounted for growing emphasis on fashion as a whole have been responsible for acceleration of the fashion tempo.

## THE FASHION CYCLE

Style change is of increasing importance not only to consumers, but also to manufacturers and distributors, including retailers. Unforeseen changes in style and failure of particular styles to attain vogue, and hence to become fashions, may result in severe losses to businessmen. Outmoded or unacceptable merchandise may become unsalable or disposable only at prices which result in heavy losses. It becomes essential, therefore, for businessmen to understand the circumstances under which fashions are created, placed on the market, bought by consumers, and finally abandoned. The several phases through which a fashion passes represent What is generally known as the *style or fashion cycle,* referring to the wavelike regularity of movement that generally characterizes a fashion.

If a style is widely enough accepted to become a fashion, its history or cycle is marked by the following *stages or phases:* creation, showing, adoption, adaptation, popularization, mass production, and abandonment. From the standpoint of consumer reaction the cycle is characterized by the stages of adoption by style leaders, followed, in order, by first imitators, white collar masses, lower income groups, and finally by those on the subsistence level. The fashion cycle may be portrayed by a simple curve of a wavelike nature showing point of inception, point of greatest popular acceptance of the product, and point of termination or abandonment. If another curve representing use, rather than purchase is placed on the same chart, it will be found that the point of greatest use is far beyond the point of largest purchases and that the use extends considerably beyond the point of abandonment. Stated otherwise, people continue to use a fashion article long after they refuse to purchase the identical product.

The fashion cycle is operative both with respect to *general fashions,* a term sometimes used to identify long-range fashion trends, and to *specific fashions,* a term pertaining to the popularization of various individual styles within a general fashion trend. For example, growing consumer preference for sportswear and casual clothing was a general fashion of enduring significance. On the other hand, consumer preference for white instead of red sweaters as an item of sportswear may be a specific fashion of only seasonal importance. Similarly, in the 1950's there was an important general fashion trend in men's suits manifested by consumer preference for single- rather than double-breasted garments, and with a narrower, trimmer, less padded appearance than was formerly popular. Within this trend, specific fashions varied considerably from season to season, as evident by the widespread demand for three-button, charcoal gray suits for a time and preferences for lighter colors with various design modifications on other occasions. While general fashions may enjoy a long period in the "mass production" phase of the fashion cycle, specific style numbers may move through the various phases of the cycle with great rapidity.

Attempts to popularize any new specific style are always experimental. No one can say with absolute assurance that it will have any wide acceptance. This is true whether the style relates to clothing, housing, home furnishings, automobiles, or food. The motif or idea underlying a new design or style may originate in such a cataclysm as war, outstanding events in the field of exploration, political upheavals, a certain part of the world coming into prominence, an outstanding play or motion picture, or in some action of an individual upon whom public attention is focused. In other words, the creation must express something—a trend, fact, or thought—that is prominent in the public mind.

Creation is followed by a showing of the new fashion to test public response. New designs in women's apparel may be brought before welldressed women by the use of manikins. Usually, showings are held by the designers at their salons for the benefit of store buyers in accordance with published announcements in leading periodicals. Furniture is exhibited at World Fairs and at such centers as Chicago and Grand Rapids at regular intervals. Showings may also be accomplished by the production of small quantities of the new style and its display by stores catering to a wealthy or influential clientele. Of the many styles created, only a minority are ever widely enough adopted to become fashions.

If the new style is adopted by well-to-do purchasers in large fashion centers such as Paris, New York, or Hollywood, it may become very popular and spread throughout the country with great rapidity. Wide acceptance will be accompanied by large-scale production and the style, first shown in models of very high unit price, will be immediately copied and adapted by producers of popular and low-priced merchandise.

## MARKETING OF FASHION MERCHANDISE

The introduction of style elements into merchandise where style was formerly negligible, the increased emphasis upon style, and the shortening of the fashion cycle have added greatly to the cost of manufacturing and marketing. Manufacturers frequently misinterpret consumer reactions and suffer severe losses which must be compensated for in the prices received for those styles which meet with wide acceptance. Merchants are forced to buy more frequently and in smaller quantities, and their risks on account of style obsolescence are greatly increased. Consumers must pay a higher price as a result of constant change in styles and because they seem to be ruled by fashion.

Whether or not consumers get value received in consequence of the rapid fashion changes and whether this is in the public interest are often debated, but it is a subject beyond the scope of this immediate discussion. There are, however, certain statements that can be made in the nature of principles that have been derived from a study of the subject overt many years, as follows:

- *A new style conception cannot be forced upon the consuming public as a fashion unless the conception or design is attractive to a large segment of the population. For example, purchases are not made by buyers for retailing organizations, the interpreters of local consumer demand, unless they are reasonably certain that the consumers will buy what they buy for resale.*
- *The higher the standard of living, the greater the mobility of the population, and the more widespread the interchange of information, the greater the emphasis upon fashion.*
- *The greater the emphasis upon fashion and the shorter the fashion cycle, the higher the costs of manufacturing and marketing goods.*

Chapter 7

# Retailing Structures

## RETAILING CONCEPTS

The terms "retailing," "retailer," and "retail store" are popularly used interchangeably and in a befuddled manner. Several questions may indicate the confusion that prevails. Is a sale "retail" because it was consummated in a retail store? Does a retail sale necessarily involve a small quantity of goods, a higher price than in a wholesale transaction, or a particular kind of merchant who effects the transaction? When a consumer buys from a business firm claiming to be a wholesaler and obtains a price lower than the ordinary retail price, is the consumer purchasing at retail or wholesale? The variety of uninformed answers to such questions points to the need for considering the meaning of important retailing terms as authoritatively recognized. Carefully formulated definitions are a necessity for meaningful discussion and analytical study, for proper classification of quantitative data, and for various legal purposes, including matters of taxation and coverage of establishments under wage and hour legislation.

### Retailing and Retail Sale

Retailing is an activity word and denotes selling at retail. Among authorities who have given the most serious study to the question, the consensus is that the only clear, sound criterion for distinguishing retailing from other business activity is the *status or motive of the purchaser. Thus, a retail sale is one in which the buyer is an ultimate consumer,* as opposed to a business or institutional purchaser, *and the motive is personal or family satisfaction stemming from the final consumption of the article being purchased,* in contrast with purchases for resale or for business, industrial, or institutional use. It is, however, impractical to obtain data pertaining to all such transactions. Insurmountable difficulties would be encountered in distinguishing retail sales from sales to business firms when a business user of a commodity makes a purchase of a small quantity of an item in a regular retail store and at the same price as paid by the ultimate consumer; consequently, such sales to business users are usually regarded as retail in character.

## Retail Establishment

The composite of its transactions gives an establishment its principal character. A *retail establishment* is, therefore, *a single or separate place of business, principally engaged in the performance of marketing functions, wherein or out of which sales are made primarily to ultimate consumers.* In borderline cases such as are encountered in attempts to classify split-function establishments (i.e., those that sell partly at retail and partly at wholesale), the classification is usually effected on the basis of the rule of more than 50 per cent of the dollar volume of business. Thus an establishment is considered as retail if more than one-half of its dollar volume of business consists of sales to ultimate consumers.

## Retail Store

Most retail establishments are *stores* or *places of business open to and frequented by the general public, and in which sales are made primarily to ultimate consumers, usually in small quantities, from merchandise inventories stored and displayed on the premises.* Some retail establishments are operated by nonstore retailing organizations. The major types in this category consist of mail order establishments, offices that serve as headquarters for house-to-house selling companies, and facilities from which vending machine operators conduct their businesses.

## Retailer

Any person or business firm can own and operate a retail

store or a retail establishment. The very great majority, however, are operated by retailers. *Retailers are merchant middlemen who are engaged primarily in selling to ultimate consumers.* Unlike manufacturers or farmers who may operate retail establishments, retailers specialize in retailing activities. They stand in the channel of distribution between manufacturers, farmers, or wholesale middlemen and ultimate consumers; they buy and assemble stocks of merchandise which they own and hold at their own risk and attempt to resell them at a profit.

### Differences in Concepts

It is evident that distinct conceptions Underlie proper use of the terms *retailing, retail establishment, retail store,* and *retailer*. Retailing, the broadest conception, is the activity of selling to consumers for personal or household use.

While most of this activity takes place through stores, it may be engaged in by anyone—for example, a farmer selling vegetables door to door, a wholesaler selling to a personal acquaintance, or a manufacturer selling direct to consumers by mail. Such retailing activities are not included within the scope of operations of retail establishments, which constitutes the basis for all Census of Business data presented in this part of the text.

On the other hand, many retail stores make some sales which are essentially wholesale because the goods are purchased by businesses for purposes of resale or for business use.

Most retail stores are operated by retailers, merchant middlemen selling primarily to consumers, but this is not universal, for some are owned and operated by manufacturers, consumers, governmental agencies, and others.

## ECONOMIC BASIS OF RETAILING

The role of retailing in our economic life is related to the values created in the retailing process and the marketing functions performed by retailing organizations as they produce such values.

## Productive Character of Retailing.

Retailing organizations add values to commodities principally through the creation of place, time, and possession utilities and, to a limited extent, by the creation of form utility. Place utility is added by bringing goods from wholesale markets to conveniently accessible stores and, in some cases, by providing delivery service to consumers. Time utility is provided by anticipating consumer wants and storing goods from time of receipt until time of consumer purchase. Retailers make a substantial contribution to possession utility by transferring the ownership from business organizations that have no use for goods other than trading, to ultimate consumers for whom value in use is high. Many kinds of retail stores engage in form utility production as is illustrated by food preparation in eating places, meat preparation and packaging in food stores, and the operation of drapery and clothing alteration workrooms in department stores. For the most part, however, the creation of form utility by retailers is incidental rather than the principal attribute of the organization.

## Marketing Functions Performed by Retailers

In the process of creating economic values, most retailers perform all basic marketing functions, at least to some extent. *Buying* is an important function of merchants since they serve as purchasing agents and assemblers for their customers. This may be relatively simple or exceedingly complex. Some small appliance stores without repair service departments may have fewer than twenty different merchandise items in stock, and all of these may be obtained from one or two local wholesale distributors. In a modern supermarket there may be as many as 4,000 to 6,000 or more different items purchased or assembled from several hundred manufacturers and wholesale middlemen. At the extreme, a few large department stores carry more than 1 million different items in a wide variety of departments, and their buyers assemble merchandise from thousands of wholesale sources in almost all trade classifications.

*Selling* is the basic reason for the operation of stores. In stores that sell merchandise of high unit value and low replacement frequency, major reliance is often placed on personal selling so that the product line can be interpreted to the consumer and selling can be adapted to circumstances that vary appreciably among individuals. Almost, all classes of stores engage in some form of advertising. Those that sell predominantly convenience or standardized goods tend to rely heavily upon nonpersonal selling effort, making sales from visual displays that permit self-selection by consumers.

The significance of the *transportation function* varies considerably. Small retailers in convenience goods lines tend to rely upon wholesalers for long-distance spatial movements from farms or factories to the local market and from the wholesaler to the retail store. Large retailers, especially chain and department store organizations, often arrange for transportation of merchandise from distant sources to their local warehousing facilities and operate their own transportation equipment for moving goods from warehouses to individual stores or departments. Consumers have tended to assume the transportation function in store-to-household movements of merchandise, as use of automobiles has increased and retail trade has become more decentralized within metropolitan areas. Delivery service remains of great significance, however, for stores that serve a large trading area or sell heavy or bulky merchandise.

The historical significance of the *storage* function is suggested by the designation retails "store." In an early era, when transportation and communication services were slow and uncertain, the major function of retailers was that of maintaining a storehouse of merchandise, but modern developments have placed more emphasis upon the retailer's role as a distributor or seller. Storage remains, however, a key function and its importance varies in relation to stock turnover which may be more than 50 times per year for meat markets but as low as once per year for some jewelry stores. The significance of storage varies also with special facilities that often must be provided. For example, while food-store turnover is high, the investment for all of the various types of refrigeration equipment required for a modern supermarket may amount to more than $50,000.

Many large retailers are concerned with *standardization* in that they set product specifications for items manufactured or packaged under their own brand names. Food stores often pre package meat and fresh fruits and vegetables in standard units of sale. Some retailers confine their *financing* activities to providing an investment in fixtures, equipment, and inventory; but this is often supplemented by credit arrangements with wholesalers, manufacturers, and financial institutions. Many retailers finance purchases by ultimate consumers through charge account and instalment sale credit. For some retailers like department stores that sell on credit, this function has assumed tremendous significance, so that much more may be invested in receivables than in merchandise inventories. Since retailers are merchant middlemen, they assume the *risk* associated with ownership of various assets including receivables and inventories. This is especially hazardous in fashion merchandising where the wants of consumers change seasonally and within seasons. Every retailer must analyze the needs of consumers by collecting and interpreting *marketing information* if his merchandise offerings are to be in harmony with their buying wants and the goods are not to stagnate upon his shelves.

The degree to which the total performance of any given marketing function is assumed by the retailer, is divided among other marketing institutions, or is assumed by consumers through self-performance of marketing activities, varies from time to time and with different kinds of business. The costs incurred and the values contributed by retailers thus shift from time to time, as some functions increase in importance and others decrease.

## TOTAL RETAIL TRADE STRUCTURE

Some appreciation of the magnitude of the total retail trade structure and changes therein may be gained from a consideration of the dollar and physical volume of sales of all retail establishments, as related to trends in population growth, disposable income, and number of stores in operation.

## CLASSIFICATION OF RETAIL STORES

The same term, retail store, is used to refer to the vast R. H. Macy and Company department store in New York City and to the smallest cigar and newsstand operated in the lobby of a public building. Such a varied structure of retail institutions limits the extent to which it is possible to generalize about the totality. For proper understanding and evaluation of this structure and changes therein, it is essential to break it down into significant components through meaningful classifications, each of which may be studied by itself and in comparison with other segments with which it comes into competitive conflict or which may be deemed as socially or economically desirable alternatives.

It is possible to classify retail stores in an almost unlimited variety of ways, as illustrated by the outline of various alternatives. All of these classes are meaningful for some purposes, but it would be an endless and repetitious task to discuss all of them in detail. In this book attention is confined to a limited number of classification bases which have been selected with care to reveal the more significant characteristics of the retailing structure and to point up the major competitive, social, and economic problems and implications resulting therefrom.

### OWNERSHIP CLASSES

Analysis of retail stores in terms of ownership classes has long been of great interest because this approach involves numerous competitive and other implications. Such a breakdown reveals what groups have an entrepreneurial interest in retailing and which tend to dominate the institutional structure. Certain legislative and tax questions are involved. Certain regulatory and tax legislation tends to preserve or fortify the status of some ownership classes while placing handicaps or limitations on others. Type of ownership often reflects differences in operation, especially with respect to financial structure, method of procuring merchandise, and the degree to which retail store operations are integrated with the performance of wholesaling and manufacturing functions. In the following paragraphs, the more unique forms of ownership are discussed at greater length than the more commonplace because subsequent chapters are devoted substantially to the latter.

## Single-Unit Independent Stores

Over a long period of years, the independent retailer who operates a single store has dominated the retailing structure. The importance of this ownership class is indicated by the fact that such stores have comprised 86 to 90 per cent of total retail establishments enumerated in the various Censuses of Business from 1929 to 1958. Even though "typical" independent merchants operate smaller stores than their chain competitors, they dominate in total sales volume. Over the same period, sales of single-unit independents have amounted to about 66 to 70 per cent of sales of all retail establishments. With only limited exceptions, single-unit independents are relatively small, family-type enterprises that operate solely or almost altogether on the retail level. In view of the visual prominence of chain retailers, as reflected by conspicuousness in shopping centers and advertising media, the persistence of the independent is indeed remarkable.

## Chains or Multiunit Retailers

The major competitor of the independent is the chain. Multiunit or chain stores comprise about 10 per cent of all retail establishments counted in the Census of Business. Prior to World War II, the proportion of chain retail stores was somewhat higher, the decline being accounted for by the operation of larger scale establishments. Relatively, sales volume of chain organizations has been fairly stable in the long run, amounting to about 30 to 34 per cent of total retail trade, with some increase in competitive position in more recent years. About one-third of the total business of chains is done by fairly small multiunit organizations (ten stores or less) whose sympathies and outlook are in most respects more closely akin to the independent than to the large chain system. All but a small part of multiunit stores are owned by *retailers,* as opposed to manufacturers and other ownership classes.

**Manufacturer-owned Stores**

In certain lines of trade, independent and chain retailers compete with manufacturers who have integrated their operations forward in the distribution channel by the use of their own retail outlets.

Several reasons account for this practice. First, some manufacturers have opened stores in the belief that complete control over the entire marketing channel constitutes their most profitable alternative. This motive accounts for the presence of various well-known, manufacturer owned chains in the men's clothing, shoe, candy, and millinery lines of trade. Second, some manufacturer-owned stores are used to supplement other forms of distribution. Three of the best-known tire manufacturers operate company-owned retail outlets, but in no case do these constitute the company's sole outlets for tires and related automotive and household products. Such locations are usually established only in communities where there is an expectation of an unusually large volume of sales or where suitable independent outlets are not available. Third, a limited number of manufacturer-owned stores serve as experimental stations for testing product innovations or for developing merchandising methods or techniques that may be adapted for use by regular retailers. Finally, some manufacturers utilize their own retail establishments at factory locations in order to dispose of off-selected, rejected, or "stale" merchandise that is not salable through regular channels.

Expansion of retailing activities by manufacturers is limited by two major principles. First, manufacturer-owned stores are feasible only for well-financed companies that produce a relatlvely full line of related products, or products which are of relatively high unit value. In the absence of this condition, adequate sales volume cannot be obtained in a single retail establishment. As a corollary of this principle it has become apparent that successful manufacturer-owned stores usually function as merchant middlemen to some extent. Leading stores owned by men's clothing and tire manufacturers sell many items which are purchased from outside sources. Such goods are bought to round out the merchandise line, thus increasing sales volume per establishment and enhancing the efficiency of operation.

Second, many manufacturers who might prefer to develop some retail outlets are restrained by independent wholesalers and retailers, who object to such ventures as introducing unfair methods of competition. On certain occasions, the animosity of retailers has been so vociferous that attempts have been made to prohibit by legislation the operation of retail stores by manufacturers. Integration in marketing channels is now widely accepted, so that such public restrictions appear highly improbable. Fear of incurring "ill will" of regular outlets remains sufficiently strong, however, that it deters many manufacturers from engaging in retailing.

It is probable that the total of manufacturers' sales distributed through their owned retail stores does not exceed 2 per cent of the total of all manufacturers' sales distributed through all channels. To the extent that manufacturers make supplementary purchases from other sources, their retailing activities differ little from those of other multiunit retailers, except with respect to the major merchandise line of their own manufacture.

## Farmer-owned Stores

Another ownership class consists of farmers, some of whom maintain roadside establishments or leased facilities in public retail markets. The character of such establishments often results in a misleading impression that they involve, principally or entirely, direct farmer-to-consumer marketing. It is practically impossible for farmers to operate a *regular* retail establishment *on a continuing basis* solely by the sale of their own produce. When an investment is made in physical facilities or when market space is leased, it is almost always necessary for the farmer to buy many items from other farmers and from regular wholesale sources. Experience has revealed that the typical farmer cannot afford to devote time and energy to retailing and expect the same returns that are afforded to him by concentrating on agricultural production and marketing his output through regular wholesale trade channels.

Genuine direct retailing of farm produce is confined largely to seasonal and sporadic efforts. There is, for example, a considerable volume of roadside marketing during the home canning season for fresh farm produce. There is also evidence that farmers are most likely to resort to retailing as a desperation measure when prices are low or declining rapidly. So long as wholesale prices are adequate to cover the costs of agricultural production and afford the farmer a fair living, he is not likely to engage in the complex of activities necessary for satisfactory retailing.

**Government-owned Stores.**

In a socialist commonwealth the government would own and operate business organizati1ons for the benefit of the state. In the United States, however, the organization of practically all productive facilities reflects the democratic ideal of private competitive enterprise. Nevertheless, there are exceptional circumstances in which governmental units engage in retailing. Certain state governments maintain liquor stores: While such stores constitute an important source of government income, that cannot be considered as the motivating factor. The state has the alternative of levying excise taxes of any reasonable amount and could probably obtain the same or greater revenue on alcoholic beverages distributed through orthodox retail channels. State operation must then be viewed primarily as a device to effect social control of the distribution of alcoholic beverages.

Another form of government stores consists of commissaries, post exchanges, and similar establishments often used in connection with military installations, for the purpose of providing a special type of "fringe benefit" to employees on military bases. It is estimated that all classes of government operated stores account for only about 1 per cent of total retail sales volume.

## Consumer Cooperatives.

A consumer cooperative is a marketing organization owned and operated for the mutual benefit of consumerowners, who have voluntarily associated themselves for the purpose. Such an organization is an attempt to substitute joint or cooperative efforts of consumers for those of private enterprise. Properly speaking, *consumer* cooperation does not embrace cooperative dealings in industrial or business goods, such as farm supplies or equipment. There are, however, many farm cooperative associations that also handle consumer goods, and thus serve the farmers' interests as individual consumers, although such organizations are primarily concerned with the advancement of the interest of farmers as owners and operators of profit-making agricultural enterprises.

The modern consumer cooperative movement dates from 1844 when a group of poverty-stricken English weavers opened a crude store in Rochdale. Out of their experience a set of basic principles was developed and these have governed most consumer cooperatives throughout the world. These so-called "Rochdale principles" highlight the character of consumer cooperation and distinguish it from retailing as carried on by private business organizations. In brief, they are as follows:

- *Membership is open to all* adult persons, without regard to political or religious affiliations or social status;
- *Democratic control* is achieved by providing all members with one vote, regardless of amount of capital stock owned;
- *Limited interest is paid* on capital investment in accordance with the view that capital is to be regarded as the servant, not the master, of the organization
- *Sales are made at prevailing market prices* to accumulate

a surplus to be distributed in lump sums to patrons;

- Services are limited, as exemplified by the policy of *selling only for cash;*
- Any surplus accruing from the spread between prevailing market prices and cost of merchandise and store operation is paid to members in proportion to their volume of purchases as *patronage dividends;*
- Consumer cooperatives are supposed to adhere to a policy of *religious and political neutrality;*
- Certain percentages of earnings are usually set aside for purposes of *education* in order that alleged benefits and ideals can be spread among nonmembers, thus expanding the scope of operations and influence. While such "principles" have been widely observed, some cooperative organizations have found it expedient to depart from them. For example, some have tried to attract a wider membership by selling at unusually low prices, offering some types of credit service, and others have worked actively for political candidates who favor consumer cooperation and by stimulating legislation favorable to the cooperative program.

In certain European countries, consumer cooperation has achieved notable success, especially in England, Scotland, Wales, Sweden, Norway, Finland, Denmark, Switzerland, and Holland. By way of contrast, in the United States*strictly consumer* cooperative establishments (i.e., excluding the operations of those primarily engaged in selling feed, farm supplies, and petroleum products for farm business use) account for only a small fraction of 1 per cent of total retail sales volume.

Considerable controversy about consumer cooperatives has resulted from the fact that "earnings" or "savings" distributed as patronage refunds are not treated as profits for purposes of income taxation. This, it is often alleged, gives the cooperative an unfair advantage compared to private enterprises that pay income taxes on all profits. Consumer cooperatives, on the other hand, have obtained judicial support for the view that patronage dividends are a refund of purchase price rather than profits, and they point out that they comply with income tax laws, the same as any other business, on profits paid to shareholders as a return on capital investment and on all other profits not distributed on the basis of patronage. In any event, the tax advantage is a relatively minor one which gives this type of organization little or no pricing advantage, even though it may operate to increase the amount of annual patronage refund accumulated on a member's total purchases.

In the light of more than a century of experience with consumer cooperation, some explanation must be offered for the negligible part of this ownership group in the United States. For one thing, cooperatives in Europe achieved notable success in a competitive environment characterized by small, inefficient, tradition-bound, retail shops. In the United States, their success has been limited because consumers have had the opportunity to patronize chains and other limited-service retailers who have succeeded in attaining all types of economies sought by cooperatives. Second, in most European countries, the population has been more homogeneous in terms of heritage, social status, and religious affiliations, which has been conducive to cooperative effort.

In our country, the population of urban areas usually reflects a variety of occupations, social interests, and cultural values. This has made it difficult to assemble large groups of people who are favorably inclined to the cooperative movement.

Third, under economic conditions favorable for the masses, the American consumer has had a higher level of real income, has felt much less need to "pinch pennies," and has preferred to shop in a wide variety of stores which afford him an exceedingly wide range of choice of novel and unusual merchandise as well as basic necessities. Indeed, the consumer cooperatives which have achieved most notable success in this country have tended to be the ones which have sought to serve their owner-patrons by having better or superior stores rather than by emphasis upon savings or economy alone.

## EXTENT AND NATURE OF THE LINE OF GOODS HANDLED

Classification of stores on the basis of the extent and nature of the line of goods handled is useful because size, location, and, to a degree, merchandising methods are greatly affected by this factor. Three broad classes of stores are discernible:

- General merchandise stores,
- Single-line stores, and
- Specialty stores.

In distinguishing stores on this basis, the terms "variety" and "assortment" may be employed to advantage. As used in retailing *variety* implies generically different kinds of goods. Variety may be present in a related line of merchandise such as foods and is indicated by such diverse products as bread, canned tomatoes, frozen peas, cheese, and so on. It may also exist without any natural relationship among items, as in the variety store where one may find candy, toilet articles, stationery, toys, hardware, apparel, and so on. *Assortment,* on the other hand, relates to the range of choice among substitutable characteristics of a given type of article. A millinery store or department may be said to have broad or extensive assortments if a woman can choose the most suitable hat for a given purpose or use from many styles, colors, materials, and prices of hats.

### General Merchandise Stores

General merchandise stores handles such an extensive variety of goods that they cannot be classified into some kind of business grouping designated by the name of a principal type of commodity. Stores within this broad group are of several distinct types, including general stores, department stores, dry goods stores, and variety stores.

*General stores* are found chiefly in areas of scattered and isolated population, often as the only retail outlet in a small town or at some rural location. Such stores are usually small and nondepartmentized. Among the principal commodities commonly sold are groceries, hardware, dry goods, notions, toilet goods, staple lines of apparel and furnishings. A gasoline pump and very limited automobile service facilities are often a part of such businesses. The general, store was once a very significant type of outlet but has greatly declined in importance due to population growth, urbanization, and increases in automobile use and highway improvements which have made larger shopping districts more accessible to rural residents.

*Department stores* are usually large urban retail institutions that handle a wide variety of lines, such as women's ready-to-wear and accessories, men's and boys' clothing, piece goods, small wares, and home furnishings. Merchandise is segregated into separate departments for purposes of promotion, service, accounting, and control. Because department stores normally serve a large trading area, they are usually located in downtown areas or in major secondary shopping districts of large cities. The distinguishing feature of department stores is *variety* of shopping goods offerings, organized departmentally. When the department store is operated on a sufficiently large scale, individual departments are as large as or larger than ordinary specialty stores and are characterized by breadth of assortment as well as variety.

*Dry goods stores* are similar to department stores in terms of merchandise handled, although home furnishings are often absent. They are classified separately because they do not meet certain department store classification criteria, including sale of all required merchandise lines, large scale operation, or departmental organization.

As the name implies, *variety stores* handle many different kinds of merchandise, mostly of low unit value. They were the first important type of institution to emphasize self-service methods of retailing. Operations are characterized by giving merchandise maximum open display, rather than by providing active personal selling assistance by salespeople. The role of the salesperson is that of maintaining the stock in order and handling the transaction for the consumer. These stores are still popularly known by their historical connotation, "5 and 10 percent stores," even though this term is no longer descriptive due to extension of price lines and greater emphasis on shopping goods. Originally, they were essentially convenience goods stores. They are generally situated at points of heavy concentrations of consumer traffic, and most of them are units of chain organizations.

## Single-Line Stores

An extensive variety of one line of merchandise that is *related in sale or use* is the basis for classification as a single-line store. Such stores are usually designated in terms of the principal line of goods, such as groceries, drugs, hardware, men's clothing, furniture, or jewelry. In a men's clothing store, for example, a consumer expects to find all kinds of men's apparel including hosiery, shoes, underwear, shirts, neckware, suits, coats, and hats. Large assortments of any one of these kinds of merchandise are found only in fairly large clothing stores. Thus it may be said that the basis for the single-line store is related variety; wide assortments are dependent upon a scale of operation that permits an extensive inventory investment.

When single-line stores operate on a very large scale, they are usually departmentized. This is especially true in the supermarket and chain drugstore fields, as well as in the furniture and apparel trades. Stores handling men's, women's, or family apparel and organized on a departmental basis are commonly known as "departmentized specialty stores." This gives rise to some confusion because the word "specialty" in this case is used to distinguish such stores from regular department stores rather than to denote the type of limited variety characterizing small specialty stores which are described in the following section.

Historically, single-line stores tended to replace general stores as small communities grew in size. While their variety of merchandise is ordinarily much more limited than in stores of the general merchandise group, it is much more extensive than in the case of specialty stores.

## Specialty Stores

This term refers to stores which handle an extremely limited variety of goods. In some trades, practically all establishments are of this highly specialized character. Examples include automobile dealers, gasoline service stations, florists, and book stores. In other instances the specialty store handles only part of a line of goods customarily sold by single-line stores. Single-line grocery stores compete with specialty stores such as baked-goods establishments, dairy stores, and meat markets. In the clothing field single-line stores divide the market with specialty stores such as shoe stores, millinery shops, lingerie establishments, maternity dress shops, and furriers. Because specialty stores confine their offerings to a narrow range of items, they have more extensive assortments than single-line stores of comparable, size. A men's shoe store, for example, is a highly specialized operation in which the consumer expects to find a wide range of styles, colors, and prices in his size. The operation of a specialty store should not be confused with the sale of specialty goods. The term "specialty" when used to designate a store implies limited variety of goods. These may be convenience goods as illustrated by cigar stands, they may be shopping goods such as apparel items, or they may be specialty goods such as automobiles, vacuum cleaners, or collectors' items as, for example, rare postage stamps.

Specialty stores often have relatively simple buying problems in that most or all merchandise is drawn from one or few suppliers in the same trade. They have a competitive advantage over single-line stores in terms of assortments, but have a more limited opportunity for related, item selling. Specialty stores, for the most part, operate in well-established shopping districts.

## Kind of Business Groupings

Single-line and specialty stores are not separately classified in Census tabulations, and it would probably be impossible to provide quantitative information about each of these twoclasses. For purposes of business use it is more desirable to classify both single-line and specialty stores within kind-of-business classifications. With the exception of the general merchandise group, all stores included in this table may be considered as single line or specialty. It is easy to distinguish certain single-line operations, such as grocery stores, from specialty establishments like meat markets or candy stores. In other cases, such distinctions are not possible. One women's dress shop may handle a large variety of apparel, and be classified as a women's clothing store; another may specialize to the extent of selling only cotton dresses within a narrow price range, but still be grouped in the same classification.

## CLASSIFICATION BY LOCATION

Classification of stores according to location indicates the extent to which retail trade is concentrated or dispersed, and it is indicative of consumer buying habits. Stores are found in

- Rural buying centers;
- Small cities or towns, in their downtown areas or in neighbourhood locations; and
- Urban areas in a wide variety of specific types of locations.

The distribution of retail establishments and sales volume corresponds rather closely with the distribution of population and disposable personal income among the largest metropolitan areas, other metropolitan areas, and the remainder of the country. Somewhat fewer estab lishments are to be found in the largest metropolitan areas than would be expected on the basis of population and income, due to the location of many stores of unusually large size in such areas. Sales volume is greater in the largest areas than would be expected on the basis of population, because of a tendency of major shopping goods stores to draw trade beyond the boundaries of the metropolitan area; it is less, however, than would be expected on the basis of income distribution, owing to a tendency for families of unusually high incomes (and with relatively low propensity to consume) to be concentrated in the largest population areas. The local character of retailing is well illustrated by the fact that outside of the 189 major metropolitan areas are to be found 43.0 per cent of the retail establishments, 32.7 per cent of the sales volume, 38.2 per cent of the population, and 30.3 per cent of the disposable personal income.

Retail trade has tended to become more localized than was formerly the case. Since 1929 the proportion of the total population residing in metropolitan areas has increased substantially, but the proportion of retail sales accounted for by such areas has remained constant. As a result, per capita retail sales in nonmetropolitan areas have risen faster than in metropolitan areas, and nonmetropolitan areas have become relatively more important as trade centers than would be expected on the basis of their population importance. Among the plausible explanations for this situation are the following conditions:

- Changes in food purchasing patterns, reflecting increasing purchases of food store products for home use by farm families, and diminishing importance of home production for home use;
- Growing importance of brands as standards of value and increasing widespread distribution of most branded items of merchandise;
- Changes in consumer tastes and shopping habits which have tended to increase the number of items purchased on a local, or convenience, basis;
- General decline of the attractiveness of shopping in the central retail districts of major cities.

The local nature of retailing is also demonstrated by the dispersion of sales volume within metropolitan areas. Between 1954 and 1959 the proportion of retail trade transacted within the main city of the ten largest metropolitan areas declined from 61.0 to 54.8 per cent while the proportion of total sales in the remainder of such areas (consisting primarily of suburban communities which accounted for most of the population growth of the period) increased from 39.0 to 45.2 per cent..

## CONSUMER SERVICE ESTABLISHMENTS

Any broad examination of the retailing structure must include some consideration of the hundreds of thousands of service establishments that market primarily to the ultimate consumer. While such establishments are not included in the Retail Trade portion of the Census of Business, they operate on the same plane of distribution and are similar to retail stores in most other respects; moreover, service establishments that market to the general consuming public are recognized as being of the same essence as retail stores, for purposes of administering the Fair Labor Standards Act and have been so judged by federal courts.

**Table. Number and Sales Volume of Selected Consumer Service Establishments: United States, 1958**

| Kind of Business | Number of Establishments | Sales Volume (millions) |
|---|---|---|
| Hotels, motels, tourist courts, camps | 85,580 | $3,888 |
| Personal services (laundry, dry cleaning, beauty shops, barber shops, photographic, shoe repair, funeral, alteration, etc.) | 411,507 | 7,394 |
| Automobile repair and other automotive services | 125,240 | 3,853 |
| Miscellaneous repair services (electrical, watch, jewelry, furniture, etc.) | 144,759 | 2,262 |
| Motion picture theatres | 16,354 | 1,172 |
| Amusement, recreation services, except motion pictures (dance halls, theatrical presentations, bowling, billiards, commercial sports, etc.) | 74,696 | 2,661 |

The sale of services produced upon the premises is the predominant characteristic of so-called "service establishments." Many, however, sell tangible commodities as well, either as part of the process of rendering a service (as supplies or parts used in shoe or automotive repair) or on a merchandising basis (as hair preparations sold in barber shops or bowling equipment and supplies sold in bowling places).

The magnitude of the structure of consumer or "retail" service establishments is suggested by the data in Table. Such establishments, for the most part, can be classified according to the various bases previously outlined for retail establishments. In terms of ownership or location, for example, the same classifications used for retail stores are appropriate for consumer service establishments. By line or kind of business, however, most partake of the attributes of specialty stores, as opposed to single-line or general merchandise establishments, due to the lack of variety of offerings at a given place of business.

### OTHER CLASSIFICATIONS

The foregoing discussion of classifications of retail stores has revealed many varied characteristics of our retailing structure. It has not been sufficiently detailed, however, to present all significant institutional developments. Consequently, additional classifications are introduced in subsequent chapters in connection with analyses of small- and large-scale retailers, department stores, chain stores and voluntary chains, supermarkets, planned shopping centers, discount houses, mail order companies, house-to-house selling organizations, and vending machine operations.

## ADAPTIVE BEHAVIOR IN RETAILING

### HISTORICAL BACKGROUND

Early in the evolution of American retailing was the fur trading post at which pioneer trappers traded furs for manufactured goods. Later the Yankee peddler brought cutlery and tinware from New England and other producing centers to the Ohio Valley and even on to the West as settlers demanded goods which they themselves could not produce. As population increased, the need for the trading post and the peddler diminished, since the general store could take their place and render more complete service. It performed many functions which the more simple institutions could not render and which became necessary as the standard of living became somewhat higher.

With further increases in the size of cities and an enhanced flow of manufactured goods, single-line stores came into being and began to dominate the retail trade structure. Specialization in merchandise continued in the largest market centers, with the advent of specialty stores.

Many single-line and specialty stores that had established a reputation by about the time of the 1860's added other merchandise lines, thus enlarging the scale of their business by the operation of a number of separate shops under the same ownership in the same establishment. In this manner department stores were born, but this was not possible until urban areas had grown in size to permit the functioning of rather large establishments and until developments in urban transportation made it relatively convenient for consumers to visit downtown areas with some frequency.

Almost paralleling the development of the department store was the mail order house which was evolved to bring large selections of merchandise to consumers in sparsely populated areas that could not support a variety of retailing establishments. Spectacular growth in mail order sales took place after 1913, with the inauguration of rural free delivery service and parcel post. As factory production increased, a number of astute and far-seeing merchants conceived the idea of applying standard operating procedures to multiunit organizations. The Great Atlantic and Pacific Tea Company was founded in 1858 and the F. W. Woolworth Company in 1880. A number of other leading chains were also formed in the nineteenth century, but their greatest expansion came with increasing urbanization which proceeded at a fast pace during the 1920's. Through the consolidation of buying strength in a large central organization and by standardized procedures for limited-service retailing, such organizations won public favor by satisfying price-conscious consumers whose wants had apparently grown faster than their purchasing power.

Corporate chain developments of the 1920's had an adverse effect upon independents and their wholesaler suppliers. These groups adapted their operations to changing conditions, partly through the defensive mechanism of the voluntary chain which was conceived to bring similar kinds of purchasing and operating economies to the independent's sphere of activity. The supermarket, a development of the 1930's, reflects the growing importance of the automobile and also the more general recognition that consumers are willing to assume responsibility for the performance of some part of the marketing functions, provided that self-service activities are accompanied by price advantages and an attractive atmosphere for shopping.

## RECENT DEVELOPMENTS

In the post- World War II era, institutional changes have taken a variety of forms. The branch store of the large city department store has arisen in response to the movement of population to the suburbs and to communities surrounding the cities. The modern type of completely planned or "controlled" drive-in shopping centers reflects also the impact of the decentralization of urban population, increased use of the automobile, and downtown traffic congestion and parking problems associated therewith.

In the early 1950's, traditional concepts regarding the gross margin of profit necessary to cover the normal costs of merchandising many types of items were shattered by "discount houses." Such stores offered nationally advertised merchandise under conditions of limited store service at substantial discounts from prevailing prices in regular outlets. Their success may be attributed to their ability to make a large volume of sales at a relatively low gross profit per unit, and cover all necessary costs from the large volume obtainable in a modern mass market dominated by middleincome classes of consumers with unparalleled levels of purchasing power. The growth of such organizations forced department stores and other retailers to re-evaluate their performance, and to bring about changes in operating methods, pricing policy, and promotional strategy so that they could compete effectively.

Conflicting trends have been observable with respect to the extent of the line of merchandise handled by stores. On the one hand, there is a tendency toward greater variety, especially in newer shopping centers. Grocery stores of the supermarket type have become strongly entrenched in merchandising nonfood lines including drugs, toilet goods, paper products, books and magazines, and many items of housewares. Variety stores have expanded price ranges and have increased their relative emphasis upon apparel and other shopping goods lines.

Many new drugstores and hardware stores, and even gasoline service stations, carry much more diversified lines than historically associated with these lines of trade. Increased variety has resulted from the desire to add items with a larger gross profit margin and to increase sales volume per store, thus reducing certain overhead expenses. It also reflects a stronger consumer orientation in retailing, as stores have departed from tradition-bound emphasis upon generic classifications of products and have sought to pull together in planned merchandise offerings a greater variety of items which consumers may seek to purchase in combination or from a given source of supply, based on their attitudes and shopping preferences.

On the other hand, higher levels of buying income in more densely populated market areas have made possible increasing degrees of specialization. While some drug chains have opened larger and more diversified establishments, many independents have reverted to the older concept of specialized ethical drugstores, without soda-fountains and miscellaneous merchandise departments. Many shopping areas now include highly specialized establishments like drapery fabric stores, sewing machine stores, toy stores, greeting card shops, floor covering establishments, and even automobile laundries. Effective specialization has often taken the form of an appeal to some specific segment of the consumer market, as opposed to mere fractionizing of a line of commodities. Common examples include hobby shops, apparel stores for tall girls, and children's stores.

# Chapter 8

# Small-Scale Versus Large-Scale Retailing

## IMPORTANCE OF SMALL- VERSUS LARGE-SCALE RETAILING

Just what constitutes small- or large-scale retailing has been debated vigorously with little resulting agreement. A precise dividing line is of dubious value for present purposes because it is easy to demonstrate that the most prevalent form of retail enterprise is the independently owned store that would be judged small by anyone's standards.

Scale of operations is reflected in part by legal form of organization and also by size of assets. Of all retailing firms, 91 per cent are unincorporated business-77.6 per cent sole proprietorships and 13.4 per cent partnerships. To this group may well be added corporations with total assets of less than $1,000,000. These categories of firms together account for 99.8 per cent of all firms classified in retail trade and account for some three-fourths of total sales volume. On the other hand, retailing corporations with assets of over $1,000,000 (most of which would be commonly regarded as large-scale enterprises) account for only 0.2 per cent of the total number of firms but handle about one-fourth of total retail sales.

The data of retail *firms* (separate business enterprises) in Table are from a new series first published in 1960 and hence cannot be evaluated historically. From other sources it is apparent that large-scale retailing has increased somewhat in significance in recent years. Chain retailers accounted for about

30 percent of total retail volume consistently over the period 1929-48. Between 1948 and 1958, however, sales of multiunit establishments increased from about 30 per cent to 33 per cent of total retail sales. Most of this gain in the sales volume of chains was accounted for by companies operating 11 or more store units. This group increased its proportion of total retail sales from 18.6 per cent in 1948 to 22.3 per cent in 1958—a gain of about 20 per cent in *share* of total retail trade. Independents or smaller retailers, nevertheless, remain dominant, accounting for all but a minute fraction of firms and some two-thirds to three-fourths of sales, depending upon what criterion one wishes to use to distinguish between small- and large-scale organizations.

In service trades, where most firms are engaged in marketing on the retail or consumer level of distribution, the preponderance of small-scale operation is even more pronounced. Corporations with assets over $1 million represent only about 0.1 per cent of the firms and handle less than 15 per cent of total service trade sales.

## SMALL-SCALE RETAILERS

Smaller independent stores, as a class of institutions, enjoy certain competitive advantages which favor the growth and development of organizations where management has the ability to capitalize opportunities. On the other hand, smaller organizations are subject to certain rather general disadvantages which limit the growth and development of weaker firms and which, by the same token, contribute to the expansion of largerscale enterprises. Knowledge of these considerations is essential in appraising the present and probable future competitive situation in retailing.

### COMPETITIVE ADVANTAGES

One advantage contributing to survival ability is that throughout the independent store field *explicit costs of doing business are generally low* in relation to sales. These costs include out-of-pocket outlays and other items, like depreciation, carried on the accounting records as costs. Selling costs are low because the proprietor and other family employees often derive their compensation in the form of "profit" rather than salary payments which are charged against business income. Often the location of such stores enables them to pay low salaries to hired employees and to utilize rather unskilled part-time help. Rental costs tend to be low, partly because large numbers of such stores are located in neighbourhood or rural areas, also because ownership of store premises by the retailer is much more common among smaller independents than it is among chains or large-scale independent operators.

Second, *in many cases a small independent store is operated by one who devotes only a part of his time to the store.* Were it not for this advantage, it would be impossible for many small retailers to continue in business. Consider the problem of operating a store with about $25,000 annual sales volume. While gross profit margins vary considerably with different lines of trade, about 25 per cent is reasonably representative. This means that about 75 per cent of sales or $18,750 would be required to cover the cost of merchandise sold and that only about $6,250 would be available as gross profit, from which all expenses must be paid before there is any residual net profit. If reasonable allowance is made for operating expenses such as rent, advertising, store supplies, telephone, heat and light, and depreciation, it is apparent that such a merchant would have a difficult time in realizing enough personal income to afford a decent standard of living.

Nevertheless, more than 600,000 retailers in the sole proprietorship category (about one-half of the total in this group) report annual sales volume of less than $25,000. It is possible for many such merchants to continue businesses only because they may be engaged in some other gainful employment, either as salaried workers or as entrepreneurs in other enterprises, or because they are able to supplement store income with disability benefits or retirement income. When due consideration is given to this point, one must refrain from passing judgment on the economic justification of such stores merely on the basis of their small size.

The advantages thus far mentioned may be thought of by

some as uneconomic or even antisocial. Yet the fact remains that a store which can operate only with the help of unpaid members of the family, or one which exists only because the owner has other income, constitutes a definite part of our distribution system, and it does have the advantages mentioned. Moreover, in its limited way it may serve urgent needs of customers who find it convenient or otherwise desirable, while at the same time supporting in part or entirely many persons who might not otherwise be gainfully employed.

Third, and undoubtedly most important, is the advantage of *convenience of location*. One of the outstanding characteristics of smaller retailers is they are to be found nearly anywhere that trade occurs. Since most of them deal in convenience goods, they are located mainly with reference to homes of customers. Only rarely does one have to go far to find a small independent store, and numerous studies of patronage motives have revealed the importance of location as a fundamental reason why consumers buy from independent merchants. A fourth common advantage is the *opportunity for close personal contact that grows out of the size of smaller independent stores.* The ability of the owner-manager to establish and maintain friendly relationships with customers and cater to their personalized tastes is a strong argument for the well-being of the independent merchant. A corollary to this advantage is the *opportunity to develop a unique store personality.*

In one survey of informed trade opinion, lack of a well-defined character was cited as a common characteristic of independent stores while, at the same time, the opportunity to create an identity or image that differentiates a given independent store from all others of like type or size was recognized as the most outstanding single opportunity for betterment of competitive situation. Unfortunately, opportunity and realization do not always go hand in hand. A strong and distinctive store personality, brought about by an integrated approach to all aspects of customer contact activities, is developed only by merchants with energy, initiative, and ability.

## COMPETITIVE DISADVANTAGES

An outstanding limitation of smaller independents is their *buying handicap*. They cannot enjoy the lower prices which come from largescale purchases unless they join some form of group-buying organization, and even then they are rarely able to offset entirely this handicap. Wholesalers who must make small and frequent deliveries cannot offer the same low prices which they can give to the larger buyers who have both the storage space and the finances to permit quantity purchases.

Second, the smaller retailer is handicapped by the *absence of specialized employees*. Generally speaking, the entreprenuer must be his own personnel manager, advertising manager, sales manager, accountant, sales person, and, all too often, janitor as well. Lack of specialized skill is often of great importance in making wise selection of goods for resale, especially in fashion merchandising. The lack of the trained accountant and the important statistical information provided by him are serious weaknesses, yet they constitute, as was so well said many years ago, "the rudder which shows which way the ship goes."

A third competitive limitation is the *inability to advertise* on a scale comparable with chain store organizations or large-scale independent stores. Small stores often spend as large or even a greater proportion of their sales volume for advertising as their larger rivals, yet the dollar expenditures are necessarily small. This limits the small merchant's ability to utilize media with large circulation. Even in small cities where such merchants may be able to afford advertising space comparable with chain units, the limited funds and lack of specialized talent often result in ineffective layouts or poor copy.

Fourth, the small independent is distinctly *limited* with respect to *ability to innovate or experiment*. A chain store can try out a new merchandising technique or idea in one unit, or a department store in one department, and if the results prove unfavorable, the loss may be easily absorbed by profits arising from other operations. The small merchant, however, does not have this favorable distribution of risks and usually must follow rather than lead in new developments.

Fifth, most smaller stores suffer from *inability to utilize personnel and capital resources efficiently*. Surveys of operating results conducted by various associations reveal that the smallest classes of stores have lower ratios of sales per employee than the medium-sized and larger stores in the same trade classification. For example, in a 1959 survey of hardware stores, the ratio of sales per person employed was $23,145 for stores with sales under $50,000 as compared with $30,745 for those with over $200,000 annual volume.

The ratio of total assets per $10,000 of sales was about one-fifth less for stores in the larger of these two sales volume classes. Ratios of sales volume per square foot of store area also vary directly with the sales volume size of establishments in most lines of trade, demonstrating that space and other capital resources are utilized more efficiently in larger firms. This disadvantage makes it necessary for small retailers to employ unskilled personnel that can be hired for low wages and to use physical facilities in low-rent locations; these conditions, in turn, contribute to continuing low levels of operating efficiency in the smallest firms.

Another common though not universal disadvantage of smaller stores is *lack of managerial ability*. Although it is impossible to measure this alleged lack of ability, it is evident that a large number of independent store owners cannot boast of great business acumen. Because of location, friendship, lack of competition from more capable merchants, or other favorable circumstances, these merchants have been able to stay in business.

But this does not constitute proof that either the individual involved or that members of his class can continue to withstand newer types of competition. A question of serious import is whether small stores can attract efficient owners or pay the going rate for capable managers. There are reasons to believe that the general level of managerial ability has risen in recent years among independent stores generally, but this does not apply to the management of the smallest such establishments. If this is true, independent store operation may prove less attractive to young men of outstanding ability and thus add to the difficulties of existing independents in meeting competition from larger-scale institutions.

## FAILURES AND SURVIVAL ABILITY

Operation of a retail store, like that of other business enterprises, involves considerable risk. Many stores are closed each year because of inability to meet financial obligations. Even more are closed because the proprietor has not been able to secure the return on his capital and invested time to justify continuation of the enterprise. When a retailer ceases to operate his store, some disturbance of normal trade relationships usually occurs. Often closing-out sales are at price levels which, if met by competitors, result in loss to them. Landlords lose tenants. Supply houses may have to take back fixtures which are no longer new. A failure, rather than voluntary cessation of store operation, involves losses to creditors. It is therefore important to note the extent of failures, some of the common causes, and possible remedies.

Numerous studies have been made of failure rates among retailers and the basic causes thereof. The most comprehensive data on this subject are those collected by the well-known mercantile credit agency, Dun and Bradstreet, Inc. Records from this source indicate that about one-half or more of business failures are usually failures of small retailing businesses. This is explained not so much by the unusually hazardous character of retailing as it is by the fact that the number of small business firms engaged in retailing (including consumer service enterprises) is so much greater than in other business classifications. Failures in retailing occur particularly in the smallest sales-volume classes of stores and in the first two or three years of their operation.

Studies of the causes of retailing failures, based on the opinions of informed creditors as reported by Dun and Bradstreet, Inc., indicate that it is relatively rare for a retail business to fail because of reasons which are beyond the realm of managerial ability or control. About 85 to 90 per cent of retailing failures are attributed to inexperience, incompetence, or other factors related to management qualifications or performance, and this situation does not change much from one year to another. Yet, as one small merchant succumbs, another usually rises to take his place, as evidenced by continuing stability of total number of independent retailers over many years. While individual merchants, especially the less well qualified, are highly vulnerable, smaller merchants *as a class* demonstrate remarkable survival ability regardless of numerous failures.

An important underlying cause of retailing failures is *relative ease of entering the field without the experience or capital* necessary for successful operation. In retailing, more than in any other field, many persons with relatively little chance for success manage to get a start. To the extent that it is desirable for the door of opportunity always to be open to all, this is encouraging. But when the costs of failure are considered, it may be that entry is too easy.

Although many students of marketing and of social progress believe this last conclusion to be sound, no effective way of preventing the opening of stores by persons unlikely to succeed has yet been devised. Proposals urging more careful credit-granting by banks, wholesalers, and manufacturers have been made for years, but there is little valid evidence that credit is harder to secure than in the past except in periods when the supply of capital is unusually limited.

Systems of licensing based upon examinations have been suggested, but it is not likely that the probabilities of success can be adequately measured by tests. If a license to open a store were required, some governmental agency would necessarily be charged with the responsibility of determining who should receive a license. It does not seem probable that any such agency could select from many applicants those with high probability of success. It must therefore be concluded that as yet the various attempts to reduce the failure rate of merchants have met with little success.

## LARGE-SCALE RETAILING

The antithesis of the small-scale retailer is illustrated by a variety of specific kinds of stores—the metropolitan department store, large departmentized stores in the apparel and home furnishings trades, mail order companies, large supermarkets and discount houses, and multiunit or chain organizations of many kinds. Each of these types has its unique problems and advantages, but all of them have attributes in common, to the extent that they arise out of scale of operation or size of enterprise.

## ADVANTAGES

One of the most important advantages of scale is the elaborate *division of labor* that results from specialization in effort. Size permits employment of experts for executive positions. Skilled buyers, advertising managers, accountants, statisticians, and personnel directors are all at the command of such big businesses.

Large firms can usually afford *extensive departmentization.* By carefully classifying merchandise and creating departments for the sale of particular lines of merchandise or for more specific appeal to differentiated groups of customers, management enjoys not only advantages of specialization on the part of buyers and salespeople but is also facilitated in discovery of profitable and unprofitable classes of goods and in a more accurate measurement of the efficiency of department or store managers.

A most important competitive advantage is *large buying power.* Since purchases are large and hence important to suppliers, large-scale retailers can often circumvent the wholesaler in an economical manner and, by so doing, can obtain the most favorable prices. Not only are large discounts from list prices secured when big quantities are purchased, but other concessions, such as advertising allowances, exclusive rights for distribution, or free goods, may also be obtained.

While manufacturers' freedom to quote more favorable prices to large buyers has been somewhat limited by legislation, particularly the Robinson-Patman Act, large-scale retailers remain in a position to purchase on much more favorable terms than their smaller rivals on purely economic grounds. Further buying advantages are realized through ability to employ experts to perform this function. The *financial strength* of large institutions often attracts investors and facilitates the acquisition of capital for expansion. Size is an advantage in making banking connections which may enable the borrower to secure loans on favorable terms. Large financial resources make it possible to take advantage of cash discounts offered by sellers and to attract vendors who may be led to offer especially favorable terms of sale.

Large retailers have the ability to *command the most favorable locations.* Many leases in retailing involve rental payments calculated as a per cent of sales volume. In such cases, the large firm, with a demonstrated capacity to generate substantial volume, is generally a preferred tenant. Shopping center developers prefer to obtain leases from large, financially strong companies because such leases can be used as security in obtaining loans from banks, insurance companies, and other sources of capital for shopping center construction.

Many large-scale retailers achieve operating economies or derive additional income from the *integration of other business activities* with retail merchandising. Many chains, department stores, and mail order companies have established their own warehouses which are operated on an efficient scale and in which are performed the distributive functions of the regular wholesaler, with the exception of personal selling activities which are largely eliminated between these two levels in the channel of distribution. Outright ownership or control of manufacturing plants is not uncommon among large organizations in the apparel, general merchandise, and food trades. Some retailing corporations have subsidiary companies which perform essentially a banking service by financing accounts receivables for the parent organizations. Real estate developments, particularly of the planned shopping center type, are also integrated into the operation of some department store groups and food chains, usually by means of separately incorporated subsidiaries.

The *prestige* which results, in part at least, from the great size of the leading chain, department store, and mail order companies is a distinct advantage in attracting patronage. The reputation of such firms is well established, either because of a long history in a given location or the publicity associated with their operations on a widespread geographic basis. This prestige, when accompanied with integration, is particularly suitable for the promotion of private brands of merchandise.

All forms of large-scale retailing benefit from a certain amount of *risk distribution.* Customers are drawn from large areas or many different lines are sold. The organization can usually assimilate severe losses in some departments or operating units, without greatly impairing the profit making possibilities of the entire organization.

Finally, *experimentation and research* represent types of activity which may prove most effective in increasing efficiency and which, while practical for the large retailer, may be too expensive to be undertaken by his smaller competitors.

## INHERENT DISADVANTAGES

The unfavorable factors incident to large-scale retailing are less numerous than the advantages and for that reason may be stated much more briefly. This should not, however, lead to an underestimation of their importance, because it is these disadvantages that contribute a great deal toward explaining the significance of small-scale operation in our retailing structure. Furthermore, each of the various forms of large-scale retailing has some disadvantages that are peculiar to it, but which are not discussed at this point.

A major weakness of large companies lies in the *absence of close personal contact between the owners or general managers and the consuming public.* Most consumers meet only the rank and file of subordinate employees, rarely the owners or major executives. While the self-interest of routine workers, together with their training and supervision, may produce some measure of efficiency, hired managers usually function with less effectiveness than do the more able owners of small businesses with their sharpened personal interest in customers.

Another disadvantage consists of *high overhead costs arising out of the complex organization structures* of large-scale enterprises. Some advantages of specialization are offset by lack of close contact between top management and subordinates and may have unfavorable effects upon efficiency. Larger concerns ordinarily have a much greater proportion of nonselling employees than smaller retail organizations. Much nonselling labor results from the need for costly methods of recording and checking the activities of the various divisions and maintaining the minute supervision necessary to fix responsibility, check performance, and minimize waste.

## LEGAL LIMITATIONS

Belief in small business as a manifestation of the American way of life has had an important bearing upon the history of trade legislation. Numerous enactments have been designed to curb some of the buying power and other advantages of large organizations and to provide, thereby, legal methods of balancing the competitive situation between the large and the small. Noteworthy are the Robinson-Patman Act, and fair trade and unfair trade practices legislation designed to curb uneconomic price-cutting tactics.

### The Robinson-Patman Act

While trade legislation is discussed in detail in later chapters, it is important to note briefly how such legislation operates to limit large organizations.

The Robinson-Patman Act, a federal law enacted in 1936, represents an attempt to curb certain uneconomic advantages of large retailers, which they enjoyed merely because of large size and great purchasing power. Numerous instances are on record in which large-scale buyers have more or less compelled manufacturers to sell to them at prices much lower than paid by wholesalers who supply small independent merchants. Supporters of this legislation contend that such manufacturers must then charge wholesalers or independent retailers a higher than normal price to compensate for abnormally low prices given to large-scale buyers. To prevent unjustifiable differences in prices, the Act makes it unlawful for sellers to discriminate in price between different buyers (of the same type or class) on goods of like grade and quality where the effect of such discrimination may be substantially to lessen competition, to tend to create a monopoly, to injure, destroy, or prevent competition. In substance, the law provides that *only those price discriminations are allowed which are justified by differences in cost to the vendor* or when done *in good faith to meet the lower price of a competitor.* Thus, in many instances large retailers are deprived of the sizable discounts and other price concessions which they once enjoyed. In some cases, however, a manufacturer may show that his economies in selling to large buyers are greater than the discounts given, but in general the effect has been to reduce the buying advantage of the large firms.

Because of their great importance to resources, large retailers have been able to secure substantial advertising allowances. Numerous manufacturers follow a policy of advertising cooperatively with their retail outlets, with part of the cost paid by the manufacturers. This established practice usually works to the benefit of both parties and is above criticism. Objections arise not from the nature of the practice but from its abuse in the form of unjustified discrimination. Chains and large department stores were able to secure substantial advertising allowances from many companies which did not grant such allowances to small independents. In essence, such discrimination amounts to a subsidization of the big retailer's advertising program at the expense of independents who are not able to obtain comparable discounts. A second major provision of the Act attempted to prevent this kind of discrimination by *prohibiting advertising and all other forms of sales promotional or service allowances, unless they are made available on proportionally equal terms to all customers.* It is perfectly legal for a manufacturer to give a large buyer an advertising allowance amounting, for example, to 3 per cent of such buyer's purchases, but it cannot do this *legally* without making the same percentage allowance available to all customers.

Another practice curbed by the Act pertains to brokerage

fees. Numerous manufacturers cannot support their own sales force and hence employ brokers who also serve other manufacturers. In performing the selling function for the manufacturer, the broker renders a valuable service for which he is entitled to reasonable compensation. Many large chains and department store buying offices set up subsidiary purchasing companies which were, in effect, *dummy* brokerage offices. Retailers required manufacturers to sell through these subsidiaries and grant to them the usual brokerage fee.

In such an instance, the dummy brokerage office is not a representative of the seller, but rather an agent of the purchaser. As a purchasing company seeking out sources of supply, it would be logical to expect that it should be compensated by the buyer rather than the seller. When an organization owned by a buyer obtains a brokerage fee from a seller whom it does not serve, this merely amounts to an unjustified price discrimination, because other purchasers must pay the manufacturer's factory price with perhaps a brokerage fee *added* rather than *deducted*. A third major provision of the Robinson-Patman Act was designed to *prohibit sellers of merchandise from paying brokerage fees to other than their own agents*. A broker may only collect a commission or fee when he acts as a bona fide third party, rather than as an employee of the buyer, for services rendered to the principal who pays the fee.

These provisions do not curb any *economic* advantages of large-scale retailers. To the extent that a seller can deal with a large buyer at lower costs of marketing than encountered when dealing with small independents, he can give a lower price. The large retailer can still obtain advertising allowances, but only if the allowances are made available to all of the vendor's customers on proportionally equal terms. It cannot obtain brokerage fees for itself, but this does not place it at a disadvantage with respect to small merchants. The effect of the Robinson-Patman Act has been substantially that of restricting *power* advantages of giant retailers, that is, benefits that they once enjoyed to a high degree because of ability to secure concessions by coercion. It does not penalize them through curbing any natural advantages they enjoy *because of ability to perform marketing functions in a more efficient and economical manner.*

## State Pricing Legislation

In many states, laws have been enacted which limit pricing freedom, thereby restricting the price appeal and price-cutting tactics of some merchants, primarily in the large-scale classification. Other laws place restrictions on price discrimination in *intrastate commerce.*

The best known of these are the so-called *fair trade* laws. The first such law was enacted in California in 1931, for the purpose of putting a floor under the resale prices of the branded items of manufacturers that chose to operate under this type of law. Eventually, 45 states passed similar laws, and they were legalized in interstate commerce originally by the Miller-Tydings Act of 1937 and later also by the McGuire Act of 1952. Constitutionality was challenged in the court systems of most states, and judicial opinion was approximately equally divided regarding the constitutionality of such laws, either in entirety or in regard to some major provision. In 1961 some 26 states still had fully operative fair trade laws with respect to nonsigners, as explained below.

Fair trade laws permit the manufacturer of a branded item to set the minimum, or in some cases the actual, price which must be observed by retailers in reselling such merchandise. To establish a resale price under the state laws, a manufacturer must ordinarily obtain a contract with one retailer who agrees to maintain the resale price. In most states, the price is then binding on all other retailers as soon as they are notified of the agreement. Fair trade legislation has been described by opponents as "handicap competition." It has been compared with a cross-country race in which handicaps are placed on the swiftest, to assure equality of opportunity for retail contestants of varying strengths vying for consumer acceptance in the market place. Protagonists, on the other hand, attribute to it all the qualities that make for healthy competitive business enterprise. Regardless of the intent, these laws have been widely utilized in only a few lines of trade. Although effectiveness has been limited, they have enabled some small merchants to compete on more nearly equal terms, in sale of fair-traded items, with price-cutting competitors.

While fair trade laws are only permissive, that is, they merely allow a brand owner to operate under them if he so elects, there are so-called *unfair trade practices acts* which are mandatory. Some 31 states have enacted such legislation and it was still operative in 1961 in 27 states where constitutionality has been upheld or uncontested. These laws directly prohibit sales below cost, or sales below cost plus some designated per cent of markup. Also, some 26 states have laws prohibiting "sales below cost" of specifically designated products (e.g., cigarettes, liquors and malt beverages, dairy products) which are commonly used as "leaders" by price-cutting stores.

About one-half of the states have specific *price discrimination laws* which are in essence state Robinson-Patman Acts. They prohibit price discrimination such as is forbidden in the federal law but apply, of course, only to transactions in intrastate commerce. The net effect of the federal and state trade legislation has been to curb buying advantages incident to mass purchasing power and to render it more difficult for large retailers to engage in price-cutting practices designed to make consumers believe they have tremendous operating advantages over independent merchants. Large organizations, however, have not been the only price cutters. This practice has been important among some small independent merchants, and the laws apply to them with equal force. Because of limited buying power, somewhat higher operating costs, and less emphasis upon price appeal among independents as a class, the laws are to be regarded primarily as limitations to large-scale operations.

## COMPENSATORY ACTIVITIES BY SMALL-SCALE AND BY LARGE-SCALE RETAILERS

Small-scale merchants and large-scale organizations have competed effectively with each other over many decades, largely because of the manner in which progressive institutions within each class have adapted to their competitive environment and compensated for their disadvantages.

## COMPENSATORY ACTIONS WITHIN SMALL-SCALE RETAILING

A host of developments has tended to make retail store operation somewhat more efficient. For the most part these developments have stemmed from innovating practices originated from experimental or research activities of large, well-financed retailers. To survive, the smaller retailer has had to improve his operations in like manner. Ordinarily, this has been very difficult to accomplish through individual efforts. Thus the burden has fallen primarily upon groups of merchants with similar interests or upon other institutions which have identified their own welfare with small-scale business enterprise. One facet of this development consists of assistance programs of wholesalers. Since small independent merchants constitute their principal group of customers, wholesalers have engaged in a variety of activities to increase their competitive efficiency. It is common for progressive wholesalers to provide various kinds of advice and store operational assistance. This may take the form of aid programs in merchandising, store arrangement and display, modernization, accounting, and sales training.

The voluntary chain concept is another device which has tended to equalize the competitive situation. By associating themselves with a wholesaler who sponsors a voluntary chain, or by pooling interests with other retailers who wish to establish a cooperative chain organization, small retailers have been able to match large chain rivals in a number of respects. Where the voluntary chain movement is analyzed at some length, such associations have enabled small retailers to attain greater buying power through a pooling of efforts, and to perform a number of retailing functions within a central office organization, much in the manner traditional within a chain store administrative office.

A third factor consists of activities of trade associations. Most progressive small merchants belong to an association which may provide them with a variety of aids. Common services include publication of magazines or newsletters which contain information that is helpful in store operation; collection and exchange of operating cost information used for planning and control of store expenses; group purchasing of items of store supplies, such as wrapping paper and gift boxes; sponsorship of special schools and clinics at which members receive information on recommended business practices; and store display and modernization services.

As previously explained, public sympathy for the small merchant has resulted in a variety of legislative controls which have curbed certain advantages and excesses of large-scale organizations. It has also resulted in various positive measures designed to enhance the market opportunities for small business organizations. While the U.S. Department of Commerce has for many years engaged in a variety of forms of aid to small firms, it was not until 1953 that a special independent government agency was established by an Act of Congress for the express purpose of advising, assisting, and encouraging small business enterprises. In the Congressional legislation which created the Small Business Administration in that year, public policy was stated as follows:

The essence of the American economic system of private enterprise is free competition. Only through full and free competition can free markets, free entry into business, and opportunities for the expression and growth of personal initiative and individual judgment be assured. The preservation and expansion of such competition is basic not only to the economic well-being but to the security of this Nation. Such security and well-being cannot be realized unless the actual and potential capacity of small business is encouraged and developed.

The principal responsibilities of the Small Business Administration of interest to retailers are:

- To help small firms gain access to adequate credit on reasonable terms,
- To assist them with their management problems, and
- To provide financial assistance when businesses have

been damaged or destroyed by disasters such as hurricanes or floods.

Much government effort has been expended in studying the peculiar problems of small retailing firms and in disseminating knowledge to help solve them. A wide variety of publications has been issued on merchandising, accounting, and store management topics, and these are distributed free or at a nominal charge. The Small Business Administration also cooperates with local organizations of businessmen and educational institutions in sponsoring courses or seminars. These are designed to fill the gaps in the businessman's knowledge so that he can acquire a better grasp of the problems of administering a business enterprise. By the end of 1960, more than 75,000 business owners or managers had participated in some 900 such courses conducted at more than 300 educational institutions.

## COMPENSATORY ACTIVITIES OF LARGE-SCALE RETAILERS

Perhaps the outstanding handicap of large retailers is their lack of flexibility in meeting the competitive challenge of small merchants who have close personal contact with their customers and employees. In order to attain some degree of this traditional small-scale advantage, large retailers have tended to increase the extent to which they delegate responsibility and authority to store managers, department managers, and service division supervisors.

Whereas it was once common for top management executives to formulate budgets, operating policies, and merchandising plans for the whole organization, it is now common to regard each department in a department store or each store in a chain store organization as a separately managed profit center. Store managers and department managers in progressive large organizations have greater responsibility than formerly with respect to the selection and training of personnel, buying and merchandising planning and control, expense budgeting and control, merchandise display techniques, and related matters. Experience with this type of decentralized management has been varied, but it is believed that it has enabled large national organizations to compete with greater flexibility and with greater effectiveness in meeting situations which vary from one locality to another.

Labor costs are the most important ingredient of the expense structure in retailing, usually making up one-half or more of total operating expense. The large firm, to a much greater extent than the small, is dependent upon the services of paid employees who have a wide variety of alternative opportunities. It is, therefore, more seriously affected by trends in labor market conditions. Wage rates and fringe benefits increased considerably in the late 1940's and 1950's. This resulted in rising personnel expense ratios while gross margins of profit, from which store operating expenses must be paid, have tended to remain stable.

Large firms especially have been in a tight cost-margin squeeze and have attempted to compensate for this by reducing the labor component of the total expense mix. By and large, innovations related to this objective are in the nature of automation. They are ordinarily posible only under conditions of fairly high specialization and ability to make substantial investment in equipment.

A few illustrations include prepackaging and prepricing of merchandise items at central or regional warehouses utilizing machinery and specialized personnel; installation of modern data processing equipment to provide more rapid, less costly, more accurate, and more refined statistical information, often permitting reductions in labor clerical costs and, at the same time, better balanced merchandise stocks maintained at a lower level of inventory investment; and streamlined store layouts, permitting exposure of a greater number of items in given floor space, facilitating maximum customer self-selection of merchandise, and handling of all transactions at a centralized cashiering station of a supermarket type, contributing to increases in the number of transactions handled per person employed.

## Chapter 9

# Departmental Stores

*Department stores are retail organizations which carry several lines of merchandise such as women's ready-to-wear and accessories, men's and boys' clothing, piece goods, small wares, and home furnishings and which are organized into separate departments for the purpose of promotion, service, accounting, and control.* Departmental organization distinguishes them from the general store. A more important distinction is their common emphasis upon shopping goods. Department stores are distinguished from specialty, single-line, and other departmentized stores by the wide range of merchandise handled; and from most variety stores, by the wider price range of their merchandise. A widely held conception is that a department store is a large organization. In conformance with this view, the Bureau of the Census limits this classification to otherwise qualifying individual establishments that have twenty-five or more employees.

## CLASSIFICATIONS AND SPECIAL CHARACTERISTICS

The department store field includes a variety of kinds of institutions when classified by ownership, method of operation, or clientele. Also, a number of unique features characterize department store retailing to a greater extent than other types of stores.

### OWNERSHIP AND OPERATIONAL TYPES

When department stores are classified on the basis of ownership and operation, several distinct groups are recognized. First are the *independents that have no ownership affiliation with other department stores.* In 1958 the stores in this group represented about 20 per cent of all department stores and accounted for about 14 per cent of total department store sales volume. This represents a substantial drop in the relative importance of this category which is explained by construction of branches by some former single unit stores, acquisition of some large independent stores by ownership groups, and greater relative expansion of chain organizations.

In the multiunit category, which accounts for 80 per cent of department store establishments and 86 per cent of their sales, several distinct types may be differentiated. *Department stores operated by regular retail chains* are centrally owned and supervised through central or district offices. Illustrative are the larger stores of Sears, Roebuck and Company, the J. C. Penney Company, and Montgomery Ward and Company.

Much of the buying is done by central office executives who, as a rule, make all resource contacts. Individual stores usually must conform to standardized company merchandising, service, and operating policies, and they tend to have somewhat similar physical appearance and layout.

Some of the larger and newer stores operated by variety store chains and "discount store" organizations meet the definition requirements of department stores and fall in this group. Chains of more than 100 stores account for nearly one-half of all department store establishments but only for about one-third of department store sales. Stores in this classification, for the most part, are operated in a much different manner than those in other classes and have a greater resemblance to regular corporate chains.

*Ownership groups* are a second type of multiunit organization. While technically qualifying as chains on the basis of ownership, they differ from regular chains in several ways. These groups, unlike regular chains, have usually expanded their interests by purchasing established independent stores which, in most cases, have retained their original identity, personality, operating personnel, executives, and operating policies. The degree of central control varies but the general manager of an individual store usually has much more freedom than managers in regular chains. Illustrative of ownership groups is Federated Department Stores, Inc. The major stores owned and operated by this company include the following: Abraham and Straus, Brooklyn; Bloomingdale's, New York; Boston Store, Milwaukee; Burdine's, Miami; Filene's, Boston; Foley's, Houston; Goldsmith's, Memphis; Harris', Dallas; Lazarus, Columbus; Rike's, Dayton; Sanger's, Dallas; Shillito's, Cincinnati; and Fedway Stores, a chain of smaller department stores in Southwestern states. In 1960, as many as eight ownership groups had sales in excess of $200 million each.

A third multiunit type consists of *branches* operated by many independent stores as well as by some of the stores in ownership groups. Branches may be distinguished from the units of regular chains in that they are satellites of a large store and are usually administered by the operating executives of that so-called main or parent store rather than by central office executives. While a few companies have operated branches for a number of decades, branches are essentially a modern development t—one that reflects accelerated decentralization in the retail trade structure of metropolitan areas. An important limitation of the classification just presented is that all stores within the various multiunit types are not "department stores." Many smaller stores operated by regular chains such as Sears, Roebuck and Company do not carry a sufficient range of departmentized merchandise to be so considered. The same is true of many stores in certain ownership groups. Some of them, including many department store branches, are more properly considered as departmentized specialty stores.

## CUSTOMER APPEAL

In larger cities it is especially difficult for a department store to make a strong appeal to all socioeconomic classes. Thus, in communities with a variety of department stores, each one tends to have a personality or character which makes a more definite appeal to some group, even though the clientele of most or all of them overlaps to some extent. Some stores emphasize quality and fashion leadership in elegant surroundings which are consistent with merchandise offerings in the higher price ranges. Such stores are in strong competition with high-class specialty stores and make their main appeal to the higher socioeconomic groups.

Other stores concentrate primarily on medium-high- and lower-priced merchandise, to appeal largely to the great middle-class group. A great increases have occurred in the size of the socalled middle-income class and in the volume of purchasing power at its command. For this reason, many department stores appealing to this group have experienced notable expansion.

A third group of department stores places major emphasis upon lower price lines of merchandise, with the objective of appealing to those in the lower-income strata, or to other families for whom price is the paramount purchasing consideration. Many so-called "discount" department stores are clearly in this category.

In order to broaden their customer appeal, most medium-sized and large department stores in the independent and ownership group classes have a "basement store" which is organized separately from the main store departments. By handling merchandise in lower price lines, featuring frequent bargain sales, purchasing and offering considerable distress or job-lot merchandise, and sometimes by offering a much more limited range of services and breadth of assortment, basement divisions compete aggressively with various forms of price-appeal and limited-service stores.

## KINDS OF MERCHANDISE SOLD

Department stores carry a wide range of merchandise, including shopping, specialty, and convenience goods. Women's and children's ready-to-wear occupies a prominent place and dry goods departments are important. Convenience goods are, in the main, those purchased by women, and specialty items are also largely those which appeal to the housewife, such as household appliances and equipment. Shopping goods are the most important class. The sale of women's ready-to-wear and accessories and of piece goods and household textiles is of greater relative importance in smaller stores. The largest department stores place more emphasis on the sale of home furnishings, and miscellaneous lines, such as toys, sporting goods, cameras, and on restaurant service.

Although department stores sell men's clothing and furnishings, a large percentage of these items is bought by women who select such goods for other family members.

## LEASED DEPARTMENTS

The practice of leasing certain departments to outside operators is common in department stores, and it is not at all unusual for more than 10 per cent of the total number of departments to be leased. Some lessees are independent business men and others are chains that operate numerous similar departments. Among merchandise departments most commonly leased are millinery, shoes, jewelry, sewing machines, and automotive accessories. Service departments such as beauty salon, jewelry repair, and photographic studio are also frequently leased.

The usual arrangement is for the leasing organization to buy all merchandise for the leased department, provide salespeople, and operate the department as part of the store. Usually the public does not know that the leased department involves separate ownership and management. The store supplies space, light, heat, credit, and delivery service, and in return receives a definite percentage (usually 10 to 20 per cent) of sales or some stipulated sum.

A number of circumstances have contributed to the leasing of departments. Often the lessee has specialized knowledge or skills which would be difficult to duplicate among store personnel. Some leasing organizations, especially large chain operators, have superior market contacts and access to preferred sources of supply, thereby affording the store more desirable merchandise assortments than could be provided through its own merchandising staff. Departments are also often leased when the cost of sending store buyers to remote wholesale markets would be prohibitive.

## DEPARTMENTIZED SPECIALTY STORE

The departmentized specialty store sells men's or women's ready-towear, or both, and a full line of accessories. Its relatively large size makes it possible to departmentize its operations and to organize it like a department store. It differs from a regular department store principally because it does not sell furniture or home furnishings and usually handles no piece goods or domestics. A number of such stores exist in all principal cities and they are usually located in the same part of the shopping districts as department stores, since both institutions compete for much of the same trade.

Due to the great similarly between regular department stores and departmentized specialty stores, the following discussion may be regarded as characteristic of both classes of establishments, with proper qualifications for the somewhat more limited range of merchandise carried by the departmentized specialty store.

## ANALYSIS OF COMPETITIVE POSITION

The competitive position of department stores can be evaluated through a consideration of their strengths and weaknesses in comparison with those of competing types of retailing institutions.

## ADVANTAGES

The competitive advantages of department stores are of two classes: those enjoyed because of status as large-scale retailers and those which are peculiar to department stores as a specific type of large-scale retailing.

### Distinctive Advantages

One advantage of distinctive institutional character is the very *wide range of merchandise sold*. Many of our largest stores have 150 or more merchandise departments, and even among the smallest department stores the number of separate departments is rarely less than 25. This facilitates consumer shopping in that the ability to buy a large variety of goods in one place is a time-saver and in other ways appeals strongly to consumers. Moreover, effective promotion of some lines of goods stimulates the sale of other related and dissimilar lines, due to the store traffic thus generated.

Another special advantage consists of benefits derived from a *wide range of customer services.* In addition to delivery, liberal adjustments, and several forms of consumer credit, which are not particularly distinctive, most department stores offer a variety of unique services including fashion shows, maintenance of lounges and rest rooms, children's play rooms, nurseries, telephones, and libraries. Some even offer rooms where women's organizations may hold meetings, or provide space for displays by local art clubs. These services build good will and prestige and bring many customers into the store. This variety of services, whether connected with the sale of goods or offered for the convenience and enjoyment of shoppers, exerts a strong appeal.

A third distinctive advantage consists of the *highly public, expositionlike character* of department stores. Everyone feels free to enter and roam about at will even when no purchase is contemplated. Department stores attempt to capitalize on the traffic thus generated by continually creating an atmosphere of buying excitement. This is done by layout planning, attractive displays, use of demonstrations, and special effects created at various seasons as at Christmas, the Easter season or at schoolopening time.

## Peculiar Advantages of Size

While the advantages of division of labor, departmentization, buying power, financial strength, integration, prestige, and experimentation and research have already been discussed in the treatment of large-scale retailing, some of these take an unusual form in the department store and deserve additional comment.

The department store type of *division of labor* differs considerably from that ordinarily found in a chain organization, unless of course the chain is composed of department stores. Because of the size of the individual establishment, a complex organization is the general rule.

Selling specialists number about one-half of total employees in medium-sized stores and only about one-third in the largest stores. By such specialization, salespeople can develop a high degree of product knowledge and selling skill.

The remainder of the organization provides for stock clerks, merchandising experts, advertising and display specialists, credit personnel, accountants and clericals, personnel specialists, training supervisors, morale managers, warehouse employees, janitors, elevator operators, tailors, carpenters, watchmen, detectives, researchers, truck drivers, appliance installation experts, comparison shoppers, and so on. In fact, almost every kind of skill may be found within department stores. Individual units operated by chains, on the other hand, are not necessarily large, and the performance of multifarious activities is often the responsibility of a single individual.

The department store also differs from many chains with respect to *risk distribution.* While risks are distributed geographically in the multiunit types of department stores, they are also widely dispersed by virtue of varying types of merchandise sold. For example, a loss in the shoe department may be offset by a particularly favorable showing in women's coats. While all large-scale retailers can engage in *extensive advertising,* department stores tend to dominate the advertising in local newspapers. Because of the large amount of space used, competitive institutions find it difficult to make a comparable impact upon the public. Many such stores also play an active role in community affairs, and because of the large sums expended for advertising, obtain much "free" publicity for these activities.

## DISADVANTAGES

Some of the most important disadvantages of department stores have already been indicated because they are primarily attributable to size of enterprise. As large-scale retailers, such stores suffer to some extent from lack of personal contact between top management and consumers and from complex supervisory procedure in the organization structure. In addition, some limitations are rather distinctively characteristic of department stores. One of the most serious of these is *a high operating expense ratio.*

A small, medium-sized, and large department stores all incur operating expenses which are typically about 33 or 34 per cent of sales. Contradictory as it may seem, the very services from which department stores derive a competitive advantage are also partly responsible for high costs of doing business. Costs are also high because of the complexity of organization structure and the accompanying high overhead costs of supervision, systems, and recording believed necessary to control operations. All expenses typically experienced by such stores must, of course, be recovered from sales, and this limits freedom in maintaining prices that are competitive with limited-service stores.

Since *customer returns* are reflected in a high operating cost ratio, they may be viewed as another disadvantage. In the largest stores, for every $1,000 of merchandise purchased by customers, nearly $90 worth is returned to the store or must for some reason be *credited* to customers' accounts. Because of liberal policies with respect to adjustments, many customers abuse the privilege. Some women complete their shopping after taking several items home "on approval." While some of these returns are unavoidable and some others are due to poor salesmanship or overselling, many of them cannot be explained on such grounds. A large part of this returned merchandise can be sold only at marked-down prices and some not at all.

Another problem relates to *markdowns.* A large portion of the merchandise is never sold at its original retail prices but must be reduced for clearance. Markdowns are not unique among department stores, for they exist in all forms of retailing. They are of greater magnitude in department stores, partly because most such institutions have policies requiring that complete assortments be carried through the peak of each selling season. On a storewide basis, the amount of reductions from original retail prices is about 6 per cent of sales. In other words, for every $1,000 of net sales the store has taken about

$60 in price reductions. In some departments, such as women's better dresses, the ratio is usually three times this amount. In large measure this is attributed to the fact that much initial pricing of high-fashion lines is experimental until the trend of demand becomes evident. The pricing process is therefore complicated by the necessity of providing some additional margin to allow for anticipated price reductions. Furthermore, the consumer's anticipation of clearance sales leads to a fairly common reluctance to purchase merchandise at original prices.

The high expense ratio and the need for allowing a sufficient margin to cover markdowns necessitates an average original markup of about 38 to 40 per cent of original prices in most regular department stores. This markup is higher than that required by many types of competitive, limited-service, price-appeal establishments. To overcome such a disadvantage, the department store must do an unusually outstanding merchandising job, anticipating consumer wants and bringing in desired offerings in broad assortments in advance of competitors who operate on a lower margin.

Downtown department stores suffer from *traffic congestion* and lack of parking facilities. It is time-consuming and often expensive for the consumer to reach the store. Because of the larger proportion of people now living in suburban areas and the increased demands upon the time of women, many of whom are employed, there is a growing trend to shop in specialty stores in outlying shopping districts.

Finally, though the location of merchandise may be clearly indicated, the very size of many department stores makes for *confusion* in shopping and for the preference on the part of many consumers to patronize smaller, more specialized establishments. The constant shifting of departments aggravates the situation. Again, the same kind of merchandise is often carried in several different departments in widely scattered locations with the result that consumers must do a large amount of in-store traveling in order to view the establishment's complete assortment. While store executives justify this rather common practice on the basis of needing separate departments for the purpose of catering to different income or style-interest groups of customers, it is nevertheless a practice that is resented by many consumers who wish to see all that the store has to offer.

## NEWER ASPECTS OF DEPARTMENT STORE COMPETITION

Until about the late 1940's most department stores found that their competitive orbit was limited substantially, although not altogether, to other department stores and shopping goods stores in the apparel and home furnishings classifications. Since that time many changes have brought the department store into more strenuous rivalry with other types of institutions.

### VARIETY-DEPARTMENT STORES

The variety store trade had its origin in 1879 when F. W. Woolworth opened his historic "Great Five-Cent Store." Success of this institutional innovation led to rapid multiplication of Woolworth stores and imitation of his methods of operation by founders of other variety chains. Early variety stores met certain social and economic needs of the era. Department stores at that time appealed primarily to medium- and high-income classes, but low-income families of industrial and agricultural workers did not feel at home in them. Variety stores were a new source of a wide range of merchandise, priced within specific limits which appealed to the minimum disposable income of such families.

From the early days of the limited-price variety store trade until the late 1930's, expansion consisted primarily of opening additional stores. By 1940 ten major variety chains were operating 4,956 stores as compared with 93 in 1900 and 1,706 in 1920. In spite of great environmental changes over six decades of variety trade history, practically all companies adhered rigidly to major policies and practices inaugurated by Woolworth. These included:

- A clearly specified maximum price limit, even though it had been advanced gradually from time to time in most companies;

- Maximum open display and customer examination of merchandise;
- Limited customer service with operations on a cashand-carry basis;
- Clear identification as a distinctive class of institution carried to the extent of use, by most variety chains, of highly similar red and gold store signs, almost identical store fixtures and layouts, and practically interchangeable merchandise offerings; and
- Dependence upon high-traffic locations, rather than advertising and promotion, as a means of attracting customers.

In the post- World War II era, and to an accelerated extent in the late 1950's, executives in the trade realized that the rigidity of several generations had unrealistically limited their potential market.

Among the environmental changes which had rendered many traditional policies obsolete were rising levels of consumer income, population growth in suburban areas, development of planned shopping centers, increased acceptance and use of consumer credit, and aggravated interindustry competition in the sale of traditional variety store items, as illustrated by nonfood sections in supermarkets and extensive general merchandise offerings in chain drug stores.

These changes eventually forced a number of innovations which were not unique in retailing but were revolutionary developments within the limited-price variety store field. The major change was abandonment of traditional policies of limited price ranges. Three forms of *trading-up* may be distinguished:

- Evolutionary trading-up, or gradual increases in offerings of higher unit value in traditional lines, to expand the range of quality or breadth of assortment for items such as school supplies, cosmetics, or costume jewelry;
- Revolutionary trading-up by adding substantially higher-priced items in traditional lines, as illustrated by $14.95 floor lamps and $29.95 power tools in

existing housewares or hardware departments; and

- Diversification of merchandise by adding entirely new categories such as furniture and major items of outerwear apparel.

Planned shopping centers afforded new and practically unlimited opportunities for additional stores which, because of merchandise item and line expansion, became much larger. In the late 1940's and early 1950's the typical new variety store was one of about 10,000 square feet, but by 1960 new establishments in larger centers were commonly in the range of 30,000 to 50,000 square feet, and some 7 per cent of new store openings were in planned centers. Increased emphasis on the sale of high-unit value and bulky items brought about the need for additional customer services like instalment credit and charge account facilities, arrangements for delivery, and "lay-away" plans.

More stress on shopping goods also stimulated variety store advertising in newspapers and other local media. In recognition of such changes, some chains adopted the term *variety-department store or junior department store* as being more descriptive than the historic designation *limited-price variety store.*

The rapidity of these innovations brought with them many serious operational problems, including pricing techniques, markdown control, and stock control procedures for fashion items; material handling problems for bulky items; and personnel development challenges incident to drastic changes in size of establishments and functions performed. The cumulative effect, however, is that the newer type of variety-department store is more sharply in direct competition with regular department stores and other types of general merchandise stores including discount houses.

A pattern of adjustment will undoubtedly continue and traditional variety store companies will almost certainly undergo further transformation, as suggested by a 1961 announcement that F. W. Woolworth Co. planned to start a new separate division for the purpose of opening and operating large new discount stores under the name "Woolco."

## OTHER NEW COMPETITION

Most of the other newer forms of department store competition are discussed elsewhere in this text; hence it is adequate merely to enumerate them at this juncture. Of substantial concern are various types of discount houses which operate in most urban areas, featuring branded merchandise at significant reductions from retail list prices. Second, with the growth of population in suburban markets, many department stores lost patronage to smaller stores located in new outlying shopping centers. Third, to a varying degree in different parts of the country, supermarket companies have expanded their activities in nonfood lines, with some aggressively merchandising selected classes of apparel and durable household goods, as well as various kinds of convenience nonfood items which are sold in practically all supermarkets. Fourth, catalog or mail order retailers have expanded their facilities, providing additional outlets for accepting orders, and offer rapid delivery service through the facilities of local retail merchants' delivery organizations.

## RESPONSE OF DEPARTMENT STORES

Some tradition-bound regular department stores have tended to ignore the newer forms of competition in the hope that their fashion minded and service-seeking customers would remain loyal. The more progressive firms have tended to respond vigorously in various ways and with considerable effectiveness.

To cope with discount stores, some department stores have held frequent or continuous warehouse sales at which appliances and other items are sold at greatly reduced prices under conditions of limited customer service. Discount house competition has also forced a re-examination of the department store operating cost structure. During the 1950's most large department stores embarked upon elaborate programs of expense control and cost reduction. This often involved a survey of traditional services to determine which are used by only a small percentage of the consuming public and, for that reason, might be eliminated or placed on a self-sustaining basis by specific charges for them. Many department stores have also reduced costs by placing a large number of merchandise lines on a self-service basis, thereby cutting payroll expense in relation to sales in some cases.

Some organizations re-evaluated their pricing policies, and decided to meet discount house prices on all items. In many cases, such a decision has been implemented by greatly expanded comparison shopping of competitive prices in all types of outlets, adjustment of store selling prices as frequently as needed to meet market situations, and aggressive advertising of a policy of refusing to be undersold.

The challenge of suburban retailing had been met by wide-scale construction of branch stores which now dominate many regional shopping centers. Many of the early post-World War II branch stores were small and caused serious operational and customer relations problems due to the difficulty of projecting the image of a major downtown store in an outlying unit which was only a small fraction of the size of the main store. More recently, branch stores have been constructed on a more elaborate scale, bringing to the suburban shopper a fuller range of department store merchandise and services, even though the number of departments and breadth of assortments are still necessarily somewhat more restricted than in parent stores. Many newer branches have a complete basement store operation, to make a strong appeal to consumers who are most price conscious, and a few department stores have specialized branches which carry only basement store merchandise.

Some of the newer branches of department stores are operated as discount stores. In 1961 several leading ownership groups of department stores announced specific plans for engaging in discount retailing in a major way, in some cases by setting up special divisions to operate such stores under separate identity, management, and control (e.g., Allied Stores Corp.), and in other instances by incorporating discounting merchandising strategy within well-established stores for those departments handling more standardized types of goods as well as in new discount stores (e.g., May Department Stores

Co.) In spite of suburban retailing trends, it has become apparent that major central business district stores hold an attraction for many consumers, particularly for items of low purchasing frequency, that cannot be rivaled in any but the very largest planned suburban shopping centers. Consequently, millions of dollars have been invested in modernization of downtown establishments. Department store executives have been among the most active civic promoters for revitalization of central business districts. This movement has become of such great national significance that the National Retail Merchants Association has a "downtown development committee" to aid local groups of department store merchants in such programs. Provision of downtown parking facilities and additional night openings in central business districts are among other related competitive methods.

To cater to consumers who wish to buy without visiting the shopping district, many department stores have expanded their telephone and mail order selling services. This has been particularly pronounced during the Christmas merchandising season, when it is common to issue large, well illustrated catalogs in which most departments are represented. With a view to obtaining more consistent patronage from a somewhat broader segment of the public, new and more flexible forms of credit services have been inaugurated. Another outstanding development has been increased attention to research in merchandising, which has resulted in better executive training along the line of offering assortments which are more in harmony with the buying wants of customers.

## FUTURE OF DEPARTMENT STORES

Department stores have certain inherent competitive advantages and are a well-established part of our retailing structure. Over the period 1955-60 they have accounted for about 20 per cent of the total market sales in the kind of goods commonly sold in such stores. This suggests that they are a mature type of institution, already serving all segments of the consuming public that wish to buy from them. For this reason, it is not expected that they will increase their share of the market for department store types of merchandise. Indeed, it is apparent that they will have to struggle to hold their own in the face of newer forms of competitive activity. The initial success of various responsive measures discussed in the preceding section suggests, however, sufficient flexibility to maintain their position. An important reason for optimism is that the top management staff of our major department stores includes much of the best merchandising talent in the United States. Still another reason is the great financial strength of most such organizations, which permits them to engage in costly experiments and in long-range research activity. Indeed, experimental efforts involving the operation of discount stores in 1961 suggests that department store companies are likely to become leaders in that field of merchandising. In relation to the total economy, it may be recalled that department stores have experienced a declining position. If high and increasing levels of consumer income extend over a span of several decades, it is likely that department stores will continue to occupy a more limited place in the total retail trade structure unless they are effective in expanding their merchandise offerings in lines of goods and services now extensively sold in such stores. Even if that cannot be done, they can expect a larger and larger absolute volume of business if they can only maintain their present share of the market for department store types of merchandise.

## Chapter 10

# Chain Stores and Voluntary Chains

Despite abundant literature on the subject, no clear-cut and universally acceptable definitions of the terms chain, chain store, or chain system have been developed. Common usage seems to relate the term chain to retail store operations and tends to neglect the existence of many chains of public utilities, banks, hotels, motion picture theatres, finance company offices, and other types which are an integral part of marketing.

Most of the best known so-called *retail* chains also operate chains of warehouses for the performance of the wholesaling functions and many also are extensively engaged in manufacturing activities. It is important, therefore, that one get an overview of the structure of chain store organizations, including the various levels on which they operate, before delving into an analysis of their competitive position and performance on the plane of retailing. Another matter of great importance is the manner in which various independent merchants have achieved certain advantages of chain operation by voluntarily integrating their interests and activities with those of other firms, both on the retail level and on other levels of the distribution channel as well.

Several criteria are useful in differentiating chain store organizations from other types which tend to resemble them in some respects. These include

- Number of establishments,
- Type of merchandise handled,
- Plane or level of operation,

- Ownership of the units, and
- Management control.

On the basis of these factors, *a chain or chain store system or organization may be said to consist of two or more centrally owned units, handling, on the same plane of distribution, substantially similar lines of merchandise.* This definition is in line with that used by the Federal Trade Commission in various of its studies of chain stores and it is also in accord with Census of Business classification procedures.

While avoiding use of the term chain, the Census considers a store as a member of a *multiunit* organization "if it is one of two or more stores in the same general kind of business operated by the same firm." Thus, for example, a firm is classified as a *multiunit* if it operates two or more food stores, or if it operates two or more apparel stores; but a firm operating one drugstore, a hardware store, and a furniture store would not be so classified, and all the individual stores in this case would be regarded as *single units.*

Emphasis is placed on central ownership rather than management control, and to that extent at least, chains are to be distinguished from the so-called cooperative or voluntary chains in which the retailer members preserve individual ownership. The regular chain has full control over its retail units, assumes full financial responsibility for such units, bears all loss when a unit is closed and retains all profit made by each store. In a voluntary chain, on the other hand, cooperation with the central organization is contractual; the individual store assumes full financial responsibility for its acts; all profit earned by the store is retained by its owner; when a store is forced to close its doors it is considered commercially and legally a failure and the total loss is borne by the owner and his creditors.

## CLASSES OF CHAINS

Two important ways of classifying regular chains are according to the extent of area served and according to the degree to which the organization has integrated retailing with other kinds of business activities.

## Geographic Basis

In terms of radius of operation, chains are generally classified as local, sectional, and national. Substantially all of the stores in *local chains* are located in or near the same metropolitan area. In almost all major cities, there are to be found local multiunit organizations in the food and drug fields. Such organizations are also rather common among department stores, clothing stores, furniture and appliance establishments, gasoline service stations, and liquor stores.

Chains are classified as *sectional* if their stores are located in some one major part of the country, such as New England, the Pacific Coast states, or any other recognized broad geographic division. Many of these are very large and are as well known to consumers within their area of operation as are the still larger national organizations.

The interests of *national* chains are much broader than any one section although they do not necessarily cover the entire country. Illustrative are the Great Atlantic and Pacific Tea Co.; Sears, Roebuck and Co.; Safeway Stores Company; J. C. Penney Company; The Kroger Company; and F. W. Woolworth Company. Some of these companies may be regarded as *international* due to extensive operations in other countries.

## Integration

Another useful classification is that based upon the degree of vertical integration. One group consists of retail chains *without wholesale distribution or manufacturing facilities,* thereby confining their activities to retailing. They procure merchandise through wholesalers or purchase directly from manufacturers, without special facilities for performing wholesaling functions within the company. In this group belong many local chains of only a limited number of units, also a substantial number of large organizations in the shoe, millinery, and apparel fields. A second group consists of chains with *warehouses or wholesale distribution centers.* This is typical in all convenience goods lines where regular wholesalers are of importance in serving independent merchants. As such chains grow in size and circumvent the wholesaler, they find it necessary to provide somewhat comparable physical facilities in which wholesaling activities are performed for the organization. In fact, there is no stronger evidence of the indispensable nature of the functions of the wholesaler than the existence of chain store wholesale warehouses.

The third type consists of chains that have integrated still farther by *the performance of manufacturing activities.* This group overlaps with the second in that its members ordinarily also operate wholesale distribution centers in addition to manufacturing establishments. Outright or partial ownership of subsidiary manufacturing companies, or strong control over the activities of supplying manufacturers by furnishing specifications and taking all or a substantial part of their output is common among the mail order companies that also operate large numbers of retail stores. In the grocery trade, 63 major chains reported that they were engaged in some forms of manufacturing in 1958, and this group operated 340 manufacturing establishments, primarily to supply private brand merchandise to company stores.

Sometimes integration has proceeded *forward* from manufacturing toward retailing, rather than *backward* from retailing toward manufacturing. Illustrative is the practice of certain major oil-producing companies whose principal business is done through bulk tank stations but which also operate some gasoline service stations. Several large shoe manufacturers have acquired chains of stores and operate them as controlled outlets. A well-known example is Genesco (formerly General Shoe Corp.). While long known as a leading shoe manufacturer, this company also diversified by acquiring firms manufacturing apparel and apparel accessory items. It operates a number of separately identified shoe chains (e.g., Jarman, Holiday, I. Miller) and apparel stores (e.g., Whitehouse and Hardy, Roger Kent).

It is thus apparent that to regard chains as purely retailing institutions is erroneous. Almost all of the medium-sized and larger organizations possess most of the characteristics of both retailing and wholesaling enterprises, and many are manufacturing as well as merchandising concerns.

## ORIGIN AND DEVELOPMENT OF RETAIL CHAINS

The modern chain store is of comparatively recent origin. The chain idea of distribution, however, has many forerunners and prototypes. As early as 200 B.C., a certain Chinese businessman owned a chain of a great many units. A poster found in Pompeii, destroyed in A.D. 79, advertised for lease a certain property consisting of 900 retail shops. The Mitsui system of apothecary shops in Japan dates from 1643, and the company has been one of the wealthiest and most powerful businesses in that country. In the Americas, the Hudson's Bay Company operated a chain of trading posts prior to 1750. But in the United States the development of the modern chain was not started until the Great Atlantic and Pacific Tea Company was founded in 1858, although the second store was not opened until a year later. The second of existing chains is Park and Tilford, which began business in 1840 but did not open a second store until 1860. The Jones Brothers Tea Company came into being in 1872, and the F. W. Woolworth Company proved the validity of the chain principle in the variety business about 1880.

While a number of chains were established during the latter half of the nineteenth century, their real growth occurred during the present century. It is estimated that in 1900 there were but 700 chains with 4,500 stores. Each succeeding year showed an increase in the number of chains and in chain stores. At first the number of chain systems increased faster than store units, but the reverse was true during the latter half of the period, indicating a possible absorption of smaller chains by larger ones and a more rapid expansion within large chain systems.

Growth in chain store volume of sales was spectacular. As late as 1919 the estimated volume of chains was less than 5 per cent of total retail sales, but by 1929 this proportion had increased sixfold to about 30 per cent. The almost phenomenal development of chain organizations during the 1920's is explained by economic and social factors. The time was ripe to apply mass methods on a more widespread basis in retail distribution where efficiency had not generally kept pace with mass production techniques in industry. The number of people living in cities was about twice that at the beginning of the century, with a large amount of the city growth coming during the 1920's. City locations are particularly desirable from the standpoint of chain store organizations, for the cost of advertising, supervision, and distribution from wholesale warehouses is low when units are highly concentrated. The development of the automobile and the improvement of roads made it possible for rural residents to shop in cities more frequently. Between 1914 and 1920 retail prices almost doubled, with the result that most consumers became extremely price conscious. Because certain operating economies were effected, in part by a transfer of marketing functions to consumers, and because chains were able to purchase merchandise on very favorable terms in a prevailing buyers' market, they were usually able to undersell independents. It is doubtful if there was any period in our previous history when price appeals were any more in harmony with the interests of consumers.

The decline in the number of chain stores in the period 1929-48 is explained by several factors. One relates to a trend toward complete food stores, as opposed to earlier greater relative importance of specialized stores such as meat markets and produce stores (once known as "green grocers"). In the 1920's, grocers tended to add meats and fruits and vegetables to their stock and thus became combination grocery stores. This trend was greatly accelerated after 1929.

A second reason has been the need for grocery chains to meet the competition of supermarkets which developed in the early 1930's, by operating fewer but larger units. Third, during the 1930's many oil refineries adopted a policy of turning over the operation of company-owned stations to independent merchants. Fourth, all of these trends and policies were stimulated by special taxes levied by some states on the stores operated by chain organizations, thus encouraging the closing of small and marginal units. In some fields, however, the number of chain stores actually increased during this period. As experience proved their worth, the number of such stores was increased in the retailing of shoes, apparel, and other kinds of business.

## Small Versus Large Chains

Multiunit firms that operate only a few stores are usually local organizations. Their interests, competitive situation, and methods of operation are often closer to those of independent merchants than they are to major chain store systems. Companies operating two to ten stores accounted for slightly more than one-half of all chain store units and about one-third of chain store sales volume in 1958. This is a lower proportion of total chain store sales than achieved by this group in 1948. Among the explanations for this decline are the acquisition of some small chains by larger organizations, expansion of some small chains resulting in reclassification, and greater sales volume expansion by chains of larger size.

Chains of 11 or more stores tend to operate establishments of greater sales volume size. They account for about two-thirds of chain store sales but operate slightly less than one-half of the chain store units. Especially significant are chains with more than 100 stores. This group, with about 27 per cent of chain store units, does about 42 per cent of chain store sales.

## Kind of Business

In some lines of business, chains dominate the trade, in others their position is not greatly different than their average share of market for total retail trade, and in still others they are of negligible importance. A chain account for more than 80 per cent of sales in the department and variety store classifications, for more than 50 per cent of the sales of grocery and food stores, and for more than 40 per cent of sales of women's ready-to-wear and tire, battery, and automotive accessory stores. By way of contrast, they do less than 20 per cent of the volume in the hardware trade, gasoline service stations, eating and drinking places, and less than 10 per cent of the business of automobile dealers.

The lines of business which are dominated to the greatest extent by chains tend also to be lines in which large chains have a much greater share of the market than do smaller companies (two to ten stores). On the other hand, small chains tend to be of as great or greater importance than large chains in lines where the per cent of sales done by all chains is low.

Between 1948 and 1958 large chains (11 or more stores) made strong advances in share of total sales in the following lines of trade: department stores, grocery stores, and women's ready-to-wear stores. These lines of trade have been affected both by acquisition of smaller companies by large organizations and by substantial expansion of chain store units in new shopping centers.

### Urban Concentration

During the early periods of development, chains tended to concentrate in large urban areas and in the most heavily populated sections of the country. While some chains are to be found in cities of any significant size, marked concentration in the largest population centers continues to be the rule. Heavy concentration in large cities is explained in part because certain prominent chains, especially in shopping goods lines, operate only in such cities; also, in convenience lines, the number of different chains competing with each other tends to be much larger than in smaller markets. The smaller the size of city, the easier it is for independents to compete with chains, especially in regard to advertising and other forms of promotional activity.

## MERGERS AND ACQUISITIONS

The economic power of certain large chains has been considerably enlarged by the acquisition of other organizations in the same or similar lines of trade. For example, in the period 1949-58, ten large food chains were particularly active in acquiring other companies. These ten corporations acquired 107 other food chains which together, in the year prior to acquisition, operated 1,474 stores with aggregate annual sales volume of $1.2 billion, 42 manufacturing establishments, and 64 wholesale distribution warehouses. Similarly comprehensive data are not available for other lines of trade, but noteworthy examples were numerous in the trade press of the late 1950's. Through a series of mergers and stock purchases, a surviving firm, McCrory Corporation, obtained ownership or control of the following companies: McCrory Stores Corporation (215 variety stores), McClelland Stores Corporation (236 variety stores), H. L. Green Company, Inc. (372 variety stores), Cassels United Stores, Inc. (18 variety stores), Oklahoma Tire and Supply Company (86 companyowned automotive accessory stores and 167 independent franchised outlets), and National Shirt Shops of Delaware, Inc. (146 men's wear stores).

Two large department store ownership groups, Federated Department Stores, Inc. and May Department Stores Co., expanded substantially by acquiring other large department store organizations. Merger activity was also conspicuous in the shoe trade, the automotive accessory field, and the apparel trades. Since most acquisitions involved mergers of chains with chains, they did not substantially affect the total competitive position of multiunit organizations, except in the department store field where some acquired firms were large single-unit stores.

The general tendency was greater concentration of ownership among the very largest firms in the trades affected. The number of such mergers would doubtless have been greater except for the fact that some were forestalled in their incipiency or dissolved through action of the Federal Trade Commission or the U.S. Department of Justice under the terms of the Clayton Act on the grounds that "the effect of such acquisition may be substantially to lessen competition, or tend to create a monopoly.

## COMPETITIVE POSITION OF LARGE, CENTRALLY MANAGED CHAINS

Since some chains operate in almost every kind of business and since almost every method of store operation or merchandising technique is used by them, no competitive advantages or disadvantages are common to all multiunit organizations. Certain competitive circumstances are, however, so widespread among large, centrally managed chains that they are characteristic of this segment of trade.

## ADVANTAGES

Most chain store advantages are basically those of large-scale retailing. Some advantages of scale nevertheless take on a distinctive form within the chain store field, and some others are peculiar to all multiunit organizations.

### Buying Power

By channeling the merchandise requirements of many retail units through a central office that negotiates with resources, the large chain is able to buy on more favorable terms than is the single-unit store in the same line of business. Since the manufacturer's selling expenses are relatively low when disposing of large quantities to one customer, the chain is able to obtain the lowest prices and to secure other allowances related to quantity buying as, for example, advertising funds, and compensation for store displays.

While this advantage is important, it can be overemphasized. Ability to obtain lower net prices is significant only when comparing such prices with the prices paid by a competitor who performs similar functions in the channel of distribution. There is no question but that chains generally pay lower prices than independent retailers. However, most chains are integrated, at least to some extent, and must incur costs in performing wholesaling activities. It is more meaningful, therefore, to compare the prices paid by chains with those ordinarily paid by wholesalers that serve independent merchants. Most large wholesalers operate on such a scale that they are able to take advantage of the maximum quantity discounts offered by well-known manufacturers selling branded goods. The chain's buying power may result in prices slightly more favorable than those paid by some wholesalers, but as a practical matter it is largely confined to situations where manufacturers are small and sell the entire output to the chain or produce only private brands of merchandise to the chain's specifications. There is no doubt that the larger chains have significant advantages in instances where they are able to contract for all of the output of manufacturers—something that cannot very well be done by the typical independent wholesaler.

## Buying Skill

Large chains also have the benefit of considerable *buying skill,* a natural result of specialization of labor. At the central or district headquarters are to be found merchandising experts who spend all of their time maintaining market contacts, collecting and interpreting marketing information, viewing offerings of vendors, determining the suitability of merchandise for sale by the company, and conducting negotiations. Unlike the manager of the independent store, the chain buyer specializes in a narrow range of merchandise and becomes thoroughly acquainted with sources of supply and current supply and demand conditions.

Unlike the "buyer" in a regular department store, the chain buyer spends practically all of his time performing the buying function; he does not have the problems of managing a retail department, preparing advertising, supervising salespeople, and other similar activities of the department manager in the large department store. Here, too, the chain's advantage is largely dissipated when compared with the wholesaler's buying organization and skill, which is similar to that of the chain.

## Low Operating Costs

Certain economies, attributable to characteristic practices among large chains, result in relatively low operating costs. One of the most significant economies among chains with warehouses is derived from the *integration of wholesaling* with retailing. A better coordination between these functions is secured, stores are supplied from or through a single chain store warehouse, no salesmen need call upon store managers to solicit business, credit *problems* are eliminated, and deliveries can be effectively scheduled. On the other hand, chain store home office and district executives must supply more supervision and assistance than is normally given to retailers by independent wholesalers. In any event, it is often possible for the chain to save part of the wholesaler's margin, particularly in lines of business where wholesalers have appreciable costs of selling to retailers and the latter do not concentrate their purchases with a single source of supply.

Another economy is *curtailment of consumer services.* As compared with its typical independent competitor, the large, centrally managed chain tends to sell to a greater extent on a cash basis; to render delivery service only for bulky or expensive items, or to make a charge for delivery when provided; and to emphasize self-service or self-selection merchandising techniques, thus limiting the assistance the consumer receives from salespeople. All of these service limitations, while making possible operating economies, may be viewed in another light, namely, that they represent successful attempts to shift performance of some marketing functions to the consumer. Many chains secure economies by *limiting the composition of their stocks.* By concentrating offerings on those items for which there is a widespread and ready demand, higher than typical rates of stock turnover are attained. As long as this is accomplished without risking loss of business on account of out-of-stock conditions, several advantages are realized. These include less risk due to merchandise deterioration or style obsolescence, less storage space required per unit of sales, lower capital costs for merchandise inventories, and lower insurance costs on inventories.

## Price Appeal

Low merchandise costs stemming from large purchasing power and the relatively low operating costs of chains, when combined with a prevalent chain store philosophy that a small percentage of net profit will maximize sales and yield large *total* dollar profits, results in a third important competitive characteristic, namely, the ability to feature price appeal. This has been an historic advantage of chainsone which accounted for significant diversion of patronage from independent to chain store in the period of rapid early growth of chains. While chains, as a general rule, tend to continue emphasis upon "low prices," the effectiveness of this appeal as a patronage-attracting device has been limited by two major factors. First, the buying advantages and pricing freedom of chains has been limited to some extent by the trade legislation of the 1930's. Second, and undoubtedly more important, is a tendency which became much more prominent in the latter 1950's, namely, the willingness of many different types of retailers to meet the lowest prices prevailing in a given local market, particularly in the case of easily identified, fast-selling, standard items. Thus, something approaching price uniformity is commonplace for such merchandise.

This tendency has become more pronounced with increased intertrade competition, as illustrated by cut-rate drugstores, supermarkets, discount houses, and variety stores, all selling similar merchandise. While the appeal of price is commonly stressed in chain store advertising and store displays, most volume-conscious independents price their merchandise at similar levels, and both groups attempt to differentiate their establishments to a greater degree through various forms of nonprice competition, such as location, character of merchandise assortments, store atmosphere, and special promotional devices.

**Advertising Advantages**

Where chain stores are in competition with neighborhood unit stores, they have marked advertising advantages. For example, a grocery chain with stores in all sections of a city can afford to use newspaper advertising space or radio and television. Neighborhood unit stores, with localized markets, cannot afford newspaper or broadcast advertising since their places of business are relatively inaccessible to most readers or listeners. Where voluntary chains have been formed, independent grocers have combined their efforts and used citywide advertising effectively. In the main, however, the chain occupies a preferred position with reference to local advertising.

## Experimentation

Chains can often undertake experiments which cannot be made without great risk by their competitors. For example, lines of merchandise can be added to or dropped from the stock at one retail unit, and the results can be used in formulating the practices and policies of all of the stores. Similar experiments can be made with respect to services, displays, stock arrangement, store layout, and other matters.

## Risk Distribution and Competitive Superiority

The wide territorial coverage of many chains reduces their risks, since a lack of local prosperity and a decline in sales or profits in one store may be offset by profits in other areas or stores. This same width of their market enables chains to transfer slow-moving stocks from some of their stores to units in which the demand for such goods is greater. By varying prices charged to consumers between different cities and sections of the country, the chain is able to average its profits and meet whatever competition may arise locally. This is an advantage which the voluntary chains cannot emulate, for a price war affects the total business of a retailer member which cannot be offset, as in the case of chains, by the profits earned in the other stores of the group.

## Location Advantage

As a form of large-scale retailing, chains are in an enviable position with respect to their ability to command the most favorable merchandising sites in established business districts and in new shopping centers. It is adequate to note at this point that the competitive position of chains was considerably enhanced during the 1950's by the preference accorded to them as the dominant tenants in most planned centers.

## COMPETITIVE] LIMITATIONS

As in the case of the favourable factors discussed above, no single disadvantage applies to each and every chain in every line of trade. A number of unfavourable factors do, however, exert a restrictive influence upon most large, centrally managed chains.

## Standardization of Operating Procedures

While standardization of merchandising and operating policies and procedures is a feature which makes it possible to operate a large chain from a central or regional headquarters office, it is also a factor which has limited chain development in certain fields where individualized management attention is of unusual importance. Large national chains are nonexistent in the hardware trade, for example, partly because of the great diversity of items which must be handled and the minute supervision and care necessary to maintain balanced stocks. Carelessness on the part of the local manager may result in a serious lack of necessary items or in excessive inventories of unsalable or slow-moving stocks. Further difficulties are found in the multiple price system which prevails in the sale of such lines as builders' hardware. Price concessions to builders often vary roughly with the volume of purchases and the bargaining power of buyer and seller. Under such circumstances chains find it particularly difficult to operate, since they may be unwilling or unable to entrust such responsibilities to local managers. In any trade in which contract work appears, chains are at a disadvantage, because each contract presents a particularized pricing problem and the need for outside sales promotion and installation introduce complications.

## Limited Service

The common practice of restricting consumer services and the limitation of stocks to articles in large demand, while reducing expenses of operation, limits the appeal of many chains. There still are and are likely to be large numbers of consumers who insist upon and are willing to pay for the wider range of services and facilities which many independent stores offer.

Limited service is not a policy inherent in chain store operation. At least some large chains provide every kind of common consumer service. Variety stores found it necessary to introduce various forms of service, such as credit, delivery, and "lay-away" plans, as they diversified their merchandise offerings by expanding into shopping goods lines. The well-managed independent store nevertheless has a distinct advantage in adjusting its own program of services to meet the particular needs of the clientele it seeks to serve within its trading area.

## Imitative Innovation

Within and between the various lines of trade in which chains are of greatest relative importance, many companies are only weakly differentiated from each other. In spite of excellent opportunities for research and experimentation in the chain store field, innovations have tended to be imitative rather than imaginative. Many chains have copied operating methods and techniques that have apparently worked well for other companies, thus contributing to a type of monotonous uniformity and a lack of exciting and dynamic merchandising. One critic has described the store units of most large chains as being characterized by bowling alley aisles with little or no interrupting note, uniformity of display, warehouse atmosphere in interior layouts, display of specialty goods as though they were staples, absence of printed selling other than manufacturers' package and price tags, and discouraging merchandise assortments. Many chains have apparently assumed a role of mere "distributor" of merchandise which is in ready demand either because of its necessary character or habitual use, or because of advance intensive demand creation activity on the part of manufacturers. This tendency among many large chains, especially in their larger and newer stores, again affords the independent an excellent opportunity to do a more outstanding promotional and personal selling job and otherwise to create a distinctive and appealing store personality.

Public Opinion. Particularly during the 1920's and 1930's and, to some extent, continuing until the present time, there have been many attempts to limit the growth of chains by arousing consumer sentiment against them. Led by some so-called representative organizations of independents and by a few individuals who perhaps saw an opportunity to further their own interests, many arguments have been made to the effect that the independent merchant, who lives and does business in the home city, deserves patronage rather than the customarily "foreign-owned" chain. It has been alleged that chains take money out of town, fail to patronize local business, pay low wages, destroy opportunities for young men to enter business for themselves, do not bear their share of the local tax burden, destroy small business, resort to unethical or unfair practices, and tend toward monopoly.

Some such allegations are obviously unfounded or exaggerated. All of them have nevertheless influenced public opinion to some degree and probably contributed to the passage of chain store tax laws and to other legal limitations. To some extent they have also doubtless contributed support to governmental policies that favor private enterprise of the small, local business firm type, as witnessed by the creation of the U.S. Small Business Administration in 1953. It is not likely, however, that such pressures upon public opinion have seriously restricted chain store patronage. While some consumers prefer independent merchants, the vast majority patronize retail stores for other kinds of reasons.

**Legal Limitations**

Most of the legal limitations in connection with large-scale retailing, were originally enacted as an aspect of the anti-chain store movement of the late 1920's and the 1930's. The chain's ability to induce discriminatory advantages in purchasing was limited by the Robinson-Patman Act, and its freedom to engage in loss-leader pricing was curtailed to some extent by the state pricing legislation discussed at that point.

In addition, many states have taxed chain store organizations in some special manner, with the intent, at least in part, of restricting the growth of chains and the multiplication of their store units. At one time chain store tax laws were in effect in 29 states. Original impetus to such laws was the Indiana statute, approved by the U.S. Supreme Court in 1931. In that decision chain stores were recognized for the first time as differing sufficiently from other types of retailing to justify a separate classification for license or occupation tax purposes. A classification for graduated license fees according to the number of stores in the state was thus held to be a valid classification based on substantial differences.

In all cases the tax is levied only on stores operated in the state in question, but the *rate of tax* is determined in two different ways. Most common is the Indiana-type law providing a graduated license fee based on a schedule of the number of stores in the same company *located within the state* and levying, for example, a fee 50 times greater for each store in a company operating more than 20 stores in the state than would apply in the case of a single unit store. Louisiana and several other states departed from this principle and based the rate on the total number of stores in the company *wherever located*—for example, a company with more than 500 stores no matter where located would pay a tax on each of its stores in Louisiana some 55 times greater than the tax applicable to a store in a company that operated not more than 10 stores.

One effect of these laws was to discourage the multiplication of chain stores in the states where rates were the highest. Another was to encourage chains to close marginal and small units, and to plan newer stores of larger sales capacity. With the passage of time, chains tended to be regarded as better neighbors. It became more widely recognized that they brought new business into many communities in which they located new and modern stores, that they employed local people, and that they purchased supplies and merchandise from all segments of the economy. As a consequence, many of the laws have been allowed to lapse or have been repealed. In 1960 there were only 12 states with chain store taxes based upon graduated license fees.

## Increasing Efficiency of Independents.

One of the major limits to the expansion of chains is the increasing efficiency of many of their independent competitors. Independents as a whole are carrying on their business much more efficiently than was formerly the case. This is due to at least two causes. The increased business of the chains has driven out many of the least efficient merchants. The better independents are the ones who have survived. Hence, the general level of merchandising ability is higher. A second reason is that many independents have learned much from the chains. Such merchandising practice as the use of open display in grocery, drug, and hardware stores, better lighting, and better entrances and fixtures have been copied, in part at least, from chains. Superfluous brands, price lines, and sizes have all been reduced. Better display and advertising practices have been adopted, and in other ways the level of independent merchandising has been raised. All of this has been accelerated through the voluntary chain movement. This fact will make it increasingly hard for chains to displace existing independents in the future. If expansion is made it will be at the expense of the type of merchant who is too old, too indifferent, or too independent and limited in ability to learn the lessons of modern merchandising. Unfortunately, there are still many such merchants, or rather, storekeepers.

## FUTURE OF CHAIN STORES

The chain store type of retailing had a phenomenal development in the 1920's. In this period many new chain organizations were brought into being and additional units were added to existing chains with the result that the chain had become a fairly mature form of retailing institution by 1929. Throughout the next two decades, the sales volume importance of chains was relatively stable at about 30 per cent of total retail trade. During the 1950's, however, chains expanded their share of total retail sales to about 33.7 per cent—a significant gain in relative competitive position. Moreover, this increase has come about principally by growth of large chain organizations, both through internal expansion and acquisition of other companies. Thus, within the chain store field, the tendency has been for a larger share of total business to be concentrated among a small number of very large firms.

Among the various factors that accounted for significant growth of chains in the 1950's, several stand out as being of unusual importance. First, the scale of operations in individual retail establishments has continued to increase, thus raising the capital requirements and level of managerial skill essential for effective competition. This, in turn, has made it somewhat more difficult for new independents to enter retailing on a level of competitive equality. Second, the 1950's were characterized by various newer forms of competition, including expansion of discount houses, branches of department stores, and the advent of the variety department store. Such inter trade rivalry resulted in intense price competition, with a tendency toward price uniformity at low margins for most types of standard, easily identified items.

Large chains, possessing the advantages of financial strength and risk distribution, have been able to withstand the onslaught of new types of rivals much better than many independents, particularly those who were weakly financed and who lacked the ability or willingness to adjust dynamically to changing times. Third, a large proportion of the total retail trade expansion in the 1950's took place in planned suburban shopping centers where chains have benefited from their status as preferred tenants. This has been especially noteworthy in the case of department stores, variety stores, apparel stores, and supermarkets—all lines in which chains have long been of high relative importance.

In the foreseeable future, it is expected that the factors just outlined will continue to favor the growth of chains. On the other hand, further expansion is restricted by a number of countervailing influences. One consists of various forms of voluntary chain and cooperative activities within the field of small scale retailing. Second, it must be remembered that the total competitive position of chains is a result of their status in specific lines of trade.

In some lines, notably department stores and variety stores, chains have reached a point of near saturation. In other lines where managerial flexibility and individualized attention to customer problems is of unusual importance, the chain method of operation is not well suited. Third, loss of share of market among independent stores has been highly concentrated among the less efficient or marginal types of stores. Further inroads by chains become increasingly difficult due to a strong survival tendency among more capable independent store operators.

When such opposing tendencies are carefully weighed, it is concluded that the growth outlook for chains, while favorable, is also likely to be limited to slow and gradual expansion. Such growth as does occur is, moreover, likely to be concentrated within the lines of trade where chains are already strongly entrenched. Within most such lines, the major rivals of an individual centrally managed chain are other similarly managed companies. Thus, to an increasing degree the competition of chains is with other chains, within and between lines of trade, and to a lesser extent with independent merchants, set apart as a different class of organizations.

## VOLUNTARY CHAINS

Independent merchants and their suppliers have resorted to a variety of competitive devices in combating chain store companies. Within lines of trade where chains have been of greatest importance, the outstanding instrument of survival has consisted of various forms of horizontal and vertical cooperation, with the objective of preserving independence while at the same time achieving certain advantages of chain operation.

### TYPES OF VOLUNTARY ASSOCIATIONS

Voluntary chains or cooperative associations of retailers assume a variety of specific forms. First, there are buying-and-advertising groups in which a small number of independent merchants combine their purchases and engage in advertising on a cooperative basis. Second, there are retailer-cooperative warehouse groups in which a number of independent merchants mutually own and buy through a common wholesaling facility. A third form consists of voluntary chains which are sponsored by a regular wholesaling organization that has assumed the initiative for cooperative action. Fourth, some of the corporate retailing chains have expanded their area of merchandising influence by licensing or franchising "associate" stores. Finally, the franchised retail outlets of certain manufacturers, who pursue an exclusive agency or selective distribution policy, often result in such a high degree of uniformity of operations on the retail level that this may be properly regarded as an aspect of the voluntary chain idea.

## POOLED BUYING AND ADVERTISING GROUPS

An early example of voluntary horizontal cooperation was the development of informal buying pools. Basing their action on the assumption that buying power was the principal if not the sole advantage of the chains, certain independent merchants, primarily grocers, druggists, and hardware dealers, developed plans for informal pooling of orders. They thus succeeded in gaining certain price concessions which, when combined with pool-cars as they often were, resulted in substantial reductions in the delivered cost of the merchandise. So long as they failed to attack the problem of effective competition with chains in other than the buying area, such groups were never very significant.

Group operations of small numbers of retailers located in the same metropolitan area became very important in the 1950's when greater emphasis was given to selling and promotion. Under the prevailing arrangement, several independent supermarket-type concerns cooperate in the use of a common name such as "Foodtown" or "Market Basket." By pooling their advertising budgets, they have been able to develop impressive advertising programs, rivaling those of major corporate chains.

Such firms have also set high standards in store appearance and merchandising. They often maintain the same prices in all stores in the cooperating group. In contrast with the forms of voluntary chains discussed below, the initiative comes from the cooperating retailers rather than from wholesalers, but the retailers do not own or operate any wholesale establishment. They usually pool certain of their buying requirements and often enter into a form of buying contract with some large independent wholesaling organization that serves them on a special cost-ofservice basis.

## RETAILER-COOPERATIVE VOLUNTARY GROUPS

Many early informal buying groups found that a logical step in their development was to purchase an existing wholesale house or to form a new one. In other cases, groups of merchants were organized for the express purpose of operating their own wholesale house. In either case, a paid manager and paid employees conduct the house just about as they would if it were owned by a private corporation. Stocks of goods are purchased, stored, sold, and delivered.

Stores operated by members of retailer cooperative voluntary groups do not account for a large proportion of total retail trade but are especially noteworthy due to their substantial influence in the grocery trade and because of their unusual significance in certain geographic areas. Some cooperatively-owned wholesale grocery facilities were established by groups of retailers prior to 1900, but the principal impetus for the movement came from increasing competition from corporate chains at a later date. About 150 retailer cooperative warehouses were in operation in 1958 and more than one-half of them were organized in the 1930's and 1940's. Between 1948 and 1958, the number of member retail stores in such organizations increased from 25,710 to 33,007, or from about 8 per cent to about 15 per cent of all grocery stores. Sales volume of member stores in the same period increased from about 11 per cent to about 15 per cent of all grocery store sales. In dollar amount, the sales increase of such member stores was 231 per cent over the 1948-58 period, a rate of gain far outstripping that of corporate chains or of wholesaler-sponsored voluntary groups. Retailer cooperatives are of greatest relative importance in the Pacific Coast States, with estimated sales of member stores amounting to more than 40 per cent of grocery trade sales in California and Arizona. Such organizations are, however, to be found in practically all sections.

Most grocery trade retailer cooperatives have from 50 to 500 members each, but a few have more than 1,000. The organization is usually of the corporate form with required minimum investment per member ranging from about $250 in some cases to several thousand dollars in others. Typically, such cooperatives are operated on the basis of one vote per member, regardless of the amount of stock ownership. Profits accruing from operations at the wholesale level are passed back to members in the form of patronage refunds. Members are usually expected or required to concentrate their purchases with the retailer-owned warehouse, thus making possible the elimination of salesmen. In some cases, individual stores are *identified* as members of a voluntary group and carry on cooperative advertising; in many instances, however, members retain a strong individual identity, engaging in no group promotional efforts, thus using the cooperative facilities solely as an economical source of supply.

In former years retailer cooperatives limited their offerings largely to staple grocery products and performed few other services for members. During the 1950's many organizations expanded their procurement services and provided a more complete source of supply. It is common for such cooperatives to supply non-food items, frozen foods, dairy items, and in numerous instances, even perishable produce and meats. Retailer cooperatives are stronger in this regard than wholesalers who sponsor voluntary chains, but they do not engage in as extensive a range of promotional, record keeping, and management advisory services as do members of the latter type.

While retailer-cooperative warehouses are predominantly associated with the grocery trade, some such organizations are encountered occasionally in other lines, notably drugs, hardware, and office supplies and stationery. In most such cases, the emphasis is primarily upon the presumed economies of group buying through an owned wholesaling facility. Outside the grocery trade, such organizations have made little effort to operate according to the voluntary chain principle by common store identification or group advertising.

## WHOLESALER-SPONSORED VOLUNTARY CHAINS

Many wholesalers attempted to offset declines in their sales volume incident to the growth of corporate chains by organizing groups of independent merchants who, in return for special services rendered to them by the sponsoring wholesaler, agree to buy a major part of their merchandise requirements from him. Such groups constitute what are known as *wholesaler-sponsored voluntary chains.* They differ from retailer-cooperatives in two ways. First, the initiative for organizing comes from the wholesaler rather than from the retailers themselves. Second, the wholesale house remains under private rather than cooperative ownership.

Although wholesaler-sponsored chains vary in many details, the essential basis of operation is one of mutual cooperation. Retailers agree to concentrate their purchases with the sponsoring wholesaler. While not all retail prices are uniform, advertised articles must be sold at the same price in every member store. The wholesaler in turn agrees to furnish certain merchandising advice and to be alert in his search for favorable opportunities to buy merchandise, the sale of which can be promoted by the group. Moreover, because there is some degree of concentration, the buying power of the wholesaler is usually increased through the sponsorship of a voluntary chain. Resulting savings are passed on to member stores as an aid to them in meeting the competition of the corporate chain.

In 1958 some 330 grocery wholesaling companies were reported as sponsoring voluntary chains. Member stores are estimated at about 36,000 and account for some 15 per cent of total grocery trade sales. Between 1948 and 1958 the rate of sales increase for such member stores was considerably less than for retailer cooperatives, but it was just about the same as that for corporate chains in the food trade. The importance of wholesaler-sponsored groups varies considerably in different geographic areas, with approximately one-half of the affiliated stores located in a group of eight contiguous states in the Middle Atlantic and East North Central divisions of the country.

Operating costs of voluntary group wholesalers have been traditionally somewhat higher than those incurred by retailer-owned warehouses because a larger part of total sales volume is made to small independent stores not members of the sponsored voluntary group, regular salesmen or "store supervisors" are employed to call on and assist members with operational and merchandising problems, credit accommodations are sometimes provided, and because a wider range of advertising, display, store planning, and managerial services is offered to members of the voluntaries than is received from retailer cooperative warehouses by their owners.

While wholesaler-sponsored voluntary chains have attained the highest form of development in the grocery business, they are not limited to this field. Butler Brothers, the leading wholesaler of variety goods, sponsors a voluntary chain of Ben Franklin variety stores located in all sections of the United States. Such stores are operated under a franchise agreement which calls for a payment by the retailer of a yearly fee which depends on store size. In return for this fee, the wholesaler provides: a complete warehouse service for all merchandise items needed to operate a variety store; a detailed stock control system; automatic store shipments of new merchandise items; a planned promotional program tied to the seasonal requirements of each month of the year; professionally prepared sales plans, display signs, price tags, and store decorations; assistance from specially trained field advisors; cooperative rebates on store purchases based on the annual volume of buying from the wholesaler; and permission to use the Ben Franklin name.

Another example of a wholesaler-sponsored voluntary consists of Rexall Drug Stores that are to be found in almost all communities. They are supplied with merchandise items from wholesale warehouses operated by the Rexall Drug and Chemical Company, are identified to the public as Rexall stores by the familiar orange and blue signs of the company, and participate in a variety of special promotional events, including the nationally advertised Rexall 1-cent sales. Through a subsidiary corporation, Rexall Realty Corp., assistance is given to franchise Rexall merchants in obtaining leases in planned shopping centers.

In the restaurant and motel field, another application of the same idea consists of Howard Johnson establishments. Such units are predominately independently owned, have a uniform appearance, and are under franchise to a central wholesaling organization which furnishes equipment, supplies, and food to individual operators who agree to maintain uniform standards of quality and service.

## COORDINATED GROUPS OF VOLUNTARIES

A majority of the wholesale grocers who sponsor voluntary chains are members of a national federation of such wholesalers. In order to secure certain advantages of group action, such as large-scale buying and promotion of private brands, it became necessary for voluntary group wholesalers to operate jointly.

One of the best known of these central organizations is the Independent Grocers Alliance of Chicago. More than 50 wholesaler members serve about 4,500 stores in all parts of the country. It assigns a franchise to a wholesaler who in turn grants the retailer the right to display the I.G.A. sign, carry the private brands of the organization, and receive merchandising aids. The central office buys goods to be packed under the I.G.A. labels and advertises such brands nationally. Red and White Stores, Clover Farm Stores, Food Merchandisers of America, and United Buyers Corp. are other well-known groups providing similar services.

Some 85 retailer cooperative groups are linked together through indirect ownership of National Retailer-Owned Grocers, Inc. (NROG). Three large regional affiliates of this organization carry on large-scale buying and promotional activities. Another affiliate, Shurfine, Inc., owns some 30 registered trademarks for various food product lines which are purchased by the three regional affiliates for exclusive sale in member stores.

## VOLUNTARY AFFILIATES OF CORPORATE CHAINS

The forms of voluntary chains discussed up to this point may be viewed as defensive measures undertaken by independent merchants or their suppliers in order to compete with corporate chains more effectively. A third form consists of companies that own and operate chains of retail stores and also serve as headquarters for a similarly identified group of independent "associate" stores. When a corporate chain undertakes such action, its motive is not to promote competition with itself. Quite to the contrary, independent affiliates are usually selected from merchants located in places that do not offer sufficient volume potential to be attractive from the standpoint of chain ownership. By selling through associate stores, the chain can add substantially to its purchasing power, increase the volume of its wholesaling facilities, reduce costs or expand the extent of advertising, spread the costs of corporate administration over a broader base, and realize a profit on wholesale sales to affiliated stores.

Probably the best known example is the Western Auto Supply Company which operates 16 wholesale houses, a chain of 376 completely owned retail stores located in medium-sized and large cities, and has some 3,600 affiliated independent merchants who are identified to the public as "Western Auto Associate Stores." For the most part these independents are located in smaller communities, and the typical establishment is considerably smaller than that of the company-owned stores. The independents concentrate their purchases with Western Auto wholesale houses, participate in company advertising, and benefit from the company's merchandising advice and physical assistance in store operation. Additional examples of the same method of operation in the automotive accessory business are provided by numerous independent merchants affiliated with tire manufacturers, such as Firestone, Goodyear, and Goodrich. Each of these companies operates a chain of company-owned stores, performs wholesaling functions, buys and resells merchandise that it does not manufacture, and engages in voluntary chain activities with independent merchants whose stores resemble the company-owned retail outlets insofar as appearance, layout, operating policies, and advertising are concerned.

Examples in other lines of trade include some 1,800

"Walgreen Agencies" which supplement over 400 company-owned stores operated by the Walgreen Drug Company, and some 30 small-town men's clothing merchants who have been licensed by Bond Stores, Inc. to sell suits and coats merchandised in that company's chain of about 100 stores which are located, for the most part, in large cities.

## FRANCHISED RETAIL OUTLETS OF MANUFACTURERS

The similarity among the operations of individual retail outlets that are franchised by certain manufacturing companies places them at least on the fringe of the voluntary chain movement. The merchandising advice and assistance provided by some of the large shoe manufacturing companies, such as the Brown Shoe Company, Inc. and the various divisions of the International Shoe Company, together with the close working relationship maintained with merchants who buy substantially from one source is one good illustration.

Certain paint manufacturing companies, especially those that are local or regional in character, distribute through carefully selected retail paint stores, provide them with store signs and other store equipment, plan and carry out sales promotion programs for the whole group of such dealers, and in general function in accordance with the procedures followed by other classes of voluntary chains. Some manufacturers of men's clothing and men's furnishings enjoy similarly close working relationships with many of their dealers who are identified to the public primarily as outlets for the manufacturer's line of goods.

Similar arrangements are to be found in the gasoline service station trade. It is common for major petroleum refining companies to develop new locations under lease arrangements with property owners, thus permitting the construction and equipping of station facilities. Stations are then commonly subleased to independent businessmen who operate their stations in accordance with the terms of a franchise. This affords the petroleum company a "chain" of independently owned outlets for its products. All gasoline service stations, of course, are not operated in this manner, as some are company-owned stations and some are owned outright by the operator or by a wholesale distributor.

## APPRAISAL OF VOLUNTARY ASSOCIATIONS

That the various forms of voluntary chains or franchise systems have inherent strength is indicated by a long period of experience, considerable recent growth of many well-established organizations, and the emergence of new voluntary groups and franchising organizations. Enough has been accomplished to establish the principle that groups of merchants working together and with their suppliers can effectively attain many of the buying, advertising, and merchandising advantages of regular chains. Perhaps the strongest advantage is the fact that the superior planning of the sponsoring organization has raised the level of merchandising in member stores. Reference has been made to the establishment of physical standards of store operation. Some plans allow the sponsor to cancel the membership of any retailer who fails to operate his store in such a manner as to reflect credit upon the group as a whole. Possibility of such action stimulates indifferent merchants to greater endeavor.

Certain weaknesses exist, however. Lack of strong central control is perhaps most important. The sponsor or a committee of the members can go only so far in encouragement or instruction in better merchandising methods. In many voluntary plans, the sponsor has field supervisors who work with and provide counsel for affiliated retailers, thus performing essentially the same functions as a district supervisor in a regular chain. Two fundamental differences are, however, especially significant. First, the supervisor in a corporate chain has disciplinary powers whereas his counterpart in the voluntary group lacks authority to alter undesirable situations in member stores. Second, the chain store supervisor has higher organizational status and rank than the store managers working under his direction whereas the successful operator of an independent retail store often regards the supervisor as a person of inferior status. Whereas the chain company supervisor has but one loyalty, to the firm that employs him, the voluntary group counselor has two—the group sponsor and the retailer—and must devote considerable time and energy to winning and maintaining acceptance of merchandising programs by the latter.

Such weaknesses have not seriously handicapped the expansion of voluntary groups. As previously indicated, voluntary chains in the grocery trade account for a majority of the business done by independent stores and the growth of retailer cooperatives, in particular, outstripped that of corporate chains in the 1950's. Significant expansions have occurred in other lines of trade as well.Voluntary cooperation within the framework of a franchising system is attractive to a sponsor because it provides a semicontrolled network of outlets for his products or services and because administrative problems and capital investment are substantially less than would be the case if the franchiser owned and operated all outlets. It is attractive to the retailer since it gives him a national or regional identity, provides him with training and guidance in business management, supplies a merchandising program based on the successful experience of similar stores, and often affords him an opportunity to establish an enterprise which could hardly be started without the sponsor's aid. It appears that the concept of voluntary association has wide application, that it has strengthened the position of independent merchants who have taken advantage of the opportunities thus offered, and that future expansion is limited almost solely by the number of qualified leaders and merchants who develop an appreciation for the benefits that such group activities may hold for them. As is evident from the context of this discussion, voluntary chains have developed primarily in lines of merchandise where merchants can utilize one principal source of supply on the wholesale level. Up to this time, little voluntary chain activity, other than group buying, has been observed in the case of fashion merchandising which involves assembling from numerous sources located in markets at a distance from the typical dealer.

## Chapter 11

# Supermarkets and Shopping Centers

Three notable and relatively recent institutional developments in retailing have been the increased influence of supermarket merchandising methods, the rapid expansion of planned shopping centers, and the birth and attainment of an aura of respectability by discount houses. Each of these developments has made an important contribution and exerts a real influence on channels of distribution, competition, and on our way and standard of living.

### SUPERMARKETS

Supermarkets have revolutionized the distribution of food. Their phenomenal success in the grocery trade has also had a persuasive influence upon the marketing of consumer goods of all classes. Supermarket merchandising techniques have been applied to some extent throughout almost all segments of the retail trade structure.

The term *supermarket* is very loosely used in marketing discussions. In general the concept conveyed is that of a very large, departmentized retail store dealing in dry groceries, produce, meats, baked goods, and dairy products. Such a store usually handles certain drugs, toilet goods, hardware, houseware items, and a variety of other classes of merchandise. Emphasis is placed on large volume of sales, mass appeal, complete assortments, and price. Up to about 1937 supermarkets were usually located outside the downtown or neighborhood areas, in a factory or a barnlike structure which had formerly been used for industrial or recreational purposes. Such a concept has been greatly modified because almost all the supermarkets constructed since that time have been of an altogether different type. Supermarkets are now to be found in all types of retailing locations; better buildings are used than in the earlier years; more emphasis is placed on display, service and assortments, and less on price.

In view of the nature of these developments a useful and inclusive definition of a supermarket is that it is a large, departmentized, retail establishment offering a relatively broad and complete stock of dry groceries, fresh meat, perishable produce, and dairy products, supplemented by a variety of convenience, nonfood merchandise and operated primarily on a self-service basis.

## IMPORTANCE

Any quantitative evaluation of supermarkets depends upon the precise criteria selected for classification purposes. The Bureau of the Census has refrained from defining the term *supermarket* owing to lack of agreement within the food trade and among marketing authorities as to precise definition. Unfortunately, the Bureau of the Census is the only organization in a position to make complete enumerations for the whole country. Other organizations, such as the national trade association, the Super Market Institute, collect statistics from members, but no such reporting agency obtains figures from all stores that might be classed as supermarkets.

The most serious problem encountered in attempting a statement regarding quantitative importance is that almost all definitions have included a minimal annual sales volume requirement which has varied, according to the viewpoint of the defining authority, from as low as $100,000 to as much as $1 million. [1] This is disheartening when attempts are made to effect historical comparisons. Because of changes in the price level—which for grocery store items increased by 147 per cent over the period from 1940 to 1959—a store classified as a supermarket in one year might not be so classified in another, even though the physical volume of business had not changed significantly. In most trade sources some criterion of minimum sales volume size has been used, although changed from time to time to reflect major changes in the level of prices. The criteria is undoubtedly reasonably representative of stores commonly regarded as supermarkets. As shown in this chart, supermarkets accounted for some 70 per cent of grocery store sales in 1959—a share of market nearly three times that which they enjoyed in 1940. The number of stores classified as supermarkets grew from 6,200 in 1940 to 22,500 in 1959 more than a threefold increase—but was still less than 10 per cent of the total number of grocery stores in operation in the latter year.

## HISTORY OF SUPERMARKETS

There are random early examples of very large food stores, such as Tiedke's in Toledo, Ohio, certain public market stores, and the L-type or drive-in markets which originated in California in 1918. During the 1920's the Ford Motor Company operated several commissary stores of unusual sales volume size. Their operations reflected some attributes of supermarkets, such as limited service and fast turnover, but they were not set up on the basis of self-service, a characteristic that was later to become one of the distinguishing aspects of supermarkets.

The first true self-service supermarket did not appear until the early 1930's when "King" Cullen opened his first market in an abandoned Long Island garage with empty ginger-ale cases for display tables. The first "Big Bear" market was opened near Newark, New Jersey, in December, 1932, and in one year sold $3.6 million in goods. [4] The supermarket at once became the sensation of the food industry and a problem to manufacturers, wholesalers, and chain and independent retailers alike.

The depression-born supermarket was stimulated by the severity of the economic crisis. Operators were able to occupy huge buildings for low rent, to obtain merchandise in large quantities from distressed sources. They had an almost inexhaustible market, consisting of consumers with depleted purchasing power. Being anxious to stretch every dollar, they responded readily to the appeal of low prices. There was little need for a convenient location, fancy fixtures, displays, or service. Hence some of these early markets incurred operating expenses of as little as 6 or 8 per cent of sales and were able to operate satisfactorily with a gross margin of profit in the range of 9 to 12 per cent of sales, which was considerably lower than the average gross profit in the then typical chain or independent counter-type store where clerks waited upon customers and where, especially in the case of independents, many orders were delivered and a large proportion of sales was made on a credit basis. These early supermarkets reduced by about one-half the margins prevailing in the food industry and, as a consequence, brought great turmoil into the market.

The first supermarkets were opened by independent merchants. Large grocery chains did not follow their lead until it became clear that something more than selling food from empty boxes and in an abandoned barn was involved. When the validity of the principles upon which the supermarket is based became clearly established, chains entered into active competition with pioneer independents and today this type of store is of outstanding importance in their operations. The chains, and successful independents as well, soon began to build stores upon modern lines, using fixtures, lights, and other specially designed equipment.

Chain store organizations now dominate the supermarket industry for two reasons. First, many original independent supermarket operators were highly successful and became multiunit organizations as profits from the first units were reinvested in new locations. In all parts of the country are to be found important local chains which can be traced to the birth of the supermarket as a retailing institution. Second, the large, well-established chains were quick to adapt to this new method of merchandising as soon as its soundness became apparent. Since 1933 the operations of the older and larger chains have been characterized by the policy of closing down small units and replacing them with larger and fewer stores of the supermarket type.

It must not be inferred, however, that supermarkets today are altogether of the chain variety, as there is a considerable number of independent markets of this type, many with annual sales over $2 million. According to one trade study, independent supermarkets and superettes —medium-sized stores that have adopted supermarket methods to a high degree—accounted for more than one-fourth of the total number of independent food stores and more than 90 per cent of their sales volume. Many of these are affiliated with some type of voluntary chain organization.

## MERCHANDISING STRATEGY

During the earlier years of the supermarket industry, when grocery trade competition was mostly between supermarkets and counter-type traditional grocery stores, rather than among supermarkets themselves, certain fundamental policies rather clearly differentiated supermarkets from their older rivals. First, self-service, though used prior thereto on occasion, has been a characteristic of supermarkets since their inception.

Second, due to the absence of personal selling, emphasis was largely upon national brands rather than upon unknown or private brands which were commonly "pushed" by clerks in service stores. Third, price appeal was a pervasive promotional attribute, both in the case of special promotions and in the emphasis on "everyday low prices." Fourth, the typical supermarket carried a very wide range of merchandise, commonly five to ten times the number of individual items found in ordinary grocery stores.

A fifth characteristic, high average sale, arose out of the large number of merchandising items, mass display and quantity pricing, a tendency for week-end rather than everyday shopping, increased use of the automobile for shopping trips, and better facilities for home storage of food, particularly items requiring refrigeration. An additional attraction was the provision of automobile parking facilities, often in amounts equal to three to four times the total area of the store.

## DYNAMICS IN SUPERMARKET OPERATION

The basic character of supermarket merchandising strategy was well established, in terms of the features outlined above, prior to the 1940's. The supermarket business has, however, continued to be one of the most dynamic of any in our retailing structure. Operators in this field have been hard pressed to keep abreast of new developments and to adapt their businesses to changing competitive and environmental conditions. Nevertheless, they have manifested an amazing ability to cope with problems of continuing innovation, adjusting their operations to the changing requirements of customer preferences.

### Size of Store

In 1949 the "ideal" size of a supermarket was deemed to be about 11,700 square feet of total floor space, but by 1956 it had grown to 20,000 square feet, an increase of more than 70 per cent. In the later 1950's the *average* size of *new* stores leveled off at about 20,000 square feet, perhaps indicating that supermarkets are now about as large as they will become. Stores of larger size require a larger than average trading area to support economical operation and competitive conditions are such that it is difficult to find sites where a supermarket does not have to compete with at least several similar stores. There is, however, considerable variation from the *average* size, with many supermarkets in excess of 30,000 square feet and some larger than 50,000.

### Hours

Store hours have been adjusted to provide greater opportunity for family shopping. Between 1951 and 1960 the proportion of supermarkets open every evening increased from 27 to 66 per cent, and those open on Sunday increased from 9 to 22 per cent.

### Store Refinements

Many types of store refinements have become common in newer supermarkets. By way of contrast with the barnlike atmosphere of the early 1930's, many contemporary planners incorporate elaborate facilities, including "Kiddie Korrals," rest rooms, better lighting, striking color combinations, murals, automatic doors, parcel conveyors, in-store music, air conditioning, and a variety of other customer-pleasing devices.

## Extension of Self-Service

While self-service in the grocery department has been an attribute of supermarkets since their beginning, the trend has been to extend this method of merchandising to all departments. In 1950, 41 per cent of the supermarkets operated meat departments on a complete self-service basis and 47 per cent of the produce departments were of this nature. By 1960, these percentages had increased, respectively, to 87 per cent and 64 per cent; moreover, most stores without complete self-service in these departments were at least partially on that basis.

## Growth in Merchandise Items

While supermarkets have traditionally carried many more items than other grocery stores, the increase in the number of items handled by the typical supermarket is startling. In 1950 the average supermarket carried 2,000 items, but by 1960 this had increased to 6,000, with the middle one-half of the stores reporting between 5,000 and 7,500 items. This growth is partially explained by a larger number of nonfood items, but is attributed primarily to a steady stream of new products developed by manufacturers in traditional grocery store categories. More and more of the housewife's work in the area of food preparation has been shifted to the manufacturer of food products, thus contributing to an increase in the number of available items. In the case of frozen foods, technological innovations opened the way for a wide variety of food items previously unthinkable. To a substantial extent, the stream of new items has both contributed to and resulted from a "splintering" of former product classifications into numerous new categories. Within each of the new product classes, supermarkets have found it necessary to make merchandising decisions regarding a number of different available brands with several package sizes or types for each.

## Nonfood Merchandising

Early supermarkets specialized in selling groceries, produce, and meats, although certain nonfood household items such as paper products and soaps have traditionally been part of the grocery department. Following World War II, the picture changed radically as many companies added new classifications of goods not formerly sold in supermarkets. Sales in so-called "nonfood lines" (i.e., those not traditionally included in grocery departments) grew from almost nothing in the mid-1940's to 3.4 per cent of supermarket sales in 1954 and to 5 per cent in 1957. In 1958 and 1959, however, such sales remained stable at 5 per cent, indicating that the rate of increase was no more rapid than the growth in total supermarket sales. This apparent stability can be misleading. Actually, the increase in the dollar volume of sales of nonfood items has been substantial, owing to the fact that the number of supermarkets and their share of total grocery store sales has grown markedly. According to trade estimates in 1961, supermarkets were accounting for some 50 per cent of sales of leading health and beauty items, about 13 per cent of total phonograph record sales, and about 20 per cent of total newsstand magazine sales. The number of nonfood lines commonly stocked in supermarkets has continuously increased, as has also the proportion of supermarkets stocking each such line. Within most such lines, however, assortments are usually quite limited, with merchandising emphasis confined to products of high consumer purchase frequency and to the most popular brands.

## Hybrid Stores

In the late 1950's and early 1960's, some supermarket companies diversified substantially through the operation of so-called "hybrid" stores of some 40,000 to 60,000 square feet, of which about onehalf is devoted to general merchandise, similar to the offerings of a modern variety-department store.

A notable example is the Grand Union Company, an eastern chain of some 440 supermarkets, which by 1960 had opened some 17 such hybrid grocery—general merchandise stores, identified as "Grand Way Discount Centers." Success of these establishments plus scattered examples of similar ventures by other supermarket chains provoked considerable speculation about the possibility of the supermarket eventually becoming a complete one-stop shopping center within itself. The outlook for such a development is not promising, for two major reasons. First, it takes at least several times as many families to support a given sales area devoted to general merchandise as it does to support a food store of comparable size, owing to the much greater relative importance of food expenditures in the typical family budget. Thus, a hybrid store of the kind described above must draw families from a much larger trading area than required to support an ordinary supermarket. Second, the hybrid supermarket must compete aggressively for general merchandise business with strongly entrenched competitors, such as variety stores, department stores, discount houses, and many kinds of single-line stores.

Supermarkets have been somewhat concerned about a tendency of certain discount houses to add large grocery departments to attract more patrons to their general merchandise departments, and to some extent ventures into general merchandise retailing by supermarkets have been regarded as defensive measures. Certainly some supermarket organizations will build large hybrid stores, and the number of them will increase. In view of the reasons explained above, it seems evident, however, that the large hybrid store will be the more exceptional case and that the typical supermarket will continue to be predominantly a food store.

## Promotional Practices

As the number of supermarkets has grown, and as most supermarket companies have demonstrated increasing willingness to meet the lowest competitive prices prevailing in their area, price in itself has become somewhat less important as a patronage-attracting feature. Emphasis has tended to shift to various promotional strategies which tend to induce the consumer to purchase from a given store on a continuing basis. The use of trading stamps, grew from 13 per cent of supermarkets in 1953, to 40 per cent in 1955, and to 67 per cent in 1959. The cost of using trading stamps is commonly about 1.5 to 1.8 per cent of store sales volume, but is regarded as a competitive necessity in metropolitan areas where such stamps have wide consumer acceptance and where their distribution is widespread. Regular continuous premium plans other than trading stamps were used by 8 per cent of the supermarkets in 1959.

### Efficiency Programs

Supermarkets have made extensive application of scientific work simplification programs and have made great strides in the use of mechanized equipment in receiving and handling merchandise, prepackaging of meat and fresh produce, price-marking, and check-out stand operation. As a consequence, great strides have been made in the productivity of store employees. Over the period 1951-56, when retail food store prices were relatively constant, sales per full-time store employee equivalent increased from $29,700 to $43,400. This is an increase of 46 per cent in sales per employee, a record which, it is believed, cannot be matched by any other type of store. Since 1956, however, sales per employee have remained virtually stable, indicating that efficiency measures and forms of mechanization have been carried about as far as is practical under existing conditions.

### Expenses of Operation

As a consequence of some of the above factors, especially those pertaining to merchandise line expansion, trading stamps, and increased customer facilities, and because of rising wage rates, operating expenses and gross margins in supermarkets have tended to increase. In 1955 operating expenses amounted to 14.72 per cent of sales, but increased to 15.96 per cent in 1957, and to 16.27 per cent in 1959—a marked contrast with the 6 to 8 per cent achieved by some supermarkets in the early 1930's. Nevertheless, the supermarket continues to be one of the most economical forms of retailing.

## FUTURE OF THE SUPERMARKET IN THE GROCERY TRADE

In the early years of supermarket merchandising in the food field, this form of retailing grew rapidly, at the expense of the relative market position of traditional clerk-service-type food stores. By the late 1950's it was apparent that supermarkets were rapidly approaching a more stable relative market position. In 1940 there was about one supermarket to 5,700 families, but by 1960 the ratio was one for 2,300 families. Practically all consumers who wish to buy in this type of store now have the opportunity to do so. Supermarket chains are now hard pressed to find desirable locations for new establishments because supermarkets are to be found in most market areas where the population potential is adequate to support a large volume store. The major competition for supermarkets is now with other supermarkets rather than with smaller stores, and the smaller stores that remain use supermarket merchandising methods to a high degree. This suggests that supermarket expansion in food sales will, in the future, be at a less rapid rate, more in line with increases in population and buying income. As a point of saturation is approached, the supermarket will be able to increase its share of total consumer expenditures only by continuing to expand activities in nonfood merchandising. The opportunity for doing this on a large scale does not seem particularly encouraging because of the manner in which retailers in other lines have adapted their operations to supermarket merchandising strategy. Nevertheless, it is expected that the supermarket industry will be one of continued growth and development, merely because of the long-run market increases attributable to population expansion and rising incomes. As population grows, especially in suburban market areas, many new, large, and ultra-modern supermarkets will be opened to serve the needs of people in these areas.

## GENERAL IMPACT OF SUPERMARKET MERCHANDISING METHODS

Merchandising methods developed in the supermarket industry have provided a strong attraction for the modern consumer for a variety of reasons. First, self-service methods are commonly associated with the ability to purchase at lower prices. Second, well-designed impersonal store layouts enable consumers to shop quickly, which seems to be in character with the pace of contemporary living; still, it is also conducive to relaxed, "look around" shopping, and so is in harmony with another aspect of modern times. Third, the opportunity to serve one's self relieves the consumer from some distrust of salespeople, particularly when people wish to avoid "high-pressure" salesmanship. Another thesis sometimes advanced to explain the popularity of self-service is that this type of buying provides the consumer with the opportunity to engage in a creative, absorbing, problem-solving type of activity which may be contrasted with being dependent upon the aid of a salesman.

The way in which the consumer has responded to the various appeals of supermarket merchandising strategy has resulted in imitative modifications of operating practices which are visually evident among newer or modernized stores in almost all lines of retailing.

In department stores the prevailing tendency has been to avoid the "limited-service" connotations of "self-service" operation, but many such stores have approached supermarket merchandising strategy by increasing the extent of open display and by utilizing conspicuous "transaction processing stations." These are, in reality, a modification of the supermarket check-out counter, and are often identified with signs such as "Bring Your Own Selection Here for Quick Service." Applications of this type of merchandising have been most common in departments that handle easy-to-select types of items, such as greeting cards, notions, housewares, books, and toys. Some leading department store organizations have engaged in self-service merchandising on an extensive scale, particularly in many of the newer branch stores, and more especially in those engaging in discount retailing to the greatest extent.

Most of the newer stores operated by major variety and drugstore chains are of unusually large size, utilize open display fixtures that expose merchandise items in the majority of the classifications, and have a number of regular check-out counters concentrated at the front of the stores in a manner almost identical to that of the grocery supermarket. The layout of new or modernized hardware and automotive accessory stores reflects a similar trend, with emphasis upon self-selection and a greater diversification of visually displayed merchandise than characterized such stores in the past.

Modern discount houses utilize supermarket methods to a high degree and have sometimes been described as general merchandise supermarkets. Even in the apparel field, the supermarket has had considerable influence. The Robert Hall chain of clothing stores has grown from a relatively small to a nationally known organization by utilizing, to a high degree, selfservice methods. Many other apparel retailers have made similar adaptations in their methods. Even in the shoe field, a limited number of stores are operated on a self-service basis, to the extent of allowing consumers to do their own fitting and taking their merchandise to the check-out stand. So extensive has been the influence that many establishments in nonfood lines are publicized as "supermarket" drugstores, hardware stores, nurseries, or even lumber yards.

Many supermarket adaptations have been experimental and have failed because the need for some type of personal selling assistance was overwhelming, at least for some merchandise items or for some customers who prefer personal assistance. Successful innovations in nonfood stores have usually rested upon a new approach to the handling of the retail sales transaction. Under traditional clerk-service forms of retailing, the consumer is totally dependent upon the service of a regular salesperson for all phases of the transaction. The influence of supermarket merchandising has been essentially that of dividing sales transactions into two components—first, the merchandise selection aspect and, second, the recording aspect. The first can be handled *either* by the consumer through the process of self-selection *or* by the salesperson who assists the consumer with personal selling advice. The recording phase is handled at some kind of a centralized check-out counter or transaction processing station which is equipped for this purpose and manned by specialized personnel.

The majority of retailers who have attempted well-planned modifications of their operations by utilizing supermarket merchandising strategy have derived substantial advantages. The prevailing tendency has been for sales to increase when clerk-service stores are converted to a self selection basis. This is attributed to several factors. First, the influence of store modernization which is in harmony with contemporary consumer buying habits undoubtedly plays a major role. Second, many more merchandise items are exposed to consumer contact and it is widely accepted that consumers buy more on impulse from open displays than they do in clerk-service stores. Third, personal selling efficiency tends to improve, because this type of selling is largely confined to merchandise classifications in which the consumer actually requires buying assistance.

Self-service methods have often had a favourable influence upon store profits. In part, this is attributable to a larger volume of sales per establishment. It is also due to a smaller amount of employee time per transaction or greater volume of sales per employee. This results from the fact that people tend to help themselves in the case of familiar "easy-to-choose" items. Trained salespeople are thus able to concentrate their efforts on higher unit value transactions where assistance is required because of the technical character of goods, or because of special compounding or fitting problems, as in the case of appliances in hardware stores, prescriptions in drugstores, and suits in men's clothing and furnishings establishments. As a result of these factors, many retailers have found that they can handle a considerably larger volume of sales in an establishment of given size without adding to the number of employees required to care for the greater number of transactions involved.

Stores adapting to supermarket self-service methods have encountered various new operational problems, one of which is the planning of assortments in relation to available display space. Under clerk-service arrangements, items can be added without the same kind of planning, since the salesperson presumably knows the stock and can bring forth those items which he believes will meet the expressed needs of the customer. Under self-service techniques, however, all items must be visibly displayed for customer selection.

Since there are rather rigid restrictions on the possible number of "item facings" on given display fixtures, more serious planning attention must be given to the size of inventory, the number of items contained in it, the sales potential of items, and the allocation of display space in relation to sales and profit potential of items. Just as items may vary in their price or income elasticity of demand, they may also vary in their *display elasticity of demand*. Since merchants often have more control over allocation of display space than they do over item pricing, the concept of display elasticity of demand becomes of great importance when supermarket merchandising techniques are used. As applied to manufacturers, the concept shifts channel relationships from emphasis upon obtaining personal selling support to securing preferred display locations in stores and to getting more "item facings" on display fixtures.

## PLANNED SHOPPING CENTERS

Planned shopping centers are not retailing institutions in the ordinary sense, but rather spatial arrangements of stores which have been grouped to provide a balanced shopping attraction to the area served. Each store is a tenant in common with others with respect to certain shared facilities as parking and shopping malls, and usually participates in various kinds of group promotional efforts. Thus, planned shopping centers are a type of enterprise in which tenants have joined interests with developers and with other stores to an unusual degree, giving rise to the need for considering such centers as a form of enterprise, not merely as a collection of individual stores.

## DISTINCTIVE CHARACTERISTICS

All major cities have a number of secondary business districts which have evolved gradually over a long period of years as a consequence of many individual location decisions made by a wide variety of business firms. Planned shopping centers of the modern variety differ from these uncontrolled business districts in a number of respects. All of the land and buildings in a planned center is typically owned by the developing organization which gives it an unusual measure of control over architectural, parking, store arrangement, service, and other facilities.

Second, a balanced grouping of different kinds of stores and service establishments is provided for the purpose of affording a one-stop kind of shopping. Third, the greater part of the available ground space is used for free automobile parking. Ratios of parking space to store selling area are commonly about 3 or 4 to 1. Fourth, such centers are developed according to an over-all plan prepared with the help of architects, market analysts, traffic engineers, and other specialists prior to initial construction of the first rentable units in a new center.

## TYPES OF PLANNED CENTERS

Planned centers are of several types, distinguished according to size, nature of tenants, and trading area served. At one extreme are *neighbourhood centers* usually consisting of several to a dozen or more stores of the convenience goods and service type. Most such centers have less than 50,000 feet in total store area. At the other extreme are *regional centers* which may have 50 to 100 stores, including one or more department store units, a number of almost all kinds of shopping goods stores, several variety store chains and supermarkets, and a group of convenience goods stores and service establishments. Such centers are usually developed on tracts of land in excess of 40 acres, commonly provide parking for 4,000 or more automobiles, have some 500,000 or more square feet in store area, and may draw customers from a trading area of as much as some 20 minutes' driving-time radius.

## OWNERSHIP INTERESTS

Different types of ownership interests have been involved in the development of planned shopping centers. One class consists of residential real estate developers who provide for shopping center facilities as part of the master plan for large suburban subdivisions. A second class consists of a number of organizations that specialize in building and operating centers. Some of these organizations employ a large staff of market analysts, real estate appraisers, architects and designers, and administrative personnel. One of the best known is the Don M. Casto Company of Columbus, Ohio, which has developed, owns, manages, and promotes some 30 large planned shopping centers and many small ones located in ten different metropolitan areas and in a number of small cities. A third type of ownership interest is represented by regular retailing companies that develop shopping centers in which they wish to become major tenants. Examples in the department store field include the J. L. Hudson Company of Detroit which developed famous regional shopping centers in that city; the Allied Stores Corporation, builders of Bergen Mall, near Paramus, New Jersey; and the R. H. Macy and Co., Inc., developers of the Garden State Plaza Shopping Center, also near Paramus in the New York metropolitan area. Several other examples are to be found in the food field where certain chains have formed subsidiary real estate corporations to develop centers in which the chain will have the opportunity to be the exclusive or dominant supermarket tenant.

## GROWTH OF SHOPPING CENTERS

The decade following World War II afforded a favorable environment for shopping center growth. During the war years, new home construction and commercial building had been practically at a standstill. After the war, new family formation increased markedly, and the birth rate soared, thus stimulating population growth, which was primarily concentrated in suburban areas. Such new areas, being relatively devoid of established retailing facilities, afforded a natural opportunity for the new type of center.

A second major factor consists of the more widespread ownership and greater usage of the automobile. In 1920 there were only 20 million privately owned automobiles in the United States but there were 52 million by 1955. This gave rise to serious problems of congestion and created parking difficulties in the central business districts. Longer distances to be travelled from newer residential areas to such districts discouraged frequent visits by suburbanites. Increased utilization of automobiles also adversely affected many outlying neighbourhood business districts, since it made the consumer more independent and more willing to travel appreciable distances for even ordinary items needed for daily living. Thus the planned shopping center, with its large free parking areas, presented a patronage appeal that was in harmony with contemporary living.

Another major factor is to be found in changed consumer buying habits. As a result of mass market advertising, consumers became better informed about the availability of merchandise items. Because women are busier, either at work or in a variety of social pursuits, there is greater willingness to shop from the somewhat limited assortments available in suburban shopping centers, especially when the advantages of convenience, informality, and ease of parking are set in contrast with conditions associated with trips to central business districts.

Because of the factors just enumerated, the number of planned shopping centers grew from a mere handful in the late 1940's to some 4,000 in operation in 1960. These centers in 1960 contained about 500 million square feet of store area—an amount which is adequate, based on ratios of sales per square foot used for planning purposes, to sell $35 billion annually, or about 11 per cent of total retail sales. Shopping center store capacity by lines of trade varies considerably, being relatively much higher, for example, for types such as supermarkets and variety stores, which are to be found in nearly all centers, than is the case for establishments which are not commonly an important ingredient of such centers. Most such centers, however, have a sales volume below planned capacity and could appreciably increase sales without adding to floor space.

## COMPETITIVE POSITION OF SHOPPING CENTER STORES

The controlled type of center, especially the larger ones, holds for its tenants a number of *advantages*. Some of these are obvious from the foregoing description of characteristics and reasons for growth. One is the convenience of adequate free parking. A second consists of the balanced shopping attraction which affords the consumer an opportunity for a onestop buying expedition. Third, the uniform architectural treatment is generally attractive. Fourth, all stores located in such centers are, at this early stage of development, newer and more modern than those located in competitive types of locations. Fifth, individual stores benefit from aggressive promotion of the center as a whole, at least in contrast with more limited community efforts typically associated with unplanned business districts. Sixth, most planned shopping centers provide a greater number of night openings, which has been especially attractive from the standpoint of family shopping.

## IMPACT ON CHARACTER OF RETAILING STRUCTURE

From the foregoing discussion it is readily apparent that the planned shopping center has had a significant impact on the character of retailing, particularly with reference to the distribution of trade among various types of store locations, especially as related to a diminishing share of total retail business transacted by stores located in central business districts. In addition, two common types of tenant selection policies have tended to govern the composition of planned centers and, owing to their growth, have influenced the changing competitive positions of certain types of retailers.

The first type of policy relates to preferential treatment accorded to large-scale retailers, especially chains. After a center is planned and leases have been obtained, financing is by means of long-term mortgages involving millions of dollars.

Such mortgages are usually handled by large insurance companies which approach the problem from the viewpoint of an investor of policyholders' funds. Such a financing organization often requires that the amount of rental income assured from the leases of large well-established firms be adequate to cover all fixed charges (mortgage amortization, interest, taxes, etc.). In practice, this usually requires that the developer lease about 70 per cent of the total center space to firms with a net worth of more than $1 million and with high composite credit ratings. Since large chains and major department stores are about the only types of potential tenants with this amount of net worth, independent merchants and small multiunit organizations are practically excluded from the first 70 per cent or so of the space which is leased in a large proportion of planned Shopping centers. Thus, financing arrangements have tended to favor the relative growth of large multiunit firms.

A second factor is that shopping center leases often contain provisions which place restrictions upon the kind and amount of competition within the center. Such provisions are many and varied but one of special interest relates to the strong bargaining power of the dominant tenant at the time that the center is in the lease negotiation stage. Especially in regional centers where the developer may be dependent upon some particular store in order to insure the completion of the whole project, such a prospective tenant can often obtain concessions that would give him the right to pass on the acceptability of other potential tenants. Various instances are on record where dominant tenants of an orthodox type have used their bargaining power to exclude from shopping centers innovating establishments of a low-margin or discount nature. Such a policy tends to freeze retailing in such centers into a mold which gives well-established large organizations a certain amount of nearby competitive location immunity from maverick rivals. At the same time, this drives most forms of innovating competition to other types of locations, thus intensifying the competition between large shopping centers as a whole and types of stores which, because of operational characteristics, are prevented from becoming a part of them.

## OUTLOOK FOR SHOPPING CENTERS

Growth of suburban retailing has led to various types of defensive measures on the part of downtown merchants, also by civic action. Many urban department stores have modernized their establishments, provided parking facilities, improved their merchandise assortments, and increased the aggressiveness of their advertising. Municipalities have entered the picture by providing public off-street parking, constructing expressways, placing restrictions on on-street parking, increasing the number of one-way streets, and taking other measures to increase the attractiveness of the central business district.

In spite of the disadvantages of downtown shopping, many consumers prefer to shop downtown. Advantages generally associated with consumer preferences for central business district shopping are, first, a wider range of merchandise offerings available in the larger and more numerous stores to be found there and, second, the attraction of dominant sales promotion events publicized in metropolitan area newspapers and other media. Other benefits derive from consumer thinking that this area is a better place to meet friends, to have lunch, to buy at the best prices, to obtain more numerous services including delivery, and to combine shopping with other things that one may want to do.

The growing number of planned shopping centers, together with the various defensive measures taken by central business district interests, have resulted in a highly competitive era for planned shopping centers. Whereas early centers enjoyed an almost unchallenged opportunity to serve new and rapidly growing suburban areas, many of them are now in aggressive competition with other nearby centers. Multiplication of centers in some cities has greatly curtailed the trading area that can be served advantageously by any individual center and has limited opportunities for new developers. In most large cities, the point has been reached where a new planned center can be properly developed and promoted only as a result of successful competition with rival centers. From the standpoint of future development, the need is evident for greater emphasis upon sound market analysis, the best architectural planning, a truly distinctive group of outstanding retail tenants, and the provision of various kinds of attractive community services and entertainment facilities.

## DISCOUNT HOUSES

A significant institutional development of the post- World War II era has been the expansion of "cut-price" retailing. Some of the major forms of discount selling, the principal explanations for it, its influences upon the nature of competition within retailing, and its impact upon distribution channels are examined in this section.

## DISCOUNT SELLING VERSUS DISCOUNT HOUSES

The business press of the 1950's carried many articles on the subject of "discount retailing." Some writers have regarded such retailing as a new phenomenon while others have referred to it as a continuation of the ancient art of price cutting. Estimates regarding the quantitative significance of discount retailing have varied over a wide range. Agreement is general, however, that discounting or cut-price retailing has been growing and accounts for a substantial share of total retail sales. Part of the confusion on this subject arises out of the failure to distinguish between various forms of "discount selling" which are rather widely practiced by regular retailers on a discriminatory basis and "discount houses" that consistently offer all or most of the merchandise items in their stock at prices below so-called list or regular prices. Consumers believe that they are buying at a discount under a variety of circumstances as when they:

- Negotiate a lower price by bargaining or higgling with a retailer;
- Obtain special privileges by membership in some organization or affiliation with some group;
- Buy from an establishment which actually is, or is represented to be, a wholesale place of business; or

- Purchase from a store which, as a matter of policy, consistently sells below regular or "fair trade" prices.

Discount selling has been practiced, at least to some extent, by many kinds of retailers over decades. Some gasoline service stations offer certain favored customers discounts of two or three cents per gallon from posted prices. Practically all automobile sales that involve trade-ins have been "negotiated" for many years, with the effect that the skillful and persistent bargainer obtains a "better deal" than many other purchasers. In some furniture and appliance stores, customers who manifest resistance to posted prices are turned over to another salesman who presents a more attractive offer. Drugstores commonly give "professional discounts" to physicians, especially to those who favor the store with prescription references. Many retail stores, as well as wholesale and manufacturing companies, sell to their own employees according to some discount policy.

## TYPES OF DISCOUNT HOUSES

Most discussions of discount selling have not been concerned so much with the aforementioned types of examples of occasional discriminatory selling on the part of regular stores as with a surge in the volume of business accounted for by establishments generally recognized as a regular source of discount prices. A number of such "discount houses" existed at least as early as 1930's. Most of the earlier types were located in outof-the-way places and were not widely publicized. Several major types of discount houses may be distinguished.

### Open Showrooms

Particularly in the home furnishings field, there are open showrooms, operated by manufacturers and wholesale middlemen, for the purpose of maintaining centralized displays for small dealers and decorators who cannot maintain full stocks in their own establishments. While it has been conventional to admit consumers only upon introduction from a retailer, many such establishments have willingly done business with anyone who visited them. Consumers buying from such showrooms usually believe, sometimes without justification, that substantial price concessions are obtained.

**Brokerage Buying Arrangements**

Certain appliance repairmen, upholsterers and other types of service establishments with access to wholesale sources of supply have rendered buying services to their regular customers and others. Usually they have no stocks of merchandise but may agree to purchase specified items for consumers at cost plus some brokerage or buying fee of about 10 per cent of cost. In some cases the amount of this type of brokerage buying has become such a dominant character of the business that it becomes known as a discount house.

**Closed-Door Discount Houses**

Certain large discount houses sell only to consumers who purchase a membership. The "privilege" of joining is usually restricted to certain classes of consumers, such as government employees, members of labor unions, or people with a recognized professional status. Since admission to the merchandising facilities is open only to "card-holding members," such establishments are known as *closed-door discounters*. Some such organizations operated in the 1930's, usually on a small scale as judged by size of facilities. They often did not carry much of an inventory, but ordered merchandise for customers who made buying decisions on the basis of displays of sample items or catalogs.

In the late 1950's and early 1960's this type of discount house assumed a new character and expanded rapidly. While still operating on the basis of a closed-door philosophy, thus giving the members a feeling of being "in" on something from which others are excluded, facilities have grown to stores of substantial size, often occupying as much as 100,000 square feet. These stores are usually recognizable by an abbreviated name such as FAME, GEX, GEM, or BEX which usually signifies the name of the organization and suggests the character of those eligible for membership (e.g., GEX—Government Employees' Exchange). While the membership requirement suggests the flavor of a consumers' cooperative, these organizations are private enterprises operated for profit. Many of them consist largely of a collection of leased departments, similar to arrangements common in department stores, but where each lessee agrees to operate under the cut-price philosophy of the organization and to maintain certain standards of merchandising and service. Such stores are usually to be found in "solo" or "lone-wolf" locations, along major traffic arteries in large metropolitan areas. Some 16 companies, with about 40 outlets in 1960, are members of the National Association of Consumer Organizations, a closed-door trade association formed in 1957 for the purpose of exchanging information. At least 40 additional such outlets were known to be in operation in 1960 and most such companies had announced plans for the immediate construction of more stores.

**Regular Discount Stores.**

The more common conception of a discount house is a large modern retail store which is open to the general consuming public, incorporates aspects of supermarket merchandising strategy to a high degree, prices all merchandise at a relatively low markup above cost, carries large stocks, renders only limited types of consumer services and usually on the basis of a specific extra charge, advertises regularly, occupies a good retail store location well exposed to consumer traffic, and can be distinguished from regular retailers only by its consistent emphasis upon "discount prices" and its self-designation as a *discount store.*

**Growth of Discount Houses**

A number of factors have contributed to the growth of discount stores. A redistribution of purchasing power has undoubtedly had some effect. The lower and middle income groups experienced the greatest increases in real family buying income and this brought many new families into the market for various kinds of durable goods. Many of these families were not accustomed to the wide range of services offered by department stores, furniture stores, and regular appliance dealers and were willing to purchase in the somewhat less attractive and more limited service atmosphere of the discount house.

Second, there is some relationship between the impact of supermarket merchandising methods and discount house operation. Increasing emphasis throughout the economy upon such methods contributed to greater willingness on the part of the consumer to arrive at purchase decisions without the usual services of a retail salesperson. Consumer confidence in heavily advertised brands of appliances and furniture removed some feeling of dependence upon the integrity of the retailer and made consumers more willing to purchase on a self-selection basis in almost any type of outlet.

Third, and undoubtedly of greatest importance, is the discount house's consistent appeal of substantial price savings. This was made possible, in part, by a merchandising strategy geared to the requirements of *mass market* rather than *limited market* retailing, especially in the case of the more modern promotional type of discount house. This can be understood by comparing certain characteristics of appliance marketing in the periods prior to and following World War II. The postwar era was characterized by great increases in the capacity for manufacturing, accomplished largely through more automatic methods of producing goods in highly mechanized new factories.

Durable goods poured forth from these factories in quantities that can only be described as staggering by prewar standards. They flowed, nevertheless, into a distributive system that possessed essentially the same attributes it had in the earlier years.

It consisted chiefly of a very large number of retail stores, most of which continued to appeal to limited segments of the total market, and in which a relatively large amount of personal selling and service effort was required for the consummation of the ordinary transaction. Retailer margins that had become traditional in the prewar economy were, for the most part, perpetuated in the postwar market, thus providing an umbrella of list prices under which the large-volume, limited-service organization could operate successfully at discounts.

Part of the discount house's success in underselling regular merchants is explained by its ability to operate profitably at lower expense by dispensing with some usual retail store functions. Another factor in expense reduction is that the more modern types of discount houses attempt to maximize profit by selling a large volume of items at a low percent-to-sales margin, thereby achieving high ratios of sales per dollar of inventory investment, per square foot of store space, and per employee.

Through such service limitation and operating economies, large discount houses have been able to save as much as one-half of the operating expense ratio traditionally incurred by regular or full-service retailers in the department store, furniture, home furnishings, and apparel trades. This had made it possible for discount houses to offer discounts ranging from about 12 or 13 per cent of regular list price on low-margin items to about 20 per cent on higher margin goods. Many discount houses have publicized savings amounting to much higher percentages of list prices, and these, if they exist, cannot be explained by any operating cost advantages.

Several additional factors help to explain the basis for the price appeal of the discount house. One is that many discount houses have been able to obtain discriminatory prices and other probably unearned benefits from their suppliers. In the appliance trade, manufacturers have traditionally sold to large-scale home builders at prices substantially below those prevailing in regular channels of distribution.

Some merchandise, ostensibly sold originally to the "builder market," has been diverted, ending up on the floors of large discount houses at retail prices lower than the wholesale cost to the regular dealer. Some discount houses have also been able to obtain other concessions from manufacturers, including advertising allowances and so-called "push money" for retail salesmen, which may not have been offered to regular retailers on proportionally equal terms.

## IMPACT AND FUTURE OF DISCOUNT HOUSES

It is unquestioned that discount houses have had a substantial effect upon modern retailing. Their importance in terms of sales volume is a matter of conjecture, as estimates have varied widely owing to problems of classification. According to one report, 1960 sales of regular and "closeddoor" discount houses were estimated at $5 billion. This is less than 3 per cent of total retail sales volume. The competition impact of discount houses is not, however, equal throughout the retail trade structure, and has been particularly pronounced among the various types of general merchandise stores.

In the late 1940's and the early 1950's, discount operators were commonly referred to as parasites, bootleggers, or described in even more uncomplimentary terms. In the later 1950's they had attained a semblance of more general respectability. Goaded by the success of some discount houses, other retailers have been forced to reconsider their position, to enter into more forceful and dynamic selling methods to stimulate people to buy, and to pare selling and other operating costs to meet such price competition. By 1960, it was not uncommon to find aggressive department stores, automotive accessory chains, appliance dealers, drug chains, and general merchandise departments of supermarkets regularly featuring "discount prices" of the type found in regular discount houses, thus diminishing somewhat the importance of price as a distinctive attribute of the discount house. Various well-established department store and other general merchandise chains embarked upon programs in 1961 for constructing new specialized outlets of the discount house type, thereby enlarging the scope of their customer appeal and extending the variety of kinds of companies engaged in discount merchandising.

The character of discount houses has been transformed. Many of the earlier types offered only limited assortments of merchandise, often of a distress character or of discontinued models; sold from poor physical facilities; provided practically no customer services; and were generally held in low esteem, even by many of their patrons. In order to reach a wider market, many of them have had to seek better locations; enlarge or modernize their facilities; and add various kinds of widely demanded services, such as installation, repair, delivery, and instalment credit facilities. Their success in winning customer patronage made them more desirable outlets, with the result that they are actively sought as customers by many major brand name manufacturers. As a consequence of these factors, the larger discount houses have become more or less accepted as a limited service type of departmentized store with well-established relationships with regular sources of supply for practically all classes of merchandise that they choose to handle. At the same time, many of their competitors who have adapted their operations to compete more effectively have made it difficult to distinguish clearly between discount houses and other priceappeal stores.A major effect of discount house competition has been an expansion in the market for many kinds of goods formerly sold selectively to limited segments of the market. It appears probable that a permanently lower level of gross margins on some types of goods has been brought about as a result of the pressures from this type of competition. The manner in which this is related to resale price maintenance policies of manufacturers.

# Chapter 12

# Nonstore Retailing

Thus far, the discussion of retailing has been concerned with *stores*, previously defined as establishments which are open to and frequented by the general consuming public. A small but significant proportion of retail trade is accounted for by *nonstore* retail *establishments*. These are distinguished from stores by the fact that the customer does not make his purchases at the establishment operated by the retailing organization. The principal types of nonstore retailing establishments are mail order houses, house-to-house selling organizations, and operators of vending machines.

In 1958 such nonstore retailers operated 74,679 establishments which came within the scope of Census of Business coverage and these accounted for 2.8 per cent of the sales of all retail establishments. Each of these *methods* of retail selling is of greater importance than indicated by Census data, because some manufacturers, agricultural producers, and regular store retailers utilize nonstore techniques to some degree, but are not classified in the nonstore category since their *primary* business is not that of operating a nonstore retailing enterprise.

## MAIL ORDER AND CATALOG RETAILING

The number of firms operating exclusively on a mail order basis is relatively small, but this method of operation is sufficiently widespread to justify detailed consideration. Moreover, it represents a distinctive way of doing business and illustrates the effect of changing conditions upon retailing institutions.

## TYPES OF ORGANIZATIONS

Four distinct types of organizations sell by mail. The most important are the general merchandise mail order houses which sell a great variety of consumer and farmer goods, carrying more items than are sold by any department store. Such companies are primarily retail institutions. They purchase the majority of their goods from manufacturers, although the two biggest companies in this field— Sears, Roebuck and Company and Montgomery Ward and Company—both control the manufacturing of many private brand items.

A second type consists of specialty retailers. Kinds of business in which specialty mail order operations by retailers is of some signficance include books, home furnishings, apparel and apparel accessories, food, and automotive accessories.

Manufacturers who sell by mail constitute the third type of mail order institution. Some such producers have found that their particular products can be sold directly to the consumer by mail without the use of wholesalers or retailers. The fourth type of mail order retailing is carried on by certain department and other large stores which accept orders by mail. Primarily confined to orders for merchandise currently advertised, this type of selling is a supplement to the receipt of orders over the telephone.

## HISTORY OF MAIL ORDER RETAILING

Mail order selling arose in a number of ways. Montgomery Ward and Company was founded in 1872 by a former clerk in Chicago who had also worked as a traveling salesman. The Patrons of Husbandry (the Grange) had established a number of cooperative stores and needed a wholesale connection. Mr. Ward saw the opportunity and started the business which still bears his name. The Grange stores were not generally successful so Mr. Ward's business was expanded into a mail order house to take advantage of good will among former members of the cooperative stores.

Sears, Roebuck and Company, the largest mail order firm, grew out of the efforts of Mr. Sears, a small-town station agent in Minnesota, to sell watches which had been shipped to his station on approval but rejected. The success of this venture led to a watch and jewelry mail order house in Minneapolis which was later moved to Chicago. The present largescale enterprise has grown from this small part.

Other general mail order houses had varied beginnings. Many have expanded from ordinary retail stores. Others started as specialty mail order houses and gradually expanded until they handled a more general line of merchandise.

Probably the most important reason for the success of the mail order houses in the early stages of their development is to be found in the failure of country merchants to adjust to changing conditions. In the post— Civil War period the country general store was a dominant institution. Throughout the West and South, farmers and small-town residents raised their standards of living after the period of reconstruction. Cash farm income became larger and farmers became interested in the kinds of things bought by city people. Rural and small-town merchants, however, did not appreciate such changes and continued to stock only staple merchandise which had sold well for many years. Even if such merchants had realized the significance of environmental change, the limitations of their small, local markets would have made it impossible for them to rival the assortments of the evolving mail order institution.

Another factor contributing to the development of mail order retailing was the growth of rail transportation. This made it possible to place orders by mail and to deliver merchandise to scattered areas at reasonable cost and at relatively certain dates. The spectacular and consistent development of mail order retailing began, however, with the establishment of rural free delivery service. Farmers as a class began to subscribe for city daily papers. They were thus reached by style news and by information on various changing methods of life which before had come to their attention only indirectly. Later, the moving pictures and the rotogravure supplements of the newspapers exercised their effect in creating demand for many articles not previously included in the rural standard of living.

Mail order retailing offered an opportunity for the purchase of these goods. Developments in catalog making made it possible to advertise goods effectively and to supply realistic photographs. Establishment of the parcel post system in 1913 made it possible to ship small packages more economically. Another factor in the growth of mail order houses was the recognition that this method of selling could take advantage of the economies of large-scale retailing.

The larger mail order companies engaged in programs of diversification as the country became more urbanized and opened many retail establishments of the department store type. Such stores now account for the majority of the business of both Sears' and Ward's, but mail order or catalog retailing continues to be a very large segment of their total sales volume.

## PRESENT STATUS OF MAIL ORDER ESTABLISHMENTS

In 1958 there were 2,550 retail mail order establishments, of which 1,502 had paid employees and 1,048 were small units operated exclusively by proprietors and family members. Aggregate sales volume of these establishments amounted to $20 billions, or about 1 per cent of the sales of all retail establishments. There has been practically no change in the relative sales volume importance of mail order establishments over the period 1929-58. While the 2,550 mail order establishments operated in many lines of trade, more than 75 per cent of their sales was reported by only 35 large establishments handling a complete line of department store merchandise. More than one-half of these establishments are operated by two companies— Sears' and Ward's—thus indicating high concentration in this field.

## COMPETITIVE POSITION OF GENERAL CATALOG HOUSES

The general merchandise mail order organizations have, in the main, the advantages and disadvantages of other large-scale retail enterprises. Due to the peculiar nature of their business, certain special conditions affect their competitive situation.

## Advantages

As compared with single-line and general stores in the rural districts, mail order houses offer a more complete and varied line of merchandise. Their location in the larger cities gives a certain amount of prestige to their merchandise, especially in style goods. Prices, at least for many articles, are somewhat lower than those charged for corresponding articles in the rural communities. Buying from a catalog is perhaps quicker and easier for rural people than going to stores in somewhat distant cities, and such shopping can be done at any time of day or evening that is most convenient. Convenience, moreover, is a strong appeal among urban customers who patronize catalog order offices or telephone order facilities maintained by leading mail order companies in large cities. Absence of pressure to buy, avoidance of the confusion of crowded stores, informative statements concerning products, guaranties, and a liberal returned-goods policy are other attractions. Because sales are made in all sections of the country and to different classes of consumers, sales are not greatly affected by local industrial depressions, as are those of local merchants.

Some general advantages enjoyed by all mail order vendors grow out of certain operating economies. Warehouses are located in parts of the city where rent is much lower than that which must be paid by the ordinary retailer. Expensive fixtures are unnecessary, for only equipment of the warehouse type is required. It is unnecessary to employ retail salespeople, for the catalog descriptions plus the reputation of the firm and price appeals effect sales. Hence, employees of the clerical and shipping department type are used and their work is scheduled to permit an efficient utilization of time—something difficult to accomplish in retail stores which must be staffed in accordance with daily and hourly variations in consumer traffic.

## Disadvantages

Selling by catalogs is limited by the impossibility of examining merchandise in advance of purchase. For shoes, gloves, or clothing, it may be difficult for the buyer to secure the right articles without trying them on for size and fit. Many consumers hesitate to order products where size, color, style, or texture are significant in choice making.

An important limitation is inflexibility of the merchandising program. Semi-annual catalogs published by Sears' and Ward's comprise between 1,000 and 2,000 pages. Plans must be made well in advance of the season as to the detailed composition of the line of goods and the manner in which they are to be featured and illustrated. More important, prices must be determined months before catalogs are distributed, and the firm usually must live with its pricing decisions throughout the catalog season. While the catalogs contain statements that prices are subject to change without notice, and even though special sale catalogs are issued, the companies do not have the pricing flexibility of other forms of retailing. They cannot mark down individual items of merchandise as the rate of sale becomes too slow or as costs decline; neither can they raise prices on individual items as demand increases or as wholesale costs rise. New items can be added or dropped only when new catalogs are prepared.

## DYNAMIC ADJUSTMENTS IN CATALOG RETAILING

The inception and period of rapid early development of mail order retailing was associated with the concept of a new merchandising service to the nonurban population. In modern times, with contemporary conditions of communication, transportation, and urbanization, it is indeed remarkable that catalog retailing (as measured by Census of Business data for the period 1929-58) has been able to hold a stable share of total retail sales, thus growing at the same rate as all of retailing. This is attributed to certain dynamic, and in some cases distinctive, methods and policies adopted by the general catalog houses—in large measure for the purpose of capitalizing upon their advantages, minimizing their limitations, and adjusting to changing consumer preferences. Sales promotion activities are efficiently organized. Mailing lists are prepared with care and efforts are made to keep them up to date. Careful tests are made of the success of different types of copy and appeals. Experienced copy writers know the language and the appeals which are most useful in reaching their clientele.

In order to overcome the reluctance of buyers to purchase articles which they cannot see before the order is placed, mail order houses give a very liberal guaranty, covering as a rule both quality and price. If the purchaser is dissatisfied with the commodity, it may be returned at the expense of the seller, and the purchase price is promptly refunded.

The general catalog houses have a special brand problem. To attract business, as they do in part, on a price-appeal basis, they must purchase from suppliers at lowest prices. For this reason such houses do not generally carry very many nationally advertised, branded articles. They prefer to sell unbranded commodities or those which carry their own brand. It is usually necessary to brand the specialties which they sell, in order to identify them and give them a certain distinction. Hence it is common for catalog houses to purchase such articles as vacuum sweepers, gasoline engines, washing machines, farm implements, cosmetics and drugs from suppliers who manufacture to the specifications of the catalog firm and who attach to the goods the private brand of the mail order company.

In order to reach a larger number of potential customers, the major firms have opened a large number of catalog order offices which are located in storerooms in hundreds of small cities and in many suburban shopping centers of large cities. No merchandise is available for sale over the counter in these establishments, but selected items and swatch and sample books are displayed for examination. Employees assist customers to make out and transmit orders. Many such order offices have teletype communication with a regional warehouse which services the area. Orders received prior to a certain time each day can be delivered to thc customer's home on the following day in most cities, thus rivaling the speed of delivery service available from local stores. Similar catalog departments are also found in the regular retail stores operated by mail order companies. In the typical Sears' store, the catalog order desk is usually the largest sales volume department.

Some catalog companies have expanded their customer contact points by establishing order stations in retail establishments operated by other companies. Certain small-town and cross-roads stores have displayed the general merchandise catalogs of some companies for a number of years, and accept and process orders on a commission basis. More recently some variety chains and supermarket organizations have made similar arrangements with mail order firms. For example, in 1960, Ward's established catalog order stations in certain New York state supermarkets of Loblaw, Inc., thus giving Ward's sales outlets in areas where it had no retail stores, and providing the Loblaw organization with a 100,000 item increase in its offering of nonfood merchandise lines. Another feature is the operation of telephone order offices. While confined to larger cities in which there is a considerable potential volume of daily business, this development is one of increasing significance, accounting in 1960 for more than 30 per cent of all catalog sales volume at Sears'. The catalog customer can sit in her home, order by number from the catalog, have her order dispatched by teletype as explained above in connection with catalog order offices, and receive next-day delivery in many large cities.

As a consequence of such innovations, the historic *mail order business* has evolved into a more modern conception of *general catalog retailing*, characterized by efforts to bring to the consumer wanted merchandise at various points of sales contact, using means of communication and delivery which are appropriate to contemporary conditions.

## CATALOG SELLING BY STORE RETAILERS AND MANUFACTURERS

Mail order selling is used to some extent by specialty retailers and by certain manufacturers who sell direct to the consumer. It is also used in the direct marketing of some farm products with a special appeal, such as Smoked Virginia Hams, smoked turkeys, and gift packages of fruit.

Such sellers usually do not have elaborate catalogs, but secure orders by advertising in newspapers and magazines, on radio and television broadcasts, and by direct mail addressed to the homes of consumers. Goods so ordered are shipped by parcel post, express, truck, or ordinary freight.

This type of selling brings many kinds of goods to the attention of a broad market. Items so sold are often of a novel or unusual character and are not available in local stores, especially in smaller communities. Some merchandise is sold direct to consumers by manufacturers who stress a price appeal. While specialty mail order retailing is relatively expensive, since it usually involves substantial advertising and handling and shipping costs, many consumers are nevertheless influenced by an appeal which suggests that they save money by purchasing direct rather than from a retail store.

Appeals of "lower prices," "greater values," or "substantial savings," have been used by most of the major book and record club companies that have a membership which is contacted by mail. Such savings are customarily offered in terms of "free" or "bonus" books, awarded when the member actually purchases a predetermined number of books at regular prices, in accordance with a membership agreement. Bonuses offered in this manner are largely due to low purchase prices negotiated with publishers when contracting for large numbers of copies and not to economies of selling and distributing to individual consumers on a mail order basis.

Manufacturers and retailers who sell a narrow line of goods by the mail order method are subject to most of the disadvantages enumerated above in connection with general catalog houses. In addition, they usually lack the prestige enjoyed by a large nationally known organization. Hence, such selling is relatively unimportant, and there are no reasons to believe that it will ever be of much significance in other than a very narrow range of merchandise items.

Catalog selling is also an important form of supplementary promotional effort among many regular *store retailers*, especially large department stores and departmentized specialty stores, who have a ready-made mailing list consisting of their regular charge account customers. This is especially significant for the promotion of gift merchandise during the Christmas shopping season.

## HOUSE-TO-HOUSE RETAILING

According to common: usage, the term *house-to-house selling* includes almost any type of retailing that involves contacting the consumer at his residence (or sometimes at his place of work) rather than in a retail store.

### TYPES

Several variations of house-to-house retailing are common. First, some manufacturers and retailers actually canvass on a house-to-house basis. Often solicitation is confined to residential areas or types of families which, in the experience of the individual company, have proved the most fruitful source of business. In some cases, sales coverage is haphazard because solicitation is confined largely to friends, neighbors, or other individuals who have personal contacts with the salespeople of a "house-to-house" selling organization. Some house-to-house salesmen are employees of the manufacturer who uses this method of direct distribution; others are independent dealers who buy merchandise from the manufacturer and resell as merchant middlemen, often handling the products of several organizations.

Second, some companies use what is known as the party plan. Salesmen arrange to have a housewife give a party in her home, at which merchandise is demonstrated to a group of the hostess' friends. The hostess receives merchandise prizes, awarded on the basis of the amount purchased by those attending and, in some cases, also on the basis of the number of those attending who agree to serve as hostesses for similar parties. A variation of this method is a "club" plan, according to which a consumer is awarded prizes or granted discount buying privileges by getting new customers to join the "club." The "club," of course, is the group of customers served by the selling organization and one joins by making purchases. These approaches involve something of the chain letter technique, in that each new customer is expected to obtain a number of additional new customers for the company.

Third, many companies sell to the consumer at his home on the basis of advance prospecting information. Home calls may be preceded by telephone solicitation in which women with pleasing telephone personalities are employed to call large numbers of consumers. Names of those who manifest some degree of interest are turned over to skilled salesmen who call on the consumer at home. Prospect information is also obtained in response to offers made in newspaper, car card, or other forms of advertising.

One or more of the above forms of selling are used by a large number of well-known manufacturing or distributing companies, including Avon Products, Inc. (cosmetics), Beauty Counselors, Inc. (cosmetics), Electrolux Corporation (vacuum cleaners), Fashion Frocks, Inc. (women's apparel), Fuller Brush Company (brushes, cosmetics, and household items), The Process Company (greeting cards), Real Silk Hosiery Mills, Inc. (hosiery and apparel), and Stanley Home Products, Inc. (brushes and household cleaning aids). Such methods are also widely used on a national basis in selling reference books, encyclopedias, and magazine subscriptions. Some local retailers and small manufacturers use the same approaches in selling a wide range of items, especially in the home furnishings or home improvement categories.

A fourth method coming within the general coverage of "house-tohouse" selling consists of route delivery service of perishable food items. Milk is commonly delivered to the consumer's home by a driver-salesman. In most cities some baking companies (e.g., Omar, Inc.) sell direct through route salesmen. Since this method involves frequent and continuing contacts with regular customers who are purchasing in this manner largely because of convenience, it is somewhat apart from the other methods enumerated above. Most of the following discussion is only partially applicable to the operations of such route companies.

## IMPORTANCE OF HOUSE-TO-HOUSE SELLING

House-to-house selling is the most important form of nonstore retailing. According to 1958 Census of Business data, some 64,000 direct selling "organizations" accounted for about $2.6 billion of sales, or about 1.3 per cent of total sales of retail establishments. This is believed to be less than one-half of the volume of retail sales made by this method, because the Census does not enumerate as house-to-house organizations those companies which operate a house-to-house salesforce out of a manufacturing, wholesaling, or service establishment whose principal activity is something other than retail trade in tangible goods, nor the house-to-house selling activities of regular retail stores, nor the sales of self-employed canvassers operating on a restricted part-time basis and reporting annual receipts of less than $2,500.

The Census figure of some 64,000 "organizations" is somewhat misleading, as it includes all selfemployed salesmen operating as dealers, provided annual sales of more than $2,500 are reported. Actually, there are some 180 members of the National Association of Direct Selling Companies, which is probably more indicative of the number of companies regularly distributing their products or services on a house-to-house basis. It has been estimated that some one and a half million salespeople are engaged in direct selling, about 850,000 men and 650,000 women, with a majority working on a part-time or supplementary income basis.

## REASONS FOR USE

Certain manufacturers and retailers use house-to-house selling primarily because of their ability to build a large volume of business through concentrated and specialized personal selling techniques. Trained in the art of high-pressure salesmanship, the house-to-house man gets results whether it be a small item or one involving several hundred dollars. If the salesman can interest the consumer in his offering and can, by carefully planned selling phrases, suggest that nothing like it can be had locally or that its price is very attractive, the sale is a natural outcome.

Manufacturers are interested in house-to-house distribution in some cases because an attractive margin is available but more often because they can get volume only by this method. If several hundred specialized salesmen can be recruited, trained, and assigned to territories and if the product is worthy, sales may be expected. The problem of interesting wholesalers or retailers in stocking the product and of getting their salesmen to present it to buyers through displays or face-to-face selling is avoided. It is not necessary to use extensive advertising, for personal sales effort is substituted for advertising except in the case of a few large firms who sell in all parts of the country and have found that advertising helps the salesman to gain admission and to secure an audience.

House-to-house selling is attractive to some organizations because sales costs are flexible, varying directly with volume. Salesmen are compensated, in the great majority of cases, altogether on the basis of commissions. Thus there is no expense for selling except for sales actually made.

## LIMITATIONS AND DISADVANTAGES

Lack of consumer confidence in the salesman, his firm, and his product is an important limitation to house-to-house selling. There are just enough fraudulent schemes to cause careful buyers to be wary. Better Business Bureaus have done much to limit the work of fraudulent sellers and in doing so have assisted legitimate firms.

The housewife's inconvenience or annoyance at taking time from household tasks to listen to the salesman is a disadvantage of this method of selling. To overcome the reluctance of housewives even to answer the doorbell, some companies have adopted a variety of plans to pave the way for calls, such as leaving a card saying the salesman will return at a stated time with a useful gift, or leaving an attractive catalog at the housewife's door a day or two in advance of the salesman's visit. In spite of these plans, house-to-house selling is self-limiting because it can grow only at the expense of increasing demands upon the time of the consumer.

Another disadvantage consists of the sales management

problem of recruiting, training, and supervising large numbers of salesmen or socalled agents. Usually they are of the type who need constant stimulation and close supervision, and contacts with them must be maintained frequently.

When the sale is by description only or even by sample, the salesman is handicapped, for many buyers have a definite preference for goods which can be inspected at a local store. Moreover, when an order is given to a canvasser, sufficient interest must be created to last until the delivery can be made some days later. Often desire has cooled by that time, and the order is rejected, even at the cost of forfeiting the partial payment made to the salesman.

Many cities have enacted ordinances regulating or forbidding houseto-house selling, canvassing, or soliciting of business, and thus protecting local merchants from this type of competition. The first such ordinance, which forbade this type of selling or business solicitation, except with the permission or upon the invitation of the householder, was enacted in Green River, Wyoming, in 1933; hence all comparable enactments by municipalities have become known as "Green River" ordinances. Such prohibitions tended to increase in the 1950's following a Supreme Court decision upholding their constitutionality.

For the most part, however, they have been enacted in small towns and suburban communities near major metropolitan areas. While constituting a problem, the coverage of such laws has not been sufficiently widespread to limit materially house-to-house selling on a national basis.

An important limitation is the high cost of this method of distribution. Some consumers believe that they save by buying from house-tohouse salesmen, especially when dealing with a manufacturer's salesman or agent. Experience has proved, however, that direct-selling manufacturers do not eliminate any of the retail middleman's functions but, in fact, usually incur higher costs than manufacturers who distribute through normal channels. Commissions paid to house-to-house salesmen are within the range of about 25 to 40 per cent and are often higher than the total gross margin realized by store retailers handling similar commodities. In addition, high costs of shipment or delivery are incured on items of low unit value. Unless the consumer pays in advance, there are C.O.D. ("collect-on-delivery") charges to be considered. Even among regular retailers who use house-to-house selling as a supplement to store selling, as is often done in the furniture and appliance trades, commissions paid to "outside" salesmen are usually about twice as large as those paid to salesmen who work in the store.

Because of the various problems and limitations involved in this method of distribution, it is not likely that it will ever become a larger part of total retail trade. The method is confined largely to types of items where sales volume can be expanded greatly by highly concentrated personal selling effort and to situations in which an unusually wide gross margin may be obtained so that the high costs of this method of distribution can be covered.

## VENDING MACHINES

Distribution of goods through automatic vending machines is a third distinctive form of nonstore retailing. By vending is meant the selling of goods through an automatic machine which releases an item of merchandise upon insertion of a coin or coins by the consumer, thus completing the transaction without the aid of a salesperson.

### HISTORICAL DEVELOPMENT

Crude forms of vending machines were in operation in Europe and in the United States in the nineteenth century. Early machines were restricted largely to the sale of candy, nuts, gum, tobacco products, and postage stamps. During the early part of the twentieth century, there was a great expansion in the United States in bulk vending (i.e., machines which measure out a portion of some unpackaged items such as nuts or candy), especially, "penny sale" machines. In the late 1920's and in the 1930's, new types of machines were designed to vend 5-cent confections, bottled soft drinks, and packages of cigarettes. The development of cigarette vending machines and their acceptance by the consuming public is widely heralded as the inception of the modern era of automatic merchandising. Cigarettes were the first class of commodities retailing for more than five cents and sold on a wide basis through vending machines.

## PRESENT STATUS

Outside of the tobacco, soft drink, and candy trades, vending did not attract much attention until the late 1940's, when experimental attempts were made to merchandise a wide variety of items on an automatic basis, some of which proved relatively successful. In 1958, according to the Census of Business, there were some 3,524 "merchandise vending machine operators," with sales of $842 millions, or about 0.4 per cent of the sales of all retail establishments. These are middlemen who specialize in the operation of vending machines that primarily dispense merchandise rather than provide services.

Trade estimates indicate that the total volume of vending machine sales is much greater than reported by the Census. In 1958 a trade source reported sales of $2.1 billion and in 1959, $2,4 billion. Differences between Census data and trade estimates are explained by three factors. First, some wholesalers operate retail vending machines as an adjunct to their wholesaling business, especially retail cigarette vending by tobacco jobbers. Second, many machines are owned or are serviced by local processors or manufacturers. Bottled soft drinks, ice, and milk are among the commodities often distributed through vending machines by the manufacturer rather than by a vending machine retailer. Third, many vending machines are owned and serviced by very small operators who engage in this activity only as a sideline and thus do not meet Census requirements for classification as a business establishment within the vending machine trade.

While vending machines account for only a small part of total retail trade, they are extremely important in the sale of certain commodities. Of total vending machine merchandise sales, about 44 per cent consists of sales of cigarettes, about 22 per cent of cold and hot bottled and cup drinks, and about 14 per cent of candy and gum. All other products collectively constituted less than 20 per cent of the total vending machine market in 1959.

## VENDING MACHINE OPERATORS

The vending machine firm is a rather distinctive form of enterprise in that its operations are carried on in locations owned by businesses or institutions. While there are a few large vending firms, it is predominantly a field of small operators. Some are strictly family businesses, and most of the others have only a few employees. The trend, however, has been toward a smaller number of companies of larger individual sales volume size. A few companies are exceptionally large, particularly Automatic Canteen Co., which operates nationally, and Automatic Retailers of America (ARA), which operates in a number of states.

Like other retailers, vending machine operators buy merchandise and maintain an inventory. Even though most firms are small and deal only in convenience items, it is common for them to purchase direct from manufacturers. Their business is so specialized by merchandise lines that direct buying arrangements are often feasible.

Vending machine locations are organized into routes which are served on schedule. Route men clean machines, replenish inventory, remove and audit sales receipts, and make any minor adjustments that may be necessary. Some operators have specialized service men to handle emergency calls whenever a mechanical failure occurs.

A major and distinctive problem of the operator is that of soliciting location-owners to obtain the right to place a vending machine on their premises. One type of location consists of regular retail stores, which use vending machines as a supplement to their personal selling service. Other locations include almost any kind of site at which a large number of people congregate or pass by with regularity. Examples of the more desirable types of nonstore locations include industrial plants, airports, amusement centers, apartment buildings, armed service installations, bus terminals, hospitals, office buildings, railroad stations, turnpike restaurants and service stations, schools, and theatre lobbies.

Machines are sometimes sold or leased to the owner of the location but, more commonly, the vending machine operator retains ownership and pays the location-owner a rental fee, usually determined as a percentage commission or a special amount per unit of product sold. Thus, to a considerable degree, the usual operational arrangement is analogous to that of a leased department.

## EVALUATION

Vending machines are used, in some instances, in regular stores where retailers wish to avoid certain "nuisance problems." Soft drink, candy, and cigarette sales are usually of low unit value and therefore relatively expensive to process by personal selling effort. Also, such items are often pilfered by customers or consumed by store employees who do not bother to pay for them, with resulting inventory loss. Such problems are often avoided by the use of vending machines.

Vending machines have enlarged the opportunity for marketing many items by offering them for sale at places where, and at times when, it would not be feasible to provide regular store selling service. Many items sold through vending machines are purchased for immediate consumption; hence, the quantities marketed are to a substantial measure dependent upon the vending machine as a distribution method. There has been a tendency to sell through vending machines more items in the so-called "take-home" market. Ice, ice cream, and milk have been vended profitably in many cities from nonstore locations which are accessible twenty-four hours a day, seven days a week.

One of the most rapidly growing markets for vended products consists of industrial plants where increasing interest has been devoted to machines as dispensers of foods. In some factories, vending machines supplement regular cafeteria food service by providing hot and cold beverages, sandwiches, and desserts, at a variety of in-plant locations. In many small plants that cannot provide regular in-plant food service, the vending machine has become an attractive supplement to the traditional lunch-pail.

The vending industry experienced a very favourable rate of sales growth in the period subsequent to World War II—a factor which has stimulated much discussion about this method of distribution, and one which has prompted all sorts of judgments as to its future.

Opportunities for vending machine retailing have been limited by several circumstances. First, notable success has been achieved only in the case of products possessing certain accepted "vending characteristics." These include small size, high, frequency of purchase by the average consumer, and purchase on a strictly convenience basis. Attempts to merchandise shopping goods through vending machines have not been successful, except in highly specialized situations.

Second, even though vending machine sales are effected without the aid of a salesperson, vending is still a relatively expensive form of distribution. It can be carried on profitably only at locations where a reasonable volume of regular sales can be expected. Machines in common use involve substantial investments of capital, which must be recovered by adequate depreciation charges. Servicing of the machines by route men is time-consuming and costly. In addition, the vending machine operator must cover the overhead costs of his business and pay the location-owner a fairly substantial proportion of the total receipts for rent. Vending could not have attained its present state of development if consumers were not willing, at least in many cases, to pay some premium over regular retail store prices for the added convenience of buying at nonstore locations and at odd hours.Third, vending machines have been limited historically by the use of coins, which factor restricted their application to types of items that can be bought with change carried by the average consumer. In 1960, however, new types of equipment were introduced with "bill-changing" sections. Such machines are capable of accepting currency of various denominations, rejecting counterfeits, and returning correct change to the customer.

While the eventual influence of such equipment is highly speculative, it does remove one traditional restriction in the use of vending machines as a marketing device.In summary, it is apparent that vending is a relatively high-cost method of distribution, that gross margins on goods vended must ordinarily be higher than on goods sold in large volume through ordinary retail store methods, and that vending is limited substantially to convenience goods items which may be purchased by the consumer at almost any place without advance planning. Vending is likely to remain a small factor in the total retail sales pictures, since machines for selling traditional vendible commodities are already available in nearly all types of feasible locations. New types of bill-changers, however, open additional opportunities for experimentation with products of higher unit value and suggest possibilities for rapid growth in vending, even though it is likely to remain a very small part of total retailing.

## Chapter 13

# The Buying Function

In every transaction someone engages in buying. Goods or services may be purchased for industrial or commercial use, for resale, or for ultimate consumption. The buyer may be one who specializes in performing this function, one who does buying along with many other business activities, or an ultimate consumer satisfying a personal want. In any event, there is no better indication of the importance and pervasive nature of the buying function than the fact that someone buys every time a sale is made. Buying is significant not only as a differentiated specific function but also as an economic activity, the understanding of which is basic to modern concepts of customer-oriented marketing management.

### BUYING – AN ACTIVE MARKETING FUNCTION

While buying is a basic marketing function, it is often improperly relegated to an unimportant position. It is sometimes erroneously assumed that it is of a *passive character*—merely the opposite of selling. Quite to the contrary, buying does not take care of itself, but is indeed an *active* function.

The skill used in buying has an important influence in determining the relative value of what is purchased by the consumer. The constant increase in the variety of products offered to him, the growing tendency to procure more goods and services in the market rather than to produce them in the home, the multiplicity of brands, the frequency of relatively small quality differentials, and the widely differing services offered by stores, all combine to add to the difficulty of the consumer's choice and to stress the importance of his being able to buy with intelligence. The active character of buying is especially conspicuous in the case of the consumer. Traditionally, he has taken the initiative in the exchange process. When wants are recognized and the consumer is ready to act upon them, it is customary for him to seek out a seller or sellers. When a salesperson comes into contact with the consumer-buyer, the process of exchange is often nearly completed. This is dramatically emphasized by the small proportion of retail business which is accounted for by house-to-house canvassers or other sellers who take the initiative in seeking out prospective consumer-buyers, and, by way of contrast, by the predominant proportion which is accounted for by regular retail establishments that are visited by a purchasing-minded public.

Developments in simplified selling or self-service merchandising accentuate the importance of consumer buying activity. *The more the retail selling and service functions are curtailed, the greater becomes the task and responsibility of the consumer as a buyer.* While there is a substantial amount of pre-buying stimulation in the form of aggressive retailer and manufacturer advertising and sales promotion activity, the number of items competing for consumer attention is so vast and diverse that the ordinary person must play an extremely active role in making the purchases that satisfy his wants.

Unless buying of raw materials, semimanufactures, and the many items of equipment and supplies needed for the production process is effectively accomplished, manufacturers handicap themselves in their ability to compete with those who may be more skillful in the performance of this function. Ability to select from many offerings just what will sell best and to determine the most economic quantities to be bought at a given time is one of the prime tests of the efficiency of both wholesaler and retailer.

Moreover, buying is closely related to other marketing functions. Its practices and policies are often determined, in part at least, by the financial position of the purchaser, the availability of adequate and economical transportation and storage facilities, and the degree to which standardization has been accomplished. Risk is often reduced by the adoption of proper buying policies. Skillful buyers make use of reliable and pertinent market information from a variety of sources. Goods purchased for resale must be selected primarily with reference to what the market will absorb. In short, this marketing function is closely related to the functioning of almost every part of our marketing system.

## SPECIALIZATION IN BUYING

That buying is a very active and quantitatively significant function cannot be questioned when it is considered that manufacturing companies and middlemen ordinarily employ specialists to perform this activity. In manufacturing establishments a key employee, generally known as the purchasing agent, sometimes bearing the title of Vice President in Charge of Procurement, is responsible for the function. All wholesale merchants have buyers who generally occupy the position of executives, the number depending upon the size of the business and the number of different merchandise departments involved.

Larger retail stores employ buyers who are also usually the managers of merchandise departments. Quite a number of large department stores have more than 100 buyers each. In the chain store field the buying function is either centralized or divided between the central office and the individual retail store unit. Among smaller independent stores, the buying function is usually the responsibility of the proprietor or one of the partners, but it is almost invariably one of the most important of their activities.

## WHAT BUYING INVOLVES

Like the other marketing functions, buying may be subdivided into a number of important elements or responsibilities. The most important of these:

- The selection of kinds of goods,
- The determination of quality or suitability,
- The determination of quantities,

- The selection of sources of supply.

## SELECTION OF KINDS OF GOODS

Freedom in determining the kinds of goods to be purchased varies from one type of business to another. In many lines of manufacturing the materials to be bought are fixed automatically by the nature of the product manufactured. The manufacturer of cotton textiles must buy cotton yarn or raw cotton, and the butter manufacturer must have cream. Installations and industrial equipment are determined largely by the nature of the manufacturing process, with the result that there is sometimes rather limited freedom in their purchase.

For most merchants, on the other hand, the determination of kinds of goods to be purchased is a real problem, since the firm may not constantly handle exactly the same merchandise. While within certain limits most wholesalers and retailers find their choice of merchandise circumscribed by their clientele and competition, nevertheless it is a rare mercantile business which does not have some latitude.

This problem has been aggravated considerably by a pronounced tendency for many types of stores to expand or diversify their merchandise lines. Self-service grocery stores, for example, have sought to handle any type of merchandise that is suitable for sale by self-service methods. In seeking new items to purchase, they have been attracted by the higher margins obtainable on numerous items normally handled by drug-, department, or hardware stores. As a result, numerous advertised brands of proprietary remedies, toilet preparations, cosmetics, housewares, magazines, and alcoholic beverages have been successfully added to the lines carried by many supermarkets. Drugstores, hardware stores, and other kinds of business, feeling the pressure of this competition, have also sought to expand their offerings by invading fields hitherto foreign to them. Similarly, most variety chains have abandoned their limited-price position, and some have become in essence junior department stores. Department stores, in turn, have expanded their sales volume by the addition of departments for sporting goods, cameras and photographic equipment, and other kinds of merchandise that have been sold traditionally in specialized types of establishments.

Many marketing establishments have made costly mistakes in experimental attempts to diversify their merchandise offerings. For most small establishments, experience has indicated that new items cannot ordinarily be added successfully *unless* (1) they are in keeping with the general character of the business as reflected by firm name, atmosphere, location, and advertising and promotion policies; (2) they can be sold according to the present method of sale and by present employees; and (3) sufficient space and capital investment can be devoted to the new merchandise to offer customers a reasonable range of choice within the classification to which it belongs. Obviously, these rules have not been important limiting factors for very large wholesale or retail firms where it is more feasible to add specialized personnel or facilities to handle the merchandising of items not closely related to those previously sold.

## DETERMINATION OF QUALITY

A second major buying responsibility relates to the determination of the suitability of goods for business use or for resale. This is a matter of quality, which involves consideration of materials, workmanship, grades, sizes, designs, colors, and patterns.

To a large degree manufacturers determine the quality of goods purchased by the characteristics of the products they make. For example, furniture sold in the highest price ranges demands materials far different from those used in making furniture to sell on a price basis. Although the final product depends greatly upon the skill of craftsmen assigned to its manufacture, minimum qualities of materials must be established. In many lines of manufacturing, however, there is an opportunity to exercise choice in selecting qualities for purchase. Sometimes additional labor may be applied to cheaper materials with resulting equal end results and a net cost reduction. While the specifications for materials are usually dictated by the requirements of the product being manufactured, final product design is often determined, at least in part, by the prices at which materials of varying qualities can be purchased.

Determination of quality is of especial interest in the purchase of business supplies. Good purchasing practice involves obtaining the *right quality for a particular purpose*—not the highest obtainable quality. This may be illustrated with respect to paper which is available over a wide range of quality. To purchase such a product which is either not good enough or better than necessary involves potential waste. Take the case of a large insurance company that has substantial paper requirements. For inter-office communications that are promptly read and quickly discarded, only minimum quality standards need be observed. For documents which will be kept a long time and handled often, however, much attention must be given to various quality factors which are relevant to preservation.

Retailers and wholesalers have a somewhat similar problem. Their market must be analyzed to determine the quality of merchandise which will appeal to prospective buyers. Often such a study reveals that a considerable part of the community desires either higher or lower qualities than are being supplied by stores. Not only must quality be determined, but merchants must give careful consideration to the salability of various sizes, materials, patterns, colors, and designs before entering the buying market.

Consumer demand is not, however, the sole consideration in determining just what qualities to buy. This may be illustrated with respect to the marketing of fresh peaches. Generally speaking, the consumer wants peaches which are ready to eat when purchased and prefers those that are picked from trees in a near ripe state. In the very early part of the season, however, peaches are usually quite expensive and sell rather slowly on both wholesale and retail levels of distribution. At this time, produce jobbers and retailers wish to buy peaches which are picked green because they will keep longer and can be handled with less risk of damage or spoilage.

Thus, quality considerations are dictated by cost and handling factors rather than by consumer preference. Later, as supplies become more abundant, prices decline, and the volume of sales increases markedly. Both wholesalers and retailers are then more willing to handle peaches which have been picked in a more mature state and which are more satisfactory to the ultimate consumer.

A somewhat similar situation exists in ready-to-wear apparel establishments and other stores selling style merchandise. Consumer demand may dictate quality decisions for the most part, but in some instances there are other reasons for purchasing a given quality. Some retailers will buy a few items of more expensive quality than can be readily sold to their clientele. Their reason may be that the highest priced items make the next higher priced items in the line appear less expensive by comparison. Another motive may be to use the higher quality items chiefly for prestige purposes—that is, for display to give the store more of an atmosphere of elegance and fashion leadership than it would have if it confined its offerings solely to qualities that it can merchandise profitably. All of this suggests the wisdom of not confining motivation research to consumerbuyers or to industrial users, but of extending it to buyers of consumer goods on both the retail and wholesale levels of distribution.

## Measuring Quality

While it is important to determine the desirable quality before buying, it is equally important to ascertain just what quality has actually been supplied by a seller. When quality factors are related to consideration such as flavor, visual appeal, or fashion, tests of quality are confined substantially to the judgment of the purchaser. Many aspects of quality are, however, precisely measurable. The process of analysis is used to determine the composition of an alloy or the purity of a chemical substance. Physical tests are employed to obtain the tensile strength of metal or the bursting strength of paper cartons. Precision measurements are used to find out whether the thread count of woven fibers or the thickness of sheet steel are within stated tolerances. Tests of performance are appropriate to determine how well paint will wear on a surface or how well automobile tires will last in use.

Many manufacturers utilize their own testing facilities for this purpose; others employ commercial testing laboratories. In some cases the test is made to determine the effective price, which may depend on the quality actually delivered. More often the test is made to prevent acceptance of products the quality of which is lower than was ordered. Many large retailers have installed testing laboratories for similar reasons, realizing that they must know the quality of merchandise which they sell if they are to serve their customers well. Certain trade associations perform a similar service for their members.

## DETERMINATION OF QUANTITIES

A third important buying responsibility is ascertaining the proper quantities to be purchased. In wholesaling and retailing concerns this is based upon planned sales, and in manufacturing enterprises it is based upon manufacturing schedules which are ultimately dependent upon the sales volume anticipated. In some factories scheduling is altogether or largely based on orders already received and little or no manufacturing for stock takes place. In such instances, the manufacturer may defer the purchase of materials until he has orders for his product. Most manufacturers, however, cannot defer the purchase of all materials until they have orders in hand, since to do so would mean undue delays in delivery. All merchants are forced to carry some stock, and most merchants must carry substantial inventories. For them quantitative considerations in purchasing must rest upon estimates of future sales.

The sales estimate may be made directly in terms of numbers of units of merchandise to be sold, i.e., dozens, hundreds, pounds, barrels, tons, etc., or first in terms of dollars and cents. Expressing planned sales in money is a convenient common denominator for indicating total potential sales of a diverse and varied line of merchandise. The sales estimate or plan in terms of dollars becomes a valuable "yardstick" for measuring actual sales against planned sales. Obviously, where the manufacturer or merchant begins with a sales estimate in terms of value he must convert the dollar-and-cents figures into merchandise units.

In retail stores that handle fashion merchandise, careful sales plans are made twice a year, once for the spring and summer season and again for the fall and winter season. Planned purchases are derived from such estimates. For example, a shoe retailer may anticipate sales of $150,000 for the fall and winter season. If the merchant expects to realize a gross margin of 30 per cent of sales, then 70 per cent of sales or $105,000 may be spent to purchase shoes for this season. It would ordinarily be very bad judgment to spend the entire $105,000 before the season of retail sales arrived, since that would greatly increase the expense of operating the business through higher costs in obsolescence, deterioration, interest, rent, and taxes. It is necessary, therefore, to decide just how the $105,000 in purchases is to be distributed over the period. That is, the buyer must decide how much merchandise shall be purchased or delivered before autumn and how much shall be spent for merchandise to be received during each of the autumn and winter months. If actual sales fall below the planned total, it will be necessary to curtail purchases. If actual sales exceed planned sales, then additions must be made to the sum allotted for the season's purchases.

Most retail and wholesale establishments that deal in staple commodities do not find it necessary to formulate such sales plans in order to buy intelligently. The typical grocery, hardware, or drugstore is supplied by wholesale firms in the vicinity and can obtain immediate replenishment for most items. Similarly, tobacco wholesalers reorder from manufacturers of cigarettes who maintain inventories in most major cities. Such merchants need anticipate their requirements only a short time ahead to determine quantities to be bought.

### Quantity Versus Small-Lot Buying

While the total quantity to be purchased *over a period of*

*time* is derived from anticipated sales volume, most manufacturers and merchants have considerable latitude in determining the quantity of specific products to be ordered *at a given time*. Such decisions are often a matter of policy, determined after consideration of the advantages of placing large orders and the disadvantages of such a practice.

Among the various *advantages of quantity buying*, the ability to obtain merchandise at lower cost is a foremost consideration. Many sellers quote special prices on large orders because the costs of selling and shipping are relatively less than on small orders. Price concessions may take the form of lower list price quotations, extra discounts from list prices, or "free deals" involving, for example, an offer of one dozen units of free merchandise if a merchant orders a full gross at one time rather than a mere one or two dozen. Substantial transportation economies are often associated with large orders. This is especially true if a full carload or truckload is purchased instead of an ordinary freight shipment, or if a freight shipment of 100 pounds or more is purchased instead of a considerably smaller amount. When large quantities are purchased, fewer orders are placed, which means that less time and effort may be required to perform the buying function, fewer incoming shipments need be received and checked, and a small number of invoices is to be accounted for and paid. Quantity buying is often stimulated by speculative desires. This is especially true when market prices are rising, and buyers wish to profit thereby, or when conditions of scarcity are anticipated, as in a national emergency.

While it offers many inducements, a number of *disadvantages also result from quantity buying*. The practice may lead to a decreased stockturn rate through a larger average stock on hand without a corresponding increase in sales volume. This, in turn, tends to accelerate depreciation both from physical deterioration and from style obsolescence. As against the possible speculative gains of quantity buying there must be offset the possible losses due to declining prices. Buying in smaller quantities gives more flexibility to the merchandising program, since the smaller inventories make it possible for the merchant to change his stock to bring it into conformity with changes in demand. Buying in larger quantities sometimes results in an inability to take advantage of late season bargains and other special opportunities. Furthermore, the larger stocks of goods which result from quantity buying practices spell higher costs of owning or carrying a merchandise inventory. Illustrative are greater interest costs on capital invested in inventory, larger requirements for storage space, greater insurance needs, and higher taxes on inventories, as well as greater depreciation or obsolescence losses.

## SELECTION OF SOURCES OF SUPPLY

A fourth major buying responsibility is determining the firms from which purchases are to be made. If it be assumed that decisions regarding kinds, qualities, and quantities of goods have been made, and if buying decisions were altogether objective and impersonal, it would appear that suppliers would be chosen on the sole consideration of price. The lowest price, it might be argued, would point inevitably to one particular vendor as the most logical source of supply, except where the same price is quoted by several suppliers which may be the case under conditions of either oligopoly or extremely keen competition. This sometimes holds true when an inflexible purchasing system is prescribed, as in the case of many government agencies where the purchasing agent must accept the lowest of a number of competitive bids. In business practice generally, many factors enter into the picture, often with the result of making this facet of buying very complex.

### Factors Governing the Choice of Suppliers

*Price* is obviously a very important consideration, for different vendors often quote different prices on goods of varying quality. The vendor's price quotation must be considered in relation to transportation costs, if these are to be paid by the buyer, especially if suppliers are located at a considerable distance or if the goods are heavy or economically bulky.

The ability of a supplier to make *prompt delivery* is often most important. In some cases, this may be a prime consideration, as when repair parts are needed to keep from shutting down a factory. Retailers of fashion merchandise are willing to pay premiums for immediate delivery when the demand for a specific fashion is great and stocks are depleted.

*Terms of sale* sometimes vary among vendors and are considered in the selection of suppliers. Cash discounts, which are offered to encourage the payment of bills before the expiration of a regular credit period, are often an important inducement, especially to firms that are in a healthy financial condition. The length of the credit period (i.e., whether a week, 30 days, 90 days, etc.) is important to many buyers, particularly those in weak financial condition.

The vendor's general reputation for *reliability* is often a patronagedetermining factor. This may relate to integrity in observing the terms of contracts, making deliveries on schedule, or supplying goods that conform with samples or contract grades.

Buyers are often influenced by the *distribution policies* of vendors. If a manufacturer sells direct to some retailers, some wholesalers may refuse to consider him as a source of supply. If a manufacturer operates some retail stores of his own, this may cause ill will among retailers, especially in shopping areas where the manufacturer's stores are located. Some manufacturers select only a few outlets for their products in each community, and many have only one exclusive representative. When a retailer or wholesaler is so selected, he is likely to be more favorably inclined toward the seller than in a case where a seller distributes his product widely through a large number of competing establishments.

*Sales promotion policies* of vendors also influence their selection as sources of supply. A maker of women's dresses may purchase the fabric of a particular cloth manufacturer because the latter's consumer advertising will help in the sale of the dresses made from it. Some manufacturers win the favor of retailers because of assistance provided in local cooperative advertising, point-of-sale display materials, demonstrations, direct mail advertising, or sales training programs for the buyers' employees.

The ability of a vendor to provide *continuity of supply* is often very important. Retailers do not like to patronize wholesalers who are often out-of-stock on important items and have to "back-order" them. In industrial purchasing, this factor is especially significant in connection with raw materials and supplies which are used regularly.

The selection of vendors is sometimes resolved on the basis of *reciprocity*. This is especially true in the industrial marketing field where large quantities are usually involved in a single transaction. Although this is not a scientific way of selecting suppliers, it is often rationalized by the attitude of "buying from those who buy from us, and thus we help each other." Just because a possible supplier is a customer does not mean that he is a good supplier on the basis of more rational considerations explained above. Some companies carry a policy of reciprocity to the extreme. A manufacturing company, for example, analyzes its sales to oil companies and distributes its purchases of supplies such as lubricating oil to each company in relation to the approximate volume of each oil company's purchases from it.

When a number of different potential suppliers are all satisfactory on the basis of the factors herein considered, the actual selection of sources is likely to hinge on the human equation. The personality, character, and technical proficiency of the *vendor's salesman* is frequently the factor that swings the balance of decision from some alternatives to others.

## Concentration of Purchases

The practice of buying from one source or a small number of suppliers is known as concentration of purchases. Although often a phase of quantity buying, a policy which limits the number of suppliers is practiced because of certain special advantages. Price concessions other than regular quantity discounts, better terms of credit, special help from the wholesaler or manufacturer in solving merchandising problems, and an opportunity for prior selection of desirable merchandise are often of enough importance to justify a policy of concentration. Moreover, such a policy tends to minimize the chance of overstocking, largely through a reduction in the number of brands, styles, patterns, designs, or price lines. Some retailers and wholesalers concentrate their purchases in order to secure an exclusive agency or in order to become affiliated with a voluntary chain organization.

Rigid limitations on the number of resources is not, however, always a wise policy. Some wholesalers and retailers find it necessary to buy from many sources to secure the best assortment of style goods. Good buying strategy calls for alertness for special offers which often preclude concentration, because such offerings may come from suppliers not normally patronized or from newly established sources. Many industrial purchasing agents make it a policy to develop a number of supply sources for important materials to insure continuity of procurement under circumstances that might jeopardize normal operations.

## SCIENTIFIC DEVELOPMENTS IN BUYING

The performance of the various subfunctions or elements of buying has been considerably modified by the growing use of sophisticated techniques or practices, including value analysis, vendor rating programs, determination of optimum order quantities, and automatic reordering. Such techniques are highly technical in application; hence, it is essential to limit the present discussion to an indication of their nature and significance to marketing.

### Value Analysis

As consisting of formal analytical procedures used to relate design and function of purchased products to cost, with a view to reducing cost substantially through modification of design, change in specifications, different method of manufacture, change in source of supply, possible elimination of an item, or incorporation of a new item. Value analysis differs from former buying methods in two ways—first, in the wide scope of its activities which involve participation by all departments of a business concerned with the use of resale of products being purchased and, second, in the carefully planned, methodical approach to the problem of getting the most *ultimate value* from money spent. It tends to take the emphasis away from the net cost of the item being purchased and focuses attention on eventual total costs. For example, one manufacturer had been satisfied for years with a lacquer the cost of which was substantially lower than competitive makes. One gallon covered 250 square feet. Through value analysis techniques, the purchasing department identified a much superior but higher-priced lacquer which covered nearly twice the area per gallon. While the invoice price of this lacquer was substantially greater, the ultimate cost of using it, per unit of finished product, was reduced by 30 per cent.

## Vendor Rating

Closely akin to and often considered as a part of, or a supplement to, a value analysis program are formal procedures for evaluating vendors. Traditionally, vendors have been evaluated on the basis of relatively few factors, with high priority often attached to the criteria of lowest purchase price and convenience and reliability of supply. Many business firms have developed elaborate check lists, often comprising 30 to 50 specific rating criteria, which are used periodically to evaluate alternative suppliers, with a view to identifying those who best serve the total needs of the purchaser on an over-all basis. While value analysis is concerned largely with functional attributes of a physical product, vendor analysis goes beyond, to consider the other values available from suppliers and which, therefore, are an important aspect of productive purchasing.

## Optimum Order Quantities.

From the preceding discussion of quantity versus small-lot buying, it is evident that the optimum quantity to purchase of a given item depends upon a wide range of complex variable factors including the following: risk of losses from deterioration and obsolescence; costs of storing or warehousing inventories; financial costs of carrying inventory, such as interest on investment, insurance, and taxes; risk of lost sales or interrupted manufacturing operations owing to a lack of availability; transportation costs which may vary on a per unit basis with quantity purchased; discounts or price concessions related to quantity bought; and acquisition costs such as those of processing purchase orders and handling accounts payable transactions. The number of such variables is so large, their applicability varies so much from one product class to another, and the number of items to be purchased by most businesses is so great that traditionally the determination of purchase quantities has necessarily been largely a matter of subjective judgment, often taking into account only the most obvious of such variables, such as quantity discounts and transportation economies. However, under modern conditions of automatic data processing by means of high-capacity electronic computers, it is relatively easy to use mathematical formulas which relate all of the variable factors listed above, for the purpose of determining the optimum quantity to purchase for each one of thousands of items which are *regularly* bought in substantial amounts. It is, moreover, feasible to do this as frequently as changes occur in any of the variable factors included in the formulas.

## Automatic Reordering

In many large organizations, electronic computers are used to reduce the amount of human judgment involved in routine reordering of staple items continually maintained in stock. This necessitates the prior determination of minimum stock levels for individual items, based on factors such as historical rates of sale, optimum reorder quantities (as discussed in the preceding section), normal stock replenishment time, and safety factors (stock "cushion") to allow for random or unpredictable needs (e.g., delays in transit or occasional sales in unusually large quantities). Once a minimum stock quantity for an item is determined, computers can be used to reduce reordering to a semiautomatic or completely automatic basis.

All information about changes in stock levels is fed into the computer. New purchases or receipts are added to previous balances, and all sales or use information is deducted, with the result that data are constantly available within the computer to reveal the current inventory figure for each item. A computer can be programmed so that it prepares daily a list of all items for which the amount of stock on hand, plus the stock on order, is less than the previously determined minimum. The computer can also indicate the number of units that should be ordered to bring the inventory (plus commitments) up to desired levels. This results in semiautomatic reordering, since the buyer need give attention only to computer determined replenishment requirements of those items listed on such special reports.

In some cases reordering is completely automatic in the sense that the computer is programmed to prepare an actual purchase order for a predetermined optimum purchase quantity whenever the stock on hand and on order falls below specified minimums. The buyer then needs only to signify approval of the computer-prepared purchase order by signing it.

## Marketing Significance

While the various scientific or analytical procedures discussed above have been growing in importance, their application has been confined mainly to large-scale buyers and even then principally in connection with goods which are purchased regularly. Extensive use of such procedures involves two prerequisites—specialization of a fairly high order in the buying organization and volume of sales sufficient to warrant the use of expensive data processing equipment. Such procedures are of rather limited value for new items for which there is no historical information on use or resale, for items the sale of which is relatively unpredictable owing to changing consumer tastes or fashion, and for items needed only occasionally. Nevertheless, their application has been widespread in industrial purchasing, particularly for materials used in manufacture and for supply items with a high consumption rate. It has also been extensive in wholesale distribution warehouses (whether operated by manufacturers, chain store companies, or regular wholesalers), particularly those dealing in numerous items continuously maintained in stock as, for example, groceries, hardware, drugs, and automotive supplies.

The impact of such procedures has been to place buying on a more scientific plane, with the result that the buying function is controlled more rigidly by predetermined criteria. As a consequence many sellers have been forced to adapt their marketing operations more closely to the requirements of customers who have committed themselves to any or all of the buying procedures here discussed. This has made it much more difficult for the seller, in appropriate cases, to count upon his own selling effort to bring about changes in buying practices. Such procedures have also had an important bearing upon more scientific approaches to the physical distribution of goods.

## BUYING PRACTICES

Various practices are followed in contacting resources, appraising their selections, and making purchases. Buying may be accomplished through central market visits, by negotiating with salesmen who visit the purchaser's premises, by means of trade registers and directories, in cooperation with other buyers who have similar needs, or by delegating the authority for purchases to a central agency.

### VISITING THE MARKET

In a number of lines of business, leading central markets have developed, and these are regularly visited by merchants or store buyers who wish to make purchases. New York City, for example, is both an important manufacturing and buying center for women's clothing. Other cities such as Chicago, Miami, St. Louis, Dallas, San Francisco, and Los Angeles are of importance as centers of supply for the same merchandise and are visited annually by merchants. The major market for furniture and home furnishings is in Chicago. Hundreds of exhibitors have offices and showrooms in this city in, or in the vicinity of, the Merchandise Mart, which is a famous market center with 93 acres of floor space. Other major furniture markets include New York, Dallas, Atlanta, Los Angeles, and High Point, North Carolina. A general trend in both apparel and home furnishings markets has been for the number of centers to increase with more emphasis upon regionalism. This has made it possible for larger numbers of buyers from all parts of the country to visit at least one market center, but it has also created problems for many manufacturers who now find it necessary to display merchandise in a greater variety of market centers.

A number of considerations affect the frequency of market visits. Buyers from stores located in communities remote from central or regional markets, even though interested in style merchandise, may go to market but once or twice a year or not at all, while those near at hand make frequent visits. Buyers from large firms usually visit markets more often than do representatives of the smaller houses. Retail stores which feature special sales at short intervals make frequent market trips to procure merchandise for these sales.

**Trade Shows**

A great deal of buying activity takes place at special trade shows which are held periodically, usually annually or semiannually, in many lines of business—for example, toys, housewares, hardware, office equipment, scientific instruments, packaging materials, and materials-handling equipment. Such shows are usually held in a major city with hundreds or thousands of exhibitors displaying their wares in temporary booths established for the duration of the show in hotels or exhibition halls.

Some of the well-known shows of this type are held in connection with national, regional, or state trade association conventions so that buyers can combine buying trips with allendancc at business meetings of their association. Trade shows are of such outstanding interest in lines in which they are common that considerable attention is devoted to them in trade magazines.

## BUYING ON THE PURCHASER'S PREMISES

All kinds of business firms do a large part of their buying on their own premises, either by mail orders or through suppliers' salesmen. Mail orders sent to suppliers are the least important for most organizations. They are usually based on catalogs furnished by vendors or information contained in trade registers and directories. Many retail stores and wholesalers use the mails for fill-in orders which are placed in the interval between salesmen's calls or visits to market centers. This method is also commonly used in industrial purchasing, especially for routine or occasional buying of supplies, tools, and stocks of repair parts.

Buying from salesmen is the second form of purchasing on the buyer's premises and is doubtless the most important single form of buying. Most independent dealers in convenience goods buy a large part of their stock from wholesalers' salesmen who visit the store. Much style merchandise, even that sold in the very largest department stores, is purchased from manufacturers' salesmen who visit the store with samples of ready-to-wear items supplied by New York garment houses and other similar resources. Buyers for wholesale establishments, factories, and governmental units also spend a considerable amount of time with suppliers' salesmen who call at their offices, and a large proportion of their requirements is bought in this manner.

## GROUP BUYING

The practice of *cooperative combination of orders from a number of buyers* so that relatively large purchases can be made at attractive prices is known as group buying. This practice is used occasionally by some wholesale and retail merchants in a wide variety of trades but is especially important among groups of department, dry goods, and apparel stores that have combined orders of many articles to the mutual advantage of participants. Arrangements for group buying are often made by resident buying offices. These arrangements include plans for group participants to visit the central market at the same time. Samples of the type of merchandise under consideration are collected and examined by the attending buyers who express their preferences by voting upon various offerings. Quantities desired by the participants are then pooled into a combined order and a price is negotiated with the resource.

The principal advantages of group buying lie in the lower prices usually secured from vendors, the fact that the merchandise may be produced to specifications of the group and packaged or labeled with the group's brand name, [5] and the use of the combined judgment of a group of qualified experts in selecting merchandise.

Group buying has, however, met with only limited success. For this there are several reasons. First, some lines of goods must be selected with the particular needs of each store's clientele in mind. The pooled judgment of a group of buyers from different stores does not always result in the selection of just the type or style of goods which a given store needs. Second, many buyers have failed to cooperate fully in such purchases because of the tendency of the plan, if successful, to minimize the value of their individual buying skill. Third, some manufacturers refuse to make offerings to cooperative groups because sales can be effected only at such low prices as to make the business economically unattractive or impossible to justify under the price discrimination provisions of the Robinson-Patman Act.

## CENTRAL BUYING

An important buying practice, limited substantially to large multi-unit organizations, is that of central buying. Its distinguishing feature is that *authority and responsibility for purchasing are vested in a central office rather than in the individual operating units* involved. This practice is widely used by almost all types of large retailing chains, to a limited degree by independent retailers of fashion merchandise through arrangement with resident buying offices, to a considerable extent by multi-unit wholesaling and manufacturing companies, also by various governmental units that have a central purchasing organization for different divisions or departments.

In some shoe or apparel chain stores, for example, there are no buyers in the individual stores. Local store managers are chiefly responsible for sales and have responsibility for buying only to the extent of providing the central office with daily or other frequent stock control information that indicates the sales of various items and changes in the inventory situation. The central office buyer makes all market contacts, handles negotiations with suppliers, and makes actual purchases.

On the basis of individual store stock and sales reports, merchandise shipments are made to them as directed by central office personnel, either direct from factories or from a central warehouse operated by the chain. In the grocery, variety, and drug fields the practice varies from this pattern. Store managers or other key employees check the stock periodically and requisition or order merchandise as needed, but from warehouse stocks or catalog listings that have been made available through central office negotiations.

Similar practices are sometimes followed in industrial or governmental purchasing. A large manufacturer of automotive equipment may operate a number of different factories, widely scattered geographically. If each of them requires similar equipment, materials, or supplies, the individual requirements are sometimes consolidated and purchased centrally.

Specific procedures used in central buying vary from one type of industry to another and often among different firms within a particular industry or trade. Regardless of variations in detail, central buying is generally adopted to obtain specific advantages which include the following: greater skill and specialization in the buying function than would be possible if each unit did its own purchasing; lower merchandise costs through the negotiating power which comes from consolidating the requirements of the various units; ability to take advantage of favorable market opportunities through continual contacts with suppliers; and economies in purchasing and accounting obtained by combining what would otherwise be a large number of individual transactions, each entailing the same unit costs for office procedures.

## SPECIFICATION BUYING BY CONTRACT

When a firm exercises rigid control over the quantitative and qualitative characteristics of an item being purchased, the practice is known as specification buying. This type of buying is quite frequently accompanied by a contractual arrangement in which the buyer agrees to purchase stipulated quantities of goods for delivery at periodic intervals or as requisitioned, and at prices which either are set forth in the contract or are to be established in terms of some formula which is incorporated in the agreement. Contracts sometimes involve commitments for a substantial proportion of the seller's total output and may cover all or a major part of the purchaser's requirements for a period of many months or even a year or more. Because of the rather substantial character of many such contracts, they are often negotiated through high-level executives of both parties. This buying practice is encountered in various segments of business, including retail chain and mail order companies which sell products under their own brand names, wholesaling companies that feature private brands, manufacturing companies that require materials of certain specifications for further processing or for incorporation in their end product, and governmental purchasing units, especially the military organizations.

Various considerations underlie such contractual arrangements. In the case of manufacturers, the assurance of a continuing supply of raw materials at a predetermined price is often the dominant motive. On the part of some purchasers, contracts for periodic delivery of instalments may be dictated by a desire to secure quantity prices without assuming the burdens incident to carrying heavy average inventories.

Many merchants have also attempted to secure the advantages of quantity buying without assuming the disadvantages through placing contracts for the periodic future delivery of large orders. Some large retailing concerns, for example, enter into contracts calling for the delivery of a certain number of pairs of hosiery each month for a period of months. Such contracts involve careful manufacturing specifications. Colors and shades are usually not determined at the time when the original contract is made but are furnished by the buyer from time to time during the life of the contract. The manufacturer finds such an agreement advantageous in that it enables him to plan a production program and to buy raw materials more intelligently. At the same time the purchaser profits by securing a quantity price and an assured supply without increasing his average inventory and, by supplying currently a schedule of colors and shades, he is enabled to adjust his stock to shifting consumer preferences in color and shade.

## BUYING COMMITTEES

Owing to the proliferation of new product offerings in the post- World War II era, many merchandising organizations have removed ultimate responsibility for adding or eliminating new products from an individual departmental buyer and have assigned authority for final judgment and decision on such matters to a buying committee. While such committees are used in many kinds of retailing and wholesaling establishments, they are most common in the supermarket industry where about 90 per cent of the larger organizations report their use.

Under the buying committee arrangement, a departmental buyer handles all purchasing responsibilities for items regularly stocked. He also sees salesmen for new products and collects all relevant information about new items which are presented. He may reject a new item, but if it meets with his approval he still does not have the authority to buy it. Instead, it must be presented to the buying committee which considers not only matters of departmental significance, but also reviews proposed new items in terms of corporate objectives.

Each new item presents certain problems relating to limited shelf space, capital investment in inventory, promotional requirements, warehouse storage and handling, and competitive significance. It is largely due to these overall problems that buying responsibility for new items is often assigned to buying or merchandising committees.

## SPECIALIZED BUYING AGENCIES

The dynamics of marketing is vividly illustrated by a number of agencies which have emerged as specialized buying institutions. Their economic justification rests upon ability to render a unique service at a low cost to a group of firms with common buying problems.

### Resident Buying Offices

A well-established segment of our buying structure is the resident buying office. Principally serving department, general merchandise, and apparel stores, these offices have largely supplanted private central market offices which were formerly maintained by some larger independent stores. Resident buying offices developed for the purpose of supplying central market representation for merchants and of relieving them from the necessity of making frequent trips to central markets. Such offices represent many retailers in the same line of business, and because of this fact they are able to render many services at a relatively small cost. By means of a staff of experts constantly in touch with market developments, the resident buying office is able to keep its client stores in touch with the best sources of supply. The office becomes the headquarters of visiting buyers who are guided in their purchases by office buyers of comparable lines. Style bulletins and other market information are sent to member stores at regular intervals and, in general, the office acts as their representative in the market. Some group buying and central buying is sponsored by resident buying offices, and many fill-ins are selected by its buyers for member stores.

Payment for the resident buyer's services by a fixed yearly fee is a common practice in this field, the amount being fixed by the estimated sales of the store during the period of the contract. Smaller stores are often served by resident buyers who may receive payment in the form of commissions on sales made for certain manufacturers. Resident buyers are an increasingly important factor in the distribution of ready-to-wear and certain dry goods lines. Distance from the market and the importance of style merchandise to the individual merchant are the principal factors determining the extent to which they are used. Several hundred resident buying organizations are located in New York City in the so-called "garment district" in midtown Manhattan. Many of the larger organizations have branches in other principal markets for fashion merchandise, including Chicago, Los Angeles, San Francisco, and certain foreign countries.

## Independent Purchasing Agents

Several independent business firms, known as purchasing agents or purchasing companies, provide a buying and market information service for wholesalers of consumer goods and for industrial distributors. Typical is an organization in the wholesale hardware and mill supply trade which serves many wholesalers by locating sources of new, superior, imported, or scarce merchandise and in other cases by securing attractive price quotations for them. Descriptions of thousands of items are supplied to the wholesalers in the form of a loose-leaf price book. Whenever the client believes that he can do so advantageously, he places orders with the purchasing agent, who in turn transmits them to the proper supplier for shipment. Each client pays a monthly membership fee for the services thus rendered. Similar organizations serve hundreds of wholesale grocers.

Purchasing agents of this type render an important service and constitute an important element in the distribution of certain lines of goods. [9] Their freedom to develop and operate was somewhat curtailed by the Robinson-Patman Act, for this law forbade collection of brokerage fees from sellers except for services rendered to such sellers rather than to buyers. It had been the practice of the purchasing agent to collect brokerage fees from sellers and to remit at least part to their clients, a fact which gave the clients a price advantage as compared with their competitors who bought directly from the same supplier or through the regular broker who kept his entire brokerage fee. Prevention of this and other types of price discrimination was one of the primary objects of the law. The result has therefore been that membership fees must be large enough to cover the cost of the purchasing agent's service, a fact which has somewhat reduced his importance as an agent for placing orders but which has in no way lessened the value of the market information provided.

In many trades brokers are sometimes employed by buyers to locate advantageous sources of supply, particularly for seasonal commodities or for items in short supply. When so utilized, the broker performs some of the functions of the independent purchasing agent.

### Commissioners

In purchasing goods in foreign markets buyers are frequently under the disadvantage of a lack of knowledge of good sources of supply and are further handicapped by a lack of knowledge of the language. To assist such buyers, individuals known as commissioners or commissionaires are found in foreign markets. It is the function of the commissioner to bring the buyer into contact with proper vendors and to function as an interpreter. When the American buyer is not abroad, the commissioner keeps in communication with him, furnishing him with samples and information about goods. The commissioner represents the buyer and receives his compensation from him.

## BUYING AND THE LAW

Owing to its significance as one of the two exchange functions of marketing, buying comes within the purview of certain public policy regulations. Since the whole subject of government and marketing is dealt with at a later point, it is sufficient here merely to note some of the more important legal implications.

Under the Sherman Antitrust Act, a buyer is prohibited from conspiring with other buyers whereby as a group they agree not to make purchases from certain sources of supply, when the agreement would be in restraint of trade, thus foreclosing a market or channel of distribution to one or several potential suppliers whose policies do not meet with the favor of the buyers who are in collusive agreement. Such an agreement is in violation of the law *per se*, regardless of actual effect. A buyer may also be guilty of unfair methods of competition in trade or commerce, under the Federal Trade Commission Act, if he joins with others in formulating lists or directories of buyers, where the purpose or intent of such lists is to cause suppliers to sell only to those whose names appear thereon. Under the Robinson-Patman Act it is unlawful for a buyer operating as a wholesaler (or retailer) also to presume to act as a broker and thus receive a brokerage fee on merchandise purchased for resale as a merchant. The Act limits the payment of brokerage fees to parties that are acting on behalf of, or are controlled by, the party making the payment. Also under the Robinson-Patman Act it is unlawful for a buyer knowingly to induce or to receive a discrimination in price which is prohibited by the law. As this matter has been viewed by the courts, it pertains primarily to cases in which a buyer, knowing full well that there was little likelihood of a cost saving or other legal defense by the seller for a price discrimination, nevertheless received or proceeded to exert pressure for lower prices than could be legally justified by the seller. These few illustrations are sufficient to indicate that regulations exist which, to some extent, limit the buyer as well as the seller in situations involving monopolistic, trade restraining, or unfair competitive practices.

# Chapter 14

# The Selling Function

A major function for most business firms today is that of establishing and maintaining a market for their products. In the case of such simple business enterprises as roadside markets, ordinary display and the more elementary forms of personal selling are the only expression of this function. On the other hand, many manufacturers, middlemen, and producers of business or personal services conduct elaborate campaigns to arouse or stimulate demand for their products, or to divert such demand from competitors. In each case the business organization is engaged in one of the most essential marketing functions, that of demand creation or selling.

## MEANING OF DEMAND CREATION

Throughout this book the term demand creation is used in the rather loose, broad, and very general way that has become customary in all discussions of advertising and personal selling. For example, the word demand must not be interpreted to mean a stubborn insistence upon the product advertised, for seldom is it meant to be other than a mere recognition, a favorable impression, or a preference with respect to it. More important, the word "creation" must not be interpreted to mean as bringing into existence something which has not existed before, for usually it refers to the bringing into consciousness and action motivations that have been dormant or otherwise ineffective.

Actually, then, instead of "creating demand" in the literal sense, what selling effort (including advertising) does is to arouse, stimulate, or direct a prospective buyer's conscious or dormant desire for want satisfaction that results in action with reference to a given product, service, or seller.

## METHODS OF SELLING

Two principal methods are involved in the selling function: *advertising* and *personal selling*. Advertising is any *paid* form of *nonpersonal* presentation of goods, services, or ideas to a group by an identified sponsor. Personal selling, on the other hand, is the process of personally assisting and persuading a prospect to buy a commodity or service or to act upon an idea. The presentation may be formal, in the nature of a carefully rehearsed sales talk, which is presented in substantially the same manner to all prospects, or it may be and usually is informal.

Certain other terms commonly used in the sales field, such as publicity and sales promotion, should be understood in this connection. *Publicity* is *any* form of commercially significant news items or editorial comment about products or institutions published in space or broadcast time that is *not paid* for by the sponsor, although the term is sometimes used in a broader sense to include advertising. *Sales promotion* includes those selling activities that supplement both advertising and personal selling, coordinate them, and render them more effective. It includes sampling, displays, demonstrations, and various kinds of nonrecurrent selling effort.

## RELATION OF ADVERTISING TO PERSONAL SELLING

Advertising and personal selling are not as a rule in competition but rather supplement each other. A marked characteristic of personal selling is that the message is usually delivered to a definite prospect. Advertising, except for direct mail, on the other hand, must appeal to the mass mind, or at least to the average individual within some market segment to which the appeal is directed. Moreover, personal salesmanship is adaptable. The message can be adjusted to the individual prospect and appeals can be selected which are of most importance to him. The speed of delivery and the language of the sales argument can be adjusted to the prospect's training or general intelligence. Objections can be met as they arise, and thus effective demand can be created.

Advertising is used, as a rule, to assist the salesman. It aims to give preliminary information and to break down resistance which might operate to prevent the later, effective delivery of a sales message. Advertisements in trade magazines can be used, for example, to tell the story of a certain type of business machine and to suggest that many companies have used such machines with success.

Purchasing agents and mechanical engineers are much more apt to give a careful hearing to the salesman for a machine of this kind when he calls than would be the case if they knew nothing about the machine in advance of the call. Thousands of people may receive favorable impressions about a certain kind of automobile because of the manufacturer's advertising, but as a rule it is not until after further selling effort by the dealer's salesman that a purchase is actually made.

Although commonly supplementary to each other, either of the two methods of selling may be used exclusively. Many unbranded and unadvertised raw materials and some manufactured commodities are sold without advertising. Many articles are sold by mail through advertising and without any personal salesmanship. The proportion of total goods sold by advertising alone is, however, exceedingly small. Furthermore, modern distribution is normally based on the use of both methods, neither one entirely supplanting the other.

## RATIONALE FOR THE SELLING FUNCTION

Selling effort (including advertising, personal selling, and sales promotion) is largely a phenomenon of the twentieth century. It did not exist in the conspicuous and important way that we know it today prior to the attainment of a high level of industrial production in our private enterprise economy. Moreover, selling effort as we know it in the United States is not now to be found in parts of the world characterized by low levels of industrial production; neither does it exist in areas where the buying behavior of consumers is regulated in a planned economy, ruled by a dictatorial government. Of all the marketing functions, selling is the least understood and the most maligned, even though numerous theoretical economists, marketing authorities, and business leaders have attempted to provide some rational explanation for selling costs and selling effort. Some understanding of the various theories aimed at explaining the basis for selling effort should prove helpful in evaluating the selling function from a social point of view, from the viewpoint of marketing management, and from the standpoint of the individual acting in the capacity of a consumer-buyer.

## Material Opulence

Substantial emphasis upon the selling function is ascribed by some to material opulence as reflected in the relatively high level of income and purchasing power characterizing our economy. It is claimed that "The need and the opportunity to persuade people arise only as people have the income to satisfy relatively unimportant wants, of the urgency of which they are not automatically aware."

Hence, "Our proliferation of selling activity is the counterpart of comparative opulence." According to this view, two attributes of selling are emphasized. One is its capacity to initiate the spending cycle, and the other is its contribution to the aggregate level of income which attends its widespread use.

While both of these factors are important, they do not account for the most essential characteristic of selling effort. To be sure, for example, the potential response to selling effort is determined in large measure by the level of purchasing power and to that extent this view provides a partial explanation for the emphasis placed on the selling function in our economy. But all that is thus explained is the *level* of selling expenditures in the aggregate and not the basic reason why such expenditures are made at all even in a less opulent state of economic well-being.

## Firm Differentiation

An explanation of selling effort in terms of firm differentiation is commonplace, particularly in many theoretical economic treatises. This thesis holds that selling costs arise out of the attempts of competing business units to build a protective barrier against their rivals. Selling effort, it is claimed, provides a more secure position in terms of the level of the company's sales, its degree of product acceptance, enterprise image, or some other aspect of its market standing. This conception leads to an investment approach in the management of selling costs, particularly for advertising programs intended to promote a brand or the company name. While there is substantial justification for this theory, it fails to distinguish the selling function from other aspects of business activity designed to achieve firm differentiation, such as patents, product research, and location. Moreover, it fails to account for selling effort that is not primarily of a competitive nature.

## Demand Manipulation

Selling effort has frequently been defined in terms of demand manipulation, a somewhat objectionable term because of its connotation. By implication, the buyer (commonly viewed as the ultimate or individual consumer and ignoring the status of business purchasers as targets of a large amount of selling effort) is overwhelmed by selling pressure. To use an analogy, he is swayed by the seller much like clay is shaped by the potter. This is the attitude of critics who object to the kinds of things people buy and sometimes to the idea that they buy at all. Such a concept of selling suggests a desire of the critic to impose his value standards upon the general consuming public. Obviously, a more realistic view is that sellers, by using various advertising appeals and selling techniques, can persuade buyers to respond favorably to offers of goods and services. Consequently, demand manipulation in itself, especially when used in a derogatory manner, is incomplete as an explanation because it attributes a response to selling effort but does not explain why the response occurs.

## Information

Perhaps the more widely held thesis on the rationale for the selling function is that its task is to provide information. As initially stated, the theory suggests that because buyers act rationally and should be sovereign in their decision making, the sole task of the selling process is to provide information about the product or about the seller. Any effort beyond that is unnecessary and, therefore, unproductive of an essential economic service.

Basically, this was the view of the early economic classicists who accepted demand as given (and hence not subject to change in nature, size, or direction), supply rather scarce, and man quite rational. Under such circumstances, all that a seller needs to do is to provide the necessary information concerning his product, its price, and availability, and that would comprise the totality of the selling function. It is interesting to note, however, that not all economists accepted this view of selling effort. Alfred Marshall, the developer of neoclassical economics, recognized the importance of persuasion as part of selling effort when he indicated that when a manufacturer makes a commodity, the demand for which could be increased with resulting internal economies, it may be "worth his while to sacrifice a great deal in order to push its sales in a new market." Indeed, the expenditure for this purpose may even exceed that "which he devotes directly to the manufacture.

Contemporary writers on the subject apparently overlook the views of Marshall and his followers in economic thought when they adhere to the theory that the only function of selling effort is one of providing information. In doing so, they shun the persuasion ingredient of the selling function in order to avoid buyer irrationality and ethical overtones about the seller suggested by it. This position is obviously weak theoretically and completely unrealistic. Much advertising and personal selling effort may not even impart any information but may be aimed at securing attention, reminding, or creating favorable impressions through color and symbolism.

Moreover, even so-called informative advertising and selling are designed to influence buyers and thus effect sales. Hence, an explanation of selling effort in terms of communicating information, while possessing some merit with respect to a substantial proportion of all selling activity and an essential ingredient of it, fails to capture the fundamental characteristic of most selling which is persuasion.

## Creation of Possession Utility

While all of the foregoing viewpoints cast some light on certain aspects or facets of the selling function, at least in a partial way, the clearest rationale lies in its creation of possession utility. A product consists of the satisfactions or benefits derived from its use or consumption, and production is the creation of all economic values or utilities, including those of form, time, place, and possession, as well as activities or functions that facilitate in the creation of these values.

Accordingly, the selling function is part of the productive process since it creates possession utility by affecting or effecting the exchange process. In advertising, owing to the usual remoteness from the act of title transfer, it is more a matter of affecting the process. Through personal selling, on the other hand, actual transfers of title and hence changes in legal possession are commonly effected in a direct way. Both aspects of the selling function, however, are parts of the process of exchange and consumption of goods and services.

Satisfaction in ultimate consumption or business use of goods and services issues from the selling function in a number of ways. Buyers are aided in establishing exchange contacts when sellers take the initiative, thus providing great savings in time or convenience, as compared with any possible hypothetical situation in which it would be necessary for buyers to take the initiative in all exchange activity. Under modern concepts of customer-oriented marketing management, the selling function aids in interpreting available goods and services in terms of the needs and wants of buyers. From the point of view of the individual buyer, selling activity satisfies an apparent desire for variety. This partially accounts for the wide range of selling techniques which are designed to arouse interest and provide differentiation. From an aggregate point of view, the selling function has an influence upon a variety of matters of social concern. It is generally conceded, even by its critics, that it contributes to a level of consumption and hence of total production that is much larger than would exist in the absence of selling effort. It also has an important relationship to the distribution of consumer and business expenditures by product classes. Thus it makes a contribution to the allocation of economic resources and employment in different industries and in various lines of commercial trade.

## ADVERTISING AS A BUSINESS ACTIVITY

Ultimate consumers and business purchasers are continually exposed to advertising in one form or another. Whatever the form, the advertiser's message generally appears as a simple presentation. Obscured behind the scenes, however, are a score of important business decisions that have a bearing upon the impact made on the buyer. In many companies, decisions relating to the nature of the role of advertising in the total marketing effort are a crucial aspect of marketing strategy. Various types of advertising must be considered for different specific purposes; ideas are conceived and advertisements are prepared as a result of careful plans made well in advance of publication; media are selected to convey the prepared message to the prospective recipients; and, for some or all of these decisions, a special institution known as the advertising agency is often employed.

### TYPES OF ADVERTISING

The many types of advertising may be classified in a number of ways. Furthermore, the various classes commonly recognized are not mutually exclusive but are often different ways of looking at the same thing. For example, advertising may be classified as *institutional* or *product,* depending upon whether it is aimed primarily at establishing a favorable attitude toward the advertiser or at the development of demand for a given product. It may be classified, on the basis of the advertiser's status, into *manufacturers', wholesalers', retailers', or cooperative* advertising. Again, advertising may be classified as *consumer, trade, professional,* or *industrial,* in terms of the audience to which it is directed. It may also be classified on the basis of the principal appeal, that is; whether the purpose of such an appeal is to arouse and direct demand toward a specific product or to a given general class of products.

## ADVERTISING IN THE MARKETING MIX

When a business firm has identified the market or market segment to which it wishes to make its strongest appeal, it must decide how much of its total promotional effort shall be allocated to various different elements of marketing strategy that may induce prospective customers to buy. The term *marketing mix* is commonly used to denote the amount of *relative emphasis* placed upon different components of a firm's marketing program. Possible components of such a program for many companies would include advertising, personal selling, pricing, relationships with other institutions in distribution channels, physical availability of product, aftersale service, special sales promotional activities, financing of customers, and so on.

Obviously, a firm with limited resources cannot allocate an unusually large *share* of its total marketing effort (funds) to some one component of a marketing mix without making some sacrifice or compromise about the magnitude of the expected contribution of other actual or possible components of the mix.A firm's ability or willingness to devote a substantial share of its marketing mix to advertising is influenced by two sets of factors—one relating to the characteristics of the goods or services being marketed and the other to the characteristics of advertising as they pertain to the particular firm.Factors Relating to Product. Product attributes generally accepted as favorable to heavy emphasis upon advertising in the marketing mix may be listed as follows:

- Favorable primary demand situation: Advertising is likely to be effective when there is a substantial opportunity to expand the total market for a product, as illustrated by household air conditioning, motor boats, and hearing-aid devices.

- Significant product differentiation: When a product offers benefits not readily available from close substitutes, advertising is likely to be especially productive. Differentiation may exist in the physical attributes of a product (e.g., special formula or materials) or in its application or use (e.g., shoe polish packaged for ease of application without getting one's hands or clothes soiled), or in ease of branding (e.g., Sunkist citrus products) or may take other tangible or intangible forms.
- Hidden values: Advertising appeals based upon user satisfaction are often effective to a high degree when the product has some values not readily apparent to a prospective user, as in the case of many mechanical devices and certain types of drugs and medicines.
- Emotional basis for buying: When the purchaser's motives for buying have a strong emotional basis, as illustrated by many health and personal appearance products, advertising can be a strong influence in shifting consumer preferences or in getting new potential users to try a product.

**Factors Relating to Advertising.**

Certain characteristics of advertising as one form of promotional effort either encourage or discourage heavy emphasis on it, depending upon the situation of the marketing organization. These are as follows:

- Nature of advertising expenditures: Large-scale advertising requires substantial outlays for current expense. Unlike investments made in plant or store equipment, advertising costs cannot ordinar- ily be financed through outside sources and amortized over a period of time. Thus, large-scale advertising tends to be limited to big firms with favorable working capital positions.

- Low selectivity: The more limited a firm's distribution or the thinner its market in terms of number of potential customers, the more difficult it is to utilize media in the mass communication field. Many firms encounter serious difficulty in the selection of media which reach an audience that corresponds well with the intended market, either geographically or in terms of customer characteristics.
- Inflexibility through time: Major advertising campaigns involve planning that must take place long in advance of the execution of the advertising program. This is especially true of network television, magazines, and national campaigns in newspapers. Thus, the firm that must stand ready to adjust quickly to changing market conditions finds that the potential contribution of advertising to its total marketing effort is limited.

## ADVERTISING MEDIA

The vehicle or carrier through which an advertising message is conveyed to its intended audience is known as an advertising medium. The prominence of newspapers is explained by the fact that the bulk of local retail store advertising is carried in this medium. Each of the major classes or types of media may be further subdivided; magazines, for example, can be divided into weeklies and monthlies, or into men's, women's, children's, home or "shelter," general, and so on. From the standpoint of the advertiser, the different types of media may be complementary or competitive. Each type has its value, is favored under given conditions, and is subject to certain limitations. Several types are often used simultaneously in well-rounded advertising campaigns, each supplementing the others.

The major classes of media have adjusted dynamically to changing times and each one, through innovation, has become somewhat more readily substitutable for the other. This is illustrated by the increasing availability of high-quality color illustrations in newspapers; ability of advertisers to buy pages in split-run, regional issues of certain leading magazines; magazine concept of network broadcast media, whereby the high cost of sponsoring programs is shared by a variety of advertisers; and the growth of color broadcasting in television.

## PRODUCT ADVERTISING BY MANUFACTURERS

While the details of manufacturers' advertising programs vary with the kind of product and character of the company, a common function is that of *building acceptance or preference for the advertised product,* and a common pattern of managerial decisions is followed.

First, the advertiser must be certain that the product to be promoted actually satisfies some basic need; otherwise, no amount of advertising can win acceptance for the product. Second, it is necessary to discover the uses or applications of the product, and confine the advertised uses to reasonable ones that satisfy important common needs. Third is the determination of distinctive characteristics of the product to be used as selling appeals. For advertising to be successful over a period of time, these should be real and recognizable distinctions as viewed from the customer's and not the seller's standpoint. Most manufacturers' advertising is characterized by an attempt to give the product a personality or identity which will make it stand out competitively. This requires close coordination between the planning of advertising and package or label design.

Other major management problems relate to the determination of the market for the product, whether general or highly restricted to a segment of the total market; the selection of media which will reach the consumers of the product and possibly also the trade; and the determination of an advertising appropriation that will be adequate to accomplish the objective of the program. The appropriation is likely to be large per unit of product if an item is in the introductory stage of development and, hence, is not well known to consumers or distributors; it is likely to be large in total amount, but small per unit of product, if the item is in the competitive stage and similar products are being mass-produced and mass-distributed by a number of companies.

## MERCHANDISE ADVERTISING BY RETAILERS

Retailers' merchandise advertising differs from that of manufacturers' in objective. Whereas the manufacturer usually seeks to build acceptance or preference for his brand of product, the retailer is concerned primarily with *building good will or patronage for his particular store.* Except where exclusive agencies are common, as in the automobile field, retailers' advertisements are characterized more by variety and assortments of merchandise rather than by individual items. Stress is placed upon patronage motives such as price, selection, location of stores, or services. In retail advertising there is also more of an attempt *to provoke immediate buying reaction* than is the case with manufacturers' advertising where a long program may be planned to build or sustain consumer acceptance or preference. This accounts for very marked concentrations of retail advertising at times when consumer buying urges are most active, as evidenced by heavy grocery advertising on Wednesdays or Thursdays in anticipation of week-end shopping, or unusual quantities of department store advertising at Christmas, Easter, school-opening time, and on other occasions when consumers are most likely to respond to specific advertising appeals.

## COOPERATIVE ADVERTISING

Much advertising involves the cooperative participation of a number of individual firms. Such advertising is designated as *horizontal cooperative* when the participants are functionally similar and operate on the same level of distribution. This type is particularly common where the objective is to increase primary demand for a type of product or to influence favorably public attitudes toward an industry. Illustrative are advertisements by agricultural marketing cooperatives, the cost of which is supported by charges on products marketed by members (e.g., Sunkist Growers, Inc.) and by some trade associations (e.g., American Gas Association, Pan American Coffee Bureau).

When the participants are organizations on different levels of a distribution channel, the activity is known as *vertical cooperative* advertising. It exists in a variety of forms including advertisements by manufacturers in which distributors or dealers are listed by name, and retailer advertisements featuring a manufacturer's product, for which an allowance is granted by the manufacturer to reimburse the dealer for some part or perhaps all of the cost of advertising or promoting the manufacturer's product.

The practice of granting advertising allowances to distributors or dealers is especially common among manufacturers utilizing a selective distribution policy, particularly in certain lines of appliances, household equipment, tires, paint, shoes, and men's and women's clothing. It is also prevalent in certain convenience goods lines, notably grocery products, cosmetics and toilet goods. In the grocery trade, for example, some 75 to 95 per cent of corporate chains, wholesaler sponsored voluntary chains, and retailer cooperative groups report the frequent use of advertising allowances for products in the following groups: canned foods, cooking and salad oils, crackers and cookies, frozen foods, lard and shortening, macaroni products, paper products, soaps and detergents, starches and bleaches, and tea.

Many manufacturers grant allowances to finance advertising of their products by dealers in order to guide consumers to local sources of supply, to provide a point-of-purchase tie-in with national advertising, to stimulate the cooperation of dealers, to help gain additional dealers, and to obtain a sort of automatic control over advertising expenditures, inasmuch as advertising allowances are commonly granted to dealers in direct relation to their volume of purchases during specified time periods. On the other hand, numerous manufacturers abhor cooperative advertising allowances, believing that such allowances provide a drain on their national advertising budget, reduce the quality of copy and layout when advertisements are prepared by dealers, present many nuisance problems relating to bookkeeping and control and in checking of dealer performance in relation to an advertising agreement, and cause many legal complications since under the Robinson-Patman Act, it is required that advertising allowances or special promotional services, when granted to some dealers, must be made available to all on proportionally equal terms.

Regardless of an individual manufacturer's viewpoint, it is difficult for him to avoid the granting of advertising allowances when this is a common competitive practice. From a broader point of view, the practice of granting advertising allowances has a somewhat deleterious effect upon retail advertising, inasmuch as the content of the advertising of many retail stores is determined more by the availability of advertising allowances than by careful judgments about what would constitute timely and interesting buying information for the consumer.

## THE ADVERTISING AGENCY

The growth of advertising has been associated with the development of a specialized type of institution known as the advertising agency. The first advertising agents, about the middle of the nineteenth century, were space brokers for media. At that time newspaper editors were anxious to obtain advertising revenue but had no contacts with out-of-town advertisers. The first agents recognized this situation as an opportunity for rendering an economic service. They purchased or contracted for "white space" from media and contacted advertisers in distant areas, selling the space in units suited to the requirements of advertisers. Gradually the agents began to give advice and assistance to advertisers who were seeking specialized counsel in the preparation of their copy. In time the agents developed new methods and techniques and offered new services. Eventually the advertisers rather than the media became the clients of the agents.

Today the advertising agency is a service organization composed of advertising specialists, and it shares the responsibility for advertising activities with the advertising departments of clients. It is believed that advertising agencies now assist in the creation and direction of more than 90 per cent of all national advertising, more than one-half of sectional advertising, and a considerable amount of local advertising. Between 1948 and 1958 the number of advertising agency establishments increased from 3,279 to 7,720. A large per cent of total agency business, however, is accounted for by a limited number of large agencies, most of which are located in New York City.

## Services of Agencies

The principal services of modern advertising agencies consist of planning, preparation, and placement of advertising. Planning requires a thorough knowledge of markets, products, distribution channels, and marketing policies. This often involves marketing research, which is carried on by or for the agency. Preparation includes developing a central idea or theme, production of advertisements, production or purchase of art work and printing, hiring radio and television talent and supervising or producing entertainment programs, and preparing broadcast media commercials. Placement involves selection of media; preparation of advertising schedules; purchase of broadcast time or publication space; shipment of plates, copy, and instructions to media; preparation and mailing of direct advertising; and checking publications or stations to insure that advertisements were run or broadcast properly. Some of the larger agencies also provide a marketing counseling service and go so far as to advise a client on broad management policies for his business. They may assist in product development and package design; secure patents and copyrights; prepare point-of-sale promotional aids for the client's sales force; carry on public relations and publicity work; arrange and plan demonstrations and contests; and prepare training material for dealers' and jobbers' salesmen. In fact, there is almost no type of promotional service which is not provided at least by some agencies.

## Why Agencies Are Used

Even the largest advertisers who maintain elaborate advertising departments find that there are several good reasons for using advertising agencies. First, the agency is independent of the advertiser and has an outside objective viewpoint which it can bring to bear on important decisions. Second, the agency has broad experience which results from its work with a number of clients having different products, selling in various markets, using various channels of distribution, and employing numerous types of media. Third, it must do a satisfactory job in order to hold the account. It is constantly alert to opportunities because it realizes that the advertiser can change agencies easily.

If an advertiser developed an advertising department capable of performing all agency services, such a department would be part of the organization and could not be disposed of easily. Fourth, the agency may spread the cost of certain technical services over a number of accounts. The payroll costs of advertising production specialists and marketing research experts is less than it would be if each advertiser had a staff comparable in skills to that of the agency. A fifth important reason is that all or a large part of the agency's service may not cost the advertiser anything. This is true because agencies obtain a substantial part of their revenue from media commissions which are not available to advertisers who buy space or time direct from media.

## Agency Compensation

Advertising agency compensation is largely a carryover from the early days when the principal function of an agency was selling space for media. Most agencies still obtain the greater part of their remuneration from the media, based upon the amount of space or time purchased for clients. The agency purchases publication space or broadcast time direct from the media. With only minor exceptions, it receives a discount usually amounting to 15 per cent of the list price of the space or time purchased.

For example, if the cost of a full page of space in a magazine is listed at $10,000, the recognized agency is billed for $10,000 less a 15 per cent discount, or $8,500. The agency bills its clients for a space cost of $10,000 and retains the $1,500 to defray the expense of preparing the copy, placing, and checking the advertisement. If the advertiser did not use the agency, under existing media price and discount policies, it would probably pay the magazine the full price of $10,000 and would, furthermore, have to incur the expenses of preparing and placing the advertisement.

Agency commissions from media are often supplemented by service fees paid by clients. The commission is intended to cover the service cost of preparing and placing advertising. It does not provide payment for extensive marketing research work, elaborate art work or engravings prepared outside the agency, talent for radio or television entertainment, preparation of special signs or dealer-helps, or other special services rendered or procured by the agency for the client. For such services it is customary for the agency to levy special charges based on the cost of the services plus some percentage fee agreed upon at the time the relationship is established.

The agency method of commission compensation has often been criticized as illogical, inasmuch as the services of advertising agents are rendered primarily to advertisers rather than to media which pay the commissions. It has also been criticized because the traditional pattern of commission payments became rigidly institutionalized. Various trade associations of advertising agencies and of advertising media have established criteria to be met by business firms in order for them to be recognized as accredited agencies entitled to receive such commissions. Also, it has been considered an unethical trade practice for agencies to split media commissions or to rebate any part of them to advertiser clients.

The whole agency compensation pattern was called into question in the 1950's when the Department of Justice brought proceedings against various such associations under the Sherman Antitrust Act. Early in 1956 a leading association of advertising agencies and several media associations entered into consent decrees which, among other things, prohibited practices or agreements "fixing, establishing or stabilizing agency commissions or attempting to do so" or "requiring, urging or advising any advertising agency to refrain from rebating or splitting agency commissions. These consent decrees forced a re-examination of the whole pattern of agency compensation and brought forth some experimental attempts between agencies and clients for new approaches to compensation. On the whole, however, the commission basis for agency compensation continues to be the dominant arrangement.

Agency commissions from media have not been an important factor in local or retail advertising. Newspapers and radio and television stations usually have direct contact with local advertisers. Partly because of the news value of local advertisements and partly because the large portion of revenue is obtained locally, newspapers and other local media usually have lower space or time rates for local than for nonlocal advertisers. Agency discounts do not apply to these lower local rates. This has restricted the use of advertising agencies in local advertising, because they must make a specific charge for the total value of the service rendered to local clients.

## ECONOMIC AND SOCIAL ASPECTS OF ADVERTISING

In the preceding pages advertising has been discussed as an important activity, assumed to be essential to the preponderant majority of business concerns. The broader economic and social aspects of advertising are, however, a subject of considerable controversy. The negative aspects of advertising, or those facets of it which are most readily criticized or scorned, are readily apparent and widely publicized.

On the other hand, the contributions and services of advertising are not well understood, even by many marketing and advertising executives. An appraisal of the economic, social, and public policy implications of advertising is essential for purposes of a functional analysis of marketing, both from a broad or over-all viewpoint as well as from the standpoint of marketing management, inasmuch as those who plan and carry out advertising programs can do so more effectively by understanding advertising as a part of the social scene.

## CONTRIBUTIONS AND SERVICES OF ADVERTISING

The place of advertising in our life is better understood if certain facts relating to the service of advertising to society as a whole are examined objectively. It was suggested that advertising did not become important until large-scale production made certain demand-creation activities necessary. Successful advertising campaigns have in turn *accelerated the movement toward large-scale production* by many manufacturers. As a rule, increase in the scale of form utility production is accompanied by decreasing costs per unit of output.

There are hundreds of examples of reduction in the total cost of production and distribution through successful advertising. It is equally true that advertising and a liberal use of personal selling efforts have been made necessary in order to find a large market in which to sell the increased output resulting from quantity-production methods. *Thus advertising is both a cause and effect of large-scale activity,* with emphasis probably on the latter. In either case, the result is the same. Decreased cost of manufacturing in many cases offsets wholly or in part the cost of demand-creation activities.

Another important service of advertising lies in its *beneficial effect on the standard of living.* One measure of a nation's material progress is a cross-section of the wants of the common people. In other words, advancing civilization is accompanied by increases in the quantity and variety of wants and the means of satisfying them. Advertising has done much to encourage better homes, architecturally, mechanically, and functionally. Dozens of articles are in use in the average home of today as the result of demand stimulation by advertising. Vacuum sweepers, electric refrigerators, mechanical dishwashers, and modern floor and wall coverings are illustrations. Many advertised articles help to make the modern diet more nutritious, interesting, and enjoyable than formerly.

Since advertising facilitates the profitable exploration and development of markets for new or improved products and uses, *it has tended greatly to encourage innovation and technology.* There is no doubt but that much of the technological progress in the electronic, chemical, and automotive fields recorded in modern times can be attributed to the development of potential demands for the products and uses thus made possible.

The *educational effect of advertising* is likewise important, both directly and indirectly. It is probable that advertisements of dental creams have done more to preserve the teeth of the nation than has the personal advice of thousands of dentists. Correspondence courses which have been of great aid to many people are made possible largely because of advertising. Advertising, insofar as it is truthful, educates by providing information about hundreds of articles which might be otherwise unknown or unaccepted by the average buyer. The *indirect effect of advertising upon education* is undoubtedly even more potent. Most newspapers or magazines could not be sold at prices that would make them accessible to the masses of our people in the absence of advertising which largely subsidizes them. About two-thirds to three-fourths of the average income of newspapers and magazines comes from advertising. Most radio and television programs would be virtually impossible without sponsorship by advertisers.

Constructive advertising *lessens to a great degree the necessity for buying ability*. In the days of the more simple life it was possible for buyers to be judges of the quality of the articles they purchased, since these were comparatively few in number. It is now almost impossible for the average buyer to judge with any certainty the quality of the hundreds of articles he buys. But fortunately the use of brands, which is an essential for most advertising, makes it possible to rely on the standard quality of such merchandise, and identification enables one to avoid repurchase of unsatisfactory brands.

## CRITICISMS OF ADVERTISING

Certain considerations tend in part, at least, to offset the social value of the services of advertising. Many criticisms have been made, and some of these are partially sound. Most of the criticisms are, however, at least partly the result of misunderstanding as shown by the following appraisal of some of the most commonly voiced and perhaps also the most important of these criticisms.

"Too Costly." A common criticism is that the cost of advertising is too high and that such high cost adds to the price of the advertised product. This criticism grows out of an inherent characteristic of advertising as an instrument of mass communication, necessitating expenditures of large amounts of money. It is rather common knowledge, for example, that certain large advertisers spend millions of dollars annually for advertising, that advertising pages in popular magazines are priced in tens of thousands of dollars, and that the cost of producing and broadcasting certain individual television programs may run into hundreds of thousands of dollars. Such amounts appear staggering to the person of ordinary means who forgets that expenditures for advertising are significant only when expressed in relation to some meaningful standard of comparison.

One way of judging the magnitude of advertising expenditures is in relation to total personal consumption expenditures. Advertising expenditures in 1960 amounted to $11.6 billion, but this was only 3.5 per cent of all consumer expenditures for goods and services. Over a long period of years, advertising costs of about 3 per cent to 4 per cent of consumption expenditures have been typical. This basis of comparison, however, overstates the relative importance of advertising costs. Much advertising is devoted to industrial goods and services and some to goods sold primarily to government. It is, therefore, more meaningful to compare the costs of advertising to the gross national product. Over a period of years, this basis reveals that advertising costs of about 2 per cent are the common situation. Again, advertising cost, when related to the total volume of business transacted, is less than 1 percent.

Another important approach to understanding advertising costs is in terms of units of product. In the case of cigarettes, where all important brands are highly advertised, the great amounts expended for advertising shrink into insignificance when compared to the tremendous number of units of product sold, resulting in costs of only a fraction of a cent per package. Experience varies from one industry to another. Advertising costs for certain nationally promoted brands of soap, cosmetics, and drugs amount to a significant component of final retail value. These are exceptional examples, however, and the cost of advertising for most companies is quite low when measured per unit of product sold or in relation to total sales volume involved.

The costs of advertising can also be compared with costs incurred for personal selling effort. Advertising expenses of most retail stores are only about 1 or 2 per cent of sales volume, the most notable exceptions being department stores, departmentized specialty stores, and furniture stores where advertising costs often amount to as much as 3 to 5 per cent of sales. In practically all cases this is substantially less than the expense of personal selling incurred by the same stores. Among manufacturers, advertising costs of about 1 to 3 per cent of sales volume are common experience.

While there are some exceptions to such low advertising costs, as explained in the preceding paragraph, the cost of advertising is usually low in comparison to the expense of maintaining a personal selling organization in the field. If less were spent for advertising, it would be necessary for companies to exert additional personal selling effort in order to maintain their position, and *total selling costs* would undoubtedly be considerably higher. The experience of the business community has been that advertising, when properly performed, is a *relatively* inexpensive form of selling effort and that it makes personal selling more efficient, since it paves the way for the salesman. In the last analysis, the question of how much is spent for advertising is not particularly significant.

It is much more important to inquire about *how much we get for what we spend.* A student of the subject should be more interested in the *values that are added by advertising* in relation to expenditures therefore than in costs per se. Many critics of advertising have blissfully assumed as a criterion of pure or perfect competition the existence of a state of complete and accurate knoweldge, shared equally by all buyers and sellers in the market. At the same time, such critics often fail to state or appreciate that the task of providing such an ideal state of knowledge would involve social costs perhaps hundreds or thousands of times total annual expenditures for advertising if, indeed, it could ever be achieved at all.

**Emphasizes Minor Differences**

Another criticism is that advertising has tended to develop and emphasize minor differences in the construction or formulae of advertised goods in order to have "something to advertise." It is much easier to call forth additional effective demand for a product if it is new or appears to be so than when it is just another brand of the same general type as dozens already on the market. For example, it is probably true that there are many brands of advertised toothpaste which are not essentially different and which perform the same functions as previously established brands.

It has, therefore, been necessary to emphasize minor chemical differences or new features in packages which are not always worth while. The effect of this is, in part, to reduce the scale of operations of the factories already producing toothpaste with the possibility of increased production costs. To the extent that this is true, the featuring of new brands, not essentially better than those already on the market, may be economically and consequently socially unjustifiable.

But advertising of new brands does not necessarily divert demand from older manufacturers. In many cases additional advertising has the effect of increasing the total consumption of the article under consideration. This additional consumption may or may not occur at the expense of other articles formerly purchased. When a new make of air-conditioning equipment is placed on the market, its advertising may increase somewhat the total sale of such equipment. In part it will divert to the new manufacturer sales which might otherwise have gone to existing suppliers. The effect may be to divert funds to the purchase of air-conditioning equipment which might have gone for clothing, alcoholic beverages, entertainment, insurance, or to savings accounts. In such a case, the social service of advertising must be judged by the relative social values of the alternative purchases.

## Planned Obsolescence

A somewhat related criticism is that advertising makes possible and encourages planned obsolescence. To evaluate this criticism, it is necessary to distinguish what is generally meant by planned obsolescence from other types of product obsolescence. There is, on the one hand, *obsolescence of function,* which has to do with the outmoding of a product by the introduction of another that performs the same function in a better way, as illustrated by automatic home laundry equipment to replace old-fashioned wringer-type washers. Nearly everyone welcomes and praises the obsolescence of this type and regards it as progress.

On the other hand, there is *obsolescence of quality,* or deliberate under engineering of a product, so that it will wear out quickly or be used up rapidly thus, in a sense, creating and enlarging, its own replacement demand. No sensible person can condone this type of obsolescence if the manufacturer can for the same money or for very little more provide a product that would yield more lasting benefit. Neither the obsolescence of function nor the obsolescence of under engineering of products are usually the issue when planned obsolescence is the question at debate.

Such discussions usually have to do with what has been termed the *obsolescence of desirability,* for it is this type which, to the greatest degree, is made possible and greatly facilitated by advertising. In one appraisal of the subject by a well-known advertising trade publication, this type of obsolescence was defined as "yearly or other regular superficial changes in products, styling or prestige selling appeals to persuade the public to purchase new items before the old are worn out." [15] This criticism is most frequently directed at the durable goods industries, notably automobiles and household appliances, where annual model changes are the general practice, but it also is commonly aimed at the fashion apparel industry as well. Proponents of planned obsolescence and its antagonists to some extent are engaged in a moral debate. Planned obsolescence would be morally indefensible if advertising of regular superficial changes in products brought about increased public emphasis upon material or conspicuous consumption at the expense of the attainment of higher social goals. It is certainly not clear that this is the case. The lesson of history is that the attainment of a high level of material well-being precedes rather than replaces the achievement of higher ranked social goals (e.g., better schools, medical care, or public recreation facilities).

Moreover, public response to the marketing strategy of planned obsolescence indicates that advertising of new models is a basic appeal to a rather pervasive desire for "newness" throughout our culture. In other words, advertising reflects rather than creates the social significance widely attached to innovation and change. This viewpoint is fortified by the fact that certain products are marketed on a basis where the main appeal is the absence of annual model changes, with the claim of little or no obsolescence, owing to changes in product which are confined to functional improvement (e.g., Rambler automobiles, Maytag home laundry equipment).

While nearly everyone abhors to some extent at least some aspects of planned obsolescence, even its critics see certain benefits which partially compensate for alleged wastes or abuses. Critics often seem to imply that consumers actually discard functioning products simply because they want to own a newer (but not necessarily an improved) product. Actually, second-hand automobiles, appliances, and even useful articles of clothing enter another market themselves, thus becoming worth while product acquisitions of consumers who cannot afford or who do not wish to make the monetary outlay for new items.

Moreover, there is some merit to the argument that planned obsolescence is partially a matter of planned product improvement handled on a regularly scheduled basis. Certainly it is quite frequently the case that one model of a given make of automobile is not greatly different from the preceding model. If the annual models of any make of car are compared over a long period of years, however, a much different conclusion is reached. Such a comparison brings into evidence a continuous parade of product improvement. The automobile of the early 1920's differs from the car of today by the sum of hundreds of relatively minor year-to-year advertised differences.

## Solely Competitive

Another criticism is that advertising is solely competitive and that the net result is to divert demand from one good product to another which is equally good but not superior. There can be little question as to the truth of this assertion insofar as much advertising is concerned. The potential market demand determines to a considerable degree whether or not advertising has the criticized effect. In the foregoing illustration concerning air conditioning, it was assumed that the potential demand for air-conditioning equipment is great and that a part of the effect of the advertising was to develop additional primary demand. Had the illustration referred to bread, the effect would have been vastly different.

Advertising of brands of bread has relatively little effect in increasing the demand for bread as a whole, since the primary demand for bread is well developed and is considered to be relatively stable. But who is to say that the market for bread is limited solely to the level of purchases of present users or whether it may be expansible in the sense of being only part of a larger market for starchy foods. If one describes the market for this product in terms of its present and potential uses or satisfactions rather than in terms of its generic characteristics, the possibility of increasing primary demand appears to be more reasonable.

Much advertising, nevertheless, is largely of a competitive nature wherein the selective buying or patronage appeals for a specific good or service have the effect of increasing or enhancing the market position of the advertiser rather than of increasing primary demand, even though the latter may be, to some extent, a by-product. This is, however, one of the characteristics of a competitive society. Most students of the problem recognize that much competitive effort could be eliminated were it desirable to establish a more paternalistic or dictatorial form of government. Under such circumstances it might be possible to control and even to eliminate advertising that is solely competitive. But such control would be at the expense of free competition, and freedom of competition is generally believed to be so desirable as to justify some of its inherent wastes as a necessary price for its maintenance.

## Inefficiency

Another alleged weakness of advertising as conducted at present in this country is its inefficiency. To be sure, some advertising is inefficient, and doubtless all advertising is less efficient than it could be. Even among large users of advertising, jokes are sometimes made about the efficiency of advertising. Sometime about 1910 George Washington Hill, famous president of the American Tobacco Company and an outstanding innovator in advertising methods and approaches, is reputed to have said, "I am convinced that 50 per cent of our advertising is sheer waste, but I can never find out which half." To this date, this statement is a popular quotation in advertising industry meetings and often appears in press comments about the subject.

It must be understood that advertising is a relatively new art. It is not yet a science, although scientific methods of procedure are being rapidly developed. Many valuable methods and principles have been and are being evolved as the result of the contributions of psychologists and sociologists. Such study has led to improved typography, more appealing copy, and improved layout. The more widespread practice of testing trial advertisements has eliminated considerable waste resulting from poorly conceived advertising programs. Media are now selected with more skill as a result of extensive research regarding characteristics of the circulation or audience of specific and general classes of media.

Motivation research has yielded a better knowledge of consumer buying behavior and has enabled advertisers to harmonize selling appeals with buying motives, with the effect of minimizing waste or inefficiency in the use of advertising appropriations. Other improvements in technique are constantly being developed which will no doubt lessen some of the crudities of the past. Progress in the application of more scientific procedures has indeed reached a point where many critics are more concerned about the efficiency rather than the inefficiency of advertising. This would certainly seem to be the view of some writers who regard advertising as an objectionable, manipulative art which causes people to do things they would not otherwise do, or which they should not do, if judged by the personal value standards of the critic.

### Misleading and False

An often-heard criticism of advertising is that many advertisements are misleading or definitely false. There is no doubt that this is true. Numerous advertisers have cleverly created a misleading impression even though every statement in their message, when separately considered, is literally truthful; others have quoted carefully selected findings of authoritative research studies out of context and in such a way that the quotations are construed as a product endorsement. Still others have artfully contrived to divert the reader's attention from the true nature of the terms of an offer by emphasizing headlines which give a false impression; additional advertisers have devised sensational tests which make a convincing sales argument but which have no relationship to the consumer's satisfaction from the use of the article. It is nevertheless significant that the Federal Trade Commission in its examination of hundreds of thousands of magazine, newspaper, and broadcast advertisements finds that only a very small percentage contains statements that appear to be misleading or false to a degree which justifies possible action by the Commission. No responsible citizen can condone misleading or false advertising, but to condemn all of advertising because of the objectionable practices of a deceptive minority is ridiculous. The answer, rather, is to focus attention on the control of abuses.

## CONTROL OF ADVERTISING

Popular credence in the printed word endows advertising

with great potential power. At the same time, advertising is more or less centralized and is, therefore, susceptible to control. These factors no doubt explain in part the widespread control of advertising on the one hand and the complete absence, with but rare exceptions, of control over the broader area of personal selling on the other. Control of advertising has been directed principally to the elimination of falsehood, fraud, and deceptive practices and the prevention of advertising of harmful products. More recently, partly in response to consumer pressure, attempts have been made to eliminate or minimize "bad taste" in advertising and to make advertising more informative and therefore more useful in making choices. Efforts at these various controls have been shared by many types of agencies and organizations.

## Federal Trade Commission and Advertising

Foremost in the control of advertising is the Federal Trade Commission which was created in 1914 by the Federal Trade Commission Act and was charged, among other things, with the responsibility of determining and preventing unfair methods of competition. One form of unfair competition is misleading advertising intended to deceive the public to the detriment or injury of competitors. The power of the Commission was greatly expanded by the passage of the Wheeler-Lea Act in 1938. This law amended the original Federal Trade Commission Act in three important respects. First, it broadened the Commission's jurisdiction to include practices that injure the public but which may not involve or injure a competitor. Prior to this amendment, action could be brought only upon complaint of a competitor who was presumably injured by an allegedly unfair practice. Now, the Commission may take action of its own accord if public injury can be shown.

The second major change pertained to the enforcement of orders issued by the Commission. The process of enforcement was regularized and shortened by making cease and desist orders of the Commission effective after 60 days unless appeals are made to the federal district courts.

Furthermore, it was provided that the Commission may bring action in the federal district courts in the case of violations of such orders, and substantial penalties of $5,000 were provided for each proved violation. It has been claimed that this penalty is not sufficiently severe because a violation may involve a considerable period of time. Some unethical advertisers doing a large volume of business found that such an amount is a small price to pay for the privilege of violation. For this reason, it has been advocated that the penalty be increased or made more severe so that a fine of $5,000 or more may be imposed for *each day* of violation.

The most important of the three principal changes made by the Wheeler-Lea Act is that which pertains to the *advertising other than labeling of foods and drugs*. It definitely prohibits false advertising of food, drugs, cosmetics, and therapeutic devices. Certain infractions involving these items are rendered criminal when injurious to health or when involving intent to deceive or defraud, and are punishable by both fine and imprisonment. Temporary injunctions are provided to stop these practices pending issuance of a complaint and determination of the charges. The law also permits factory inspections and forces submittal of these commodities, when required, for testing purposes; if found harmful, their sale may be prohibited.

One of the effects of this law has been greater confidence in advertising by virtue of the protection afforded. Another result is greater emphasis on specific and more informative statements in advertisements. A third result has been a re-examination of products for characteristics that could be advertised under the law. This has led to research and product improvement.

## Control by Other Federal Agencies

A number of other federal agencies have some control over advertising. One of great importance is the Pure Food and Drug Administration which operates under the authority of the Food, Drug and Cosmetic Act of 1938, which was an amendment to the Pure Food and Drug Act of 1906. Under the newer law, cosmetics and therapeutic devices were brought under control in addition to food and drugs; misbranding and misleading advertising of the specified products are banned; seizure of adulterated or contaminated foods is permitted; labels must warn of habit-forming drugs; factory inspections are permitted; and no drug can be placed on the market until after it has been tested to determine whether it is harmful. The various prohibitions may be enforced by injunction. Labeling must include the address of the manufacturer, packer, or distributor as well as facts concerning the quantity of the contents, major ingredients, and warnings against misuse of drugs. The Pure Food and Drug Administration works closely with the Federal Trade Commission. With respect to the selling function, the former agency is concerned primarily with packaging and branding. Although it watches for deceptive advertising, it usually hands over questionable cases of advertising to the Federal Trade Commission for action.

The Alcohol and Tax Division of the Treasury Department exercises powerful control over the advertising of alcoholic products. Under federal licensing regulations, this agency may require approval of all advertising and labeling of intoxicating beverages. It is very strict in the regulation of misleading advertising and has definite requirements as to the use of names for beverages and specification of exact age, type, and alcoholic content. The Post Office Department also exerts some control. Federal laws forbid the use of the mails for fraudulent purposes. While cases are relatively rare, there have been instances where the use of the mails has been forbidden to organizations that cooperated in fraudulent advertising.

## State and Local Control of Advertising

A considerable degree of control is exercised over advertising in intrastate commerce. This has become effective through the widespread enactment of the so-called Printers' Ink Model Statute which was drawn up by the advertising trade publication of that name in 1911. The purpose of this legislation was to extend the "Truth in Advertising" movement to trade not susceptible to control by federal legislation. It aims, in general, at preventing in an advertisement "any assertion, representation or statement of fact which is untrue, deceptive, or misleading," by declaring such a statement a misdemeanor. This law has been enacted in 27 states and the District of Columbia, and 17 additional states have enacted adaptations of it. Only six states have no law of this kind. In addition, many cities have ordinances relating to the use of deceptive or fraudulent local advertising.

**Control by the Business Community**

Also of great influence is voluntary control of advertising by the business community itself. Better Business Bureaus were established primarily for the purpose of promoting more truthful local advertising, especially in the retail field and in financial advertising. Operating in the principal cities, their influence in controlling local unfair advertising practices has been salutary. Newspapers and magazines often refuse to accept certain types of advertisements, exclude certain products from their pages, and otherwise censor all advertising submitted for insertion.

Following along similar lines, though much less extensively and perhaps less effectively, broadcasting companies have attempted similar controls. The efforts of certain trade and professional associations, particularly those designed to set standards for or to censor advertisements before they are printed or stated over the airways, have also been exceedingly helpful.

Finally, there are several important associations of advertising agencies, advertisers, and advertising media which have played a leading part in efforts to make advertising more useful, to place it on a higher plane, and to eliminate or minimize bad taste in advertising. This is accomplished through codes or standards of advertising practice to which the members of such associations have pledged themselves. The work of such associations is largely educational and persuasive, since they have no direct power of enforcement. Control of flagrant and intentional abuses rests necessarily with public authorities.

# Index

D



E



F



G